BUCKNELL REVIEW

Having Our Way: Women Rewriting Tradition in Twentieth-Century America

STATEMENT OF POLICY

BUCKNELL REVIEW is a scholarly interdisciplinary journal. Each issue is devoted to a major theme or movement in the humanities or sciences, or to two or three closely related topics. The editors invite heterodox, orthodox, and speculative ideas and welcome manuscripts from any enterprising scholar in the humanities and sciences.

This journal is a member of the Conference of Editors of Learned Journals

BUCKNELL REVIEW
A Scholarly Journal of Letters, Arts, and Sciences

Editor
PAULINE FLETCHER

Associate Editor
DOROTHY L. BAUMWOLL

Assistant Editor
STEVEN W. STYERS

Contributors should send manuscripts with a self-addressed stamped envelope to the Editor, Bucknell University, Lewisburg, Pennsylvania, 17837.

BUCKNELL REVIEW

Having Our Way: Women Rewriting Tradition in Twentieth-Century America

Edited by
HARRIET POLLACK

Lewisburg
Bucknell University Press
London: Associated University Presses

Associated University Presses
440 Forsgate Drive
Cranbury, NJ 08512

Associated University Presses
25 Sicilian Avenue
London WC1A 2QH, England

Associated University Presses
P.O. Box 338, Port Credit
Mississauga, Ontario,
Canada L5G 4L8

The paper used in this publication meets the
requirements of the American National Standard for
Permanence of Paper for Printed Library Materials Z39.48-1984.

(Volume XXXIX, Number 1)

ISBN 0-8387-5318-3
ISSN 0007-2869

PRINTED IN THE UNITED STATES OF AMERICA

Contents

Recent Issues of BUCKNELL REVIEW

The Senses of Stanley Cavell
John Cage at Seventy-Five
Comedias del Siglo de Oro and Shakespeare
Mappings of the Biblical Terrain: The Bible as Text
The Philosophy of John William Miller
Culture and Education in Victorian England
Classics and Cinema
Reconfiguring the Renaissance: Essays in Critical Materialism
Wordsworth in Context
Turning the Century: Feminist Theory in the 1990s
Black/White Writing: Essays on South African Literature
Worldviews and Ecology
Irishness and (Post)Modernism
*Anthropology and the German Enlightenment: Perspectives on
    Humanity*

Acknowledgments

Special thanks to the Department of English, to the Davis Library, and to Professor Joseph Flora—all at The University of North Carolina, Chapel Hill—to the Knight Foundation, to Bucknell University student readers Stephanie Paterson and Roger Hilscher, and to my much appreciated colleagues Dorothy Baumwoll, Pauline Fletcher, and Steven Styers for their contributions to the preparation of this volume.

Notes on Contributors

KING-KOK CHEUNG is an associate professor of English and Asian American Studies at the University of California, Los Angeles. She is the author of *Articulate Silences: Hisaye Yamamoto, Maxine Hong Kingston, Joy Kogawa* and the editor of *Asian American Literure: An Annotated Bibliography* and *"Seventeen Syllables": Hisaye Yamamoto.*

SUSAN FARRELL is an assistant professor of English at the College of Charleston, where she teaches courses in modern and contemporary American literature and on women writers. She is currently working on a book about ethnic American women writers in the post–civil rights era.

DEBORAH R. GRAYSON is an assistant professor of American and African American literature at the University of Rochester. She is currently working on a study of black women, beauty culture, and eating disorders.

ANDREA O'REILLY HERRERA is an assistant professor of comparative literature at SUNY, College at Fredonia. In addition to her scholarly activities, she recently completed her first novel.

BARBARA LADD is an assistant professor of English at Emory University. She has published essays in *Mississippi Quarterly, Southern Quarterly,* and *American Literature.* She is writing a book tentatively entitled *"The Direction of the Howling": Nationalism and the Color Line in the Work of George W. Cable, Mark Twain, and William Faulkner.*

AMY LING is a professor of English and director of the Asian American Studies Program at the University of Wisconsin-Madison. She is the author of *Between Worlds: Women Writers of Chinese Ancestry* (1991), a cultural literary history, and *Chinamerican Reflections* (1984), a chapbook of her poems and paintings. She has co-edited six books, including the *Heath Anthology of American Literature* and *Imagining America.*

11

MICHELLE PAYNE teaches composition and American literature at the University of New Hampshire, where she is completing her doctoral dissertation focusing on students writing (about) the body, and the professional and ethical concerns for teachers and students when students write about these issues within a college or university setting.

HARRIET POLLACK is an associate professor of English at Bucknell University. She has published articles on southern women writers in *Mississippi Quarterly, Southern Quarterly, Southern Literary Journal, Welty: A Life in Literature,* edited by Albert Devlin, and in *The Critical Response to Eudora Welty,* edited by Laurie Champion. Currently she is writing about a woman's strategic complication of the reading process in a book on Eudora Welty's fiction.

KATHERINE HEMPLE PROWN teaches English at the College of William and Mary. She has written previously on Edgar Allan Poe and is currently working on a book-length study of Flannery O'Connor and the politics of southern literary culture.

KRISTAN SARVÉ-GORHAM is completing her Ph.D. in English at Emory University. Her dissertation explores the relationship between the Western and the "medicine woman" novels of Mourning Dove, Silko, Erdrich, and Momaday.

JACQUELINE SHEA MURPHY is the author of essays on Leslie Marmon Silko and the Bill T. Jones/Arnie Zane Dance Company, and co-editor of the collection, *Bodies of the Text: Dance as Theory, Literature as Dance.* She teaches writing at the University of California, Berkeley, where she is completing a dissertation that examines how performance elements in twentieth-century U.S. multicultural narratives affect their representations of violence.

Introduction

Having Our Way is a collection of new essays on twentieth-century American women writers who meet, manage, fail to manage, revise and rewrite, engage and enter a literary tradition that has increasingly made way for and been altered by women's perceptions, issues, visions and revisions. The collection focuses on the work of ten women and brings together the voices of ten other women writers who are themselves having their way with academic tradition, revising and rewriting it, from their women's points of view. The theoretical stances here are varied and eclectic; the degree to which the writers attempt to infuse the academic with the personal also varies, but the impulse to bring together the personal, the political, and the scholarly is a marked impulse in the group as a whole. Scholarship's traditional readings and, at moments, its traditional genres are revisioned.

The scope of this issue of the *Bucknell Review* is defined by the essays that it houses. Attention to images of the body, to the power of literary establishments, to historical and cultural contextualizing, to the distance between official and unofficial definitions of "history," and to the complexity of multicultural literary encounters recur. But the central commonality among these essays is that each takes a revisionist approach to its topic.

Deborah Grayson, for example, in "Fooling White Folks, or, How I Stole the Show: The Body Politics of Nella Larsen's *Passing*" reads Larsen's novel by extending poststructuralist theories of subjectivity—specifically Foucault's notion of "the gaze" and its power to create and control "the other." Grayson's strategy for unmasking "political ideologies working obscurely within and upon the text" is to reapproach Larsen's use of the tragic mulatta convention and the act of passing to reveal race and gender issues problematized in the body of the mulatta—that space where racial demarcations assumed to be visible are blurred. Grayson shows this body, whose existence violates black/white binary "race ideology," as a place where social "inscriptions and descriptions of race" are overwritten, and she shows Larsen rewriting the conven-

tional mulatta plot in ways that destabilize it. Centering the novel
not with Irene Redfield but rather with Clare Kendry, and attending the complexity and occasional subversive comedy of crisscrossing gazes turned on Clare, Gertrude, Bellew, and Irene,
Grayson finds Larsen providing an opportunity to address how
our uses of language and its binary oppositions silence "the complexity of ourselves and of our texts," creating a legacy of reduction which "obscures the power dynamics" of the black/white
binary equation "either/or," a legacy that Grayson and Larsen put
in plain sight.

Michelle Payne also extends Foucault in her revision of Zelda
Fitzgerald's story in "5'4" × 2": Zelda Fitzgerald, Anorexia Nervosa, and *Save Me the Waltz*." While attending the Fitzgeralds' literary and personal struggle for control over the "reflection" of
themselves in language and in the "'texts' of their lives," Payne
risks reinventing Zelda. She puts Zelda forward as a possible anorexic (during a specific period of her life and marriage), arguing
that in *Save Me the Waltz* (1932) Zelda explored Alabama Beggs's
discipline (as in *Discipline and Punish*) of the female body—a narrative which F. Scott wrote out as he claimed the material of Zelda's
story for *Tender Is the Night*. In this revision, Payne goes beyond
the usual interpretation of Zelda as a victim of madness. Using
feminist psychoanalytic theories, she offers a Foucauldian analysis
of the "ritualized practices that induce women to deprive, restrict,
or punish their bodies in an effort to attain a more perfected
image of femininity." She produces a reading of anorexia itself,
which is "more than a spectacle of the state's exercise of power, of
disciplinary practices gone haywire. An anorexic's body manifests
both a cultural devaluation of femininity and a woman's desperate
attempt to overcome that devaluation"—a complex "attempt at
'self-cure,'" an exertion of control over the body in an "'effort to
ward off panic about being completely powerless.'" Payne builds
to a sustained reading of *Save Me the Waltz*, the novel in which
Alabama Beggs—having sought "identity and fulfillment . . .
through marriage and motherhood" and found herself devalued
by her artist husband's affair with a renowned ballerina—attempts to become the artist and the ballerina herself, beginning
a discipline of her body that turns obsessive and abusive and ultimately defeats her. This essay is important in its attention to anorexia (to twentieth-century women "'what hysteria was to women
of an earlier day: the crystallization in a pathological mode of a
widespread cultural obsession'") and important in its attention to
the fabrication of the Zelda mythology. The result is a reading

that makes the Fitzgeralds' story even more of an arresting cautionary tale than it has been.

"Riding the Dixie Limited: Flannery O'Connor, Southern Literary Culture, and the Problem of Female Authorship" is Katherine Hemple Prown's consideration of "how feminist theory can illuminate Flannery O'Connor's personal, professional, and literary response to the hegemonic discourses that characterized southern literary culture." Prown argues that by "revising her novels to meet the expectations of a critical establishment that considered women writers inferior, O'Connor gradually buried her female identity. . . . That the fiction so successfully conformed to the expectations of the male-dominated literary establishment of her day accounts, at least in part, for the relative ease with which she was able to earn a place in the American literary canon as well as for the relative neglect of her work by feminist critics." Prown's feminist analysis of O'Connor's work, both in manuscript and published form, is a corrective. She uncovers the writer who "played by the rules established by such influential southern writers and critics as Ransom, Lytle, Allen Tate, and Robert Penn Warren" and discovers the muted "tensions created by . . . her status as a woman." O'Connor's "very insistence on transcending femininity served . . . as a peculiarly 'female' strategy," one designed to obscure a muted, subversive, female voice. Prown asserts that while striving to be a "serious talent" and not a "lady writer" and accepting the views that "religion and art were masculine preserves, O'Connor remained acutely uncomfortable with her own desire to write." One of her "first moves as a professional writer . . . was to drop the name Mary"; another was to cultivate what she took for an "unladylike" presentation—"serious" in intent, potentially "incomprehensible" in complexity, and possibly "shocking to an audience of ladies." Prown's discussion leads to a provocative and controversial revelation: that is, the extent to which O'Connor relied on her God to authorize her authorship. "By explaining her creative drives in essentially passive terms as impulses that enjoyed the approval of the highest of masculine authorities—God himself—O'Connor could, in part, resolve the dilemma posed by her gender. Catholicism offered her a means of justifying her desire to write, allowing her to conceive of her work not as a . . . misguided usurpation of male privilege, but as a responsibility to which she must faithfully 'submit.'" From this position, Prown generalizes about the repeating patterns observable in O'Connor's fictional men and women, comparing these to others in her early manuscripts, revised as O'Connor found her way in response to the southern literary establishment.

Barbara Ladd looks at the southern literary establishment from another angle—that is, the power of its pronouncements to limit readings. "'Too Positive a Shape Not to Be Hurt': *Go Down, Moses*, History, and the Woman Artist in Eudora Welty's *The Golden Apples*" counters the persistent tendency to read Welty as an "ahistorical" writer, offering two reasons for this misperception: "gender in general and William Faulkner in particular . . . and . . . the general and the particular are intricately connected." Beginning with Welty's insistence that she wrote "from beyond . . . Faulkner's influence," Ladd shows that while Welty never emulated Faulkner, she wrote fiction that displaced his. "Her decision is not so much to avoid History out of deference to Faulkner or to the [gendered] conventions of gender role as to relocate . . . the woman's voice with respect to official History, to make the Historically invisible woman visible." Disclosing echoes of Faulkner's *Absalom, Absalom!* in Welty's early story "A Worn Path," Ladd suggests these echoes are about displacement, contrariety, resistance, and obstruction, rather than repetition. Welty "shifts the perspective to foreground the experiential reality of a black and female figure, the kind of figure who, in Faulkner's story as in official History, is hardly more than the decentered guardian of the remains of the male body. . . . Unlike Faulkner, Welty is not concerned so much with the construction or reconstruction of the tragic public History of the South—although the official History of the South is there in every scene—as with the devotion—and the forgetfulness—of a solitary old woman shaped by but strategically indifferent to that History." Ladd then settles into the similar displacement occurring between *Go Down, Moses* and Welty's most ambitious work, *The Golden Apples*. "Welty's reappropriation of women's history and women's voices . . . signifies at almost every turn upon official History, especially as it is realized in *Go Down, Moses*." It is in *The Golden Apples* that Welty launches "an intriguing, and powerful, subversion of the patriarchal aesthetic that governs [Faulkner's work] . . . by embracing the possibilities, rather than the horrors, of sexual, domestic, and literary transgressions." Ladd is both provocative and controversial as she uncovers the echoes of and yet resistance to Faulkner's text in Welty's story· cycle—where a girl's summer camp displaces Faulkner's all-male hunting camp and where "strategic indifference" to ancestor stories opposes "Ike McCaslin . . . listening with his whole being to everything . . . being said."

Jacqueline Shea Murphy in "This Holocaust I Walk In:

Consuming Violence in Sylvia Plath's Poetry" attends images of oppressed, tortured, mutilated, and consumed bodies heard throughout Plath's late poetry. She brings together the body images of Plath's 1962 work to reveal the overwhelming frequency of these images and the patterns found in them. Shea Murphy is focusing on and responding to a debate shaped by previous works which discuss the source of this violence. Where is it coming from? Is it from a sensitivity to the "horrors of a post-World War II World" (as Jacqueline Rose seems to assert in "Sylvia Plath and the Obscenity of Literary Criticism")? Or "from Plath's literal and metaphoric problems with her dead father, her poet-husband . . . and the patriarchal literary and poetic tradition in which she was immersed" (as Stephen Gould Axelrod's *Sylvia Plath: The Wound and the Cure of Words* asserts)? Shea Murphy argues that this imagery is Plath's subject itself: that is, the violence in our discourse of power. The "commonality between Nazi power and patriarchy is [in] the emphasis both place on controlling bodies. . . . Bodies violated and controlled in encounters with authority recur." Shea Murphy moves into complex space as she observes that "Plath, though, wanted authority," and her poems "show a poet grappling with authority in a world where to achieve power, as Hitler writes, 'one is either the hammer or the anvil.'" The pursuit of this speculation takes Shea Murphy through many of Plath's poems, to more extended readings of "Cut," "Fever 103°," and "Mary's Song," to poems and readings that bring together the political and the personal to explore violence and vulnerability in the discourse of power and mutilation.

In "The Dream in Flames: Hisaye Yamamoto, Multiculturalism, and the Los Angeles Uprising," King-Kok Cheung writes about Yamamoto's "A Fire in Fontana" in which the 1965 Watts riot evokes an earlier fire that also put the American Dream into flames. This autobiographical story draws on the history of a man named Short who, while Yamamoto was working as a staffwriter with the *Los Angeles Tribune,* came to enlist help. He had bought a house in a white neighborhood in Fontana and received "threatening notes from his neighbors asking him to 'get-out-or-else.' . . . Later that week his house went up in flames. Short, his wife, and two children were killed in the blaze. Though the fire 'appeared to have started with gasoline poured all around the house and outbuildings,' the police's 'official' conclusion [which the narrator reported for the *Tribune*] was that probably the man had set the gasoline fire himself, and the case was closed." Yamamoto's story's double structure juxtaposes the Watts and Short fires with the story of the Japanese American narrator's evolving racial consciousness, uncovering a story of interethnic cleavages—of the inability of people to relate to and stand up for those of another race but also of the possibility of empathy. "I wouldn't go so far as to say that I, a Japanese American, became Black. . . . But some kind of transformation did take place. . . . Sometimes I see it as my inward self being burnt black in a certain fire." Like Yamamoto's story, Cheung's essay has a double structure. It juxtaposes Yamamoto's "fires" with the 1992 Los Angeles rebellion following the acquittal of the police officers accused of brutally beating Rodney King, in which Korean American homes and stores were looted and burned and Reginald Denny beaten. And it juxtaposes the story narrator's growing racial consciousness with the story of our own multicultural classrooms—where too often we may be adding "'a week on African-Americans and another on Hispanics . . . [while] inter-group relationships remain invisible'" when we also need to teach "accountability across racial lines" as well as difference. As Yamamoto blends the personal and the public to produce her memoir, Cheung blends the personal and public to produce her scholarship. In her story, Yamamoto finds journalism a medium in which it is not possible to report the truth. She too well remembers writing "a calm, impartial story, using 'alleged' and 'claimed' and other cautious journalese," adhering to the generic rules that produced a "partial story in the name of impartiality," obliging the writer "to cite dubious 'official' sources" and preventing her from "offering her own analysis of the fire in Fontana." The narrator finds herself able "to [vindicate and reclaim] her own voice"—to write/right the wrong—only by reporting "the live incineration of the Short family" in a memoir breaking the generic rules of journalism. Similarly Cheung in her essay here presses against the generic limitations of scholarship— a medium that has often written out the personal even more than the political. Cheung's essay is one in this collection that emphasizes the collection title's reference to women scholars rewriting academic tradition—bringing to it the personal, the lived, the current, the political.

Susan Farrell in "'Who'd He Leave Behind?': Gender and History in Toni Morrison's *Song of Solomon*" brings Morrison's own advocacy of historical contextualizing to her project. "In order to fully comprehend . . . a secret between us and a secret that is being kept from us," writes Morrison, "one needs to think of the immediate political climate in which the writing took place." Farrell reads Morrison's *Song of Solomon* (1977) as a black woman's response "to quite particular and specific historical contexts: [first to] the developing dominant American literary background of postmodernism . . . [and second] to the racial and gender liberation movements of the 1960s and 1970s in America, especially the strain within the civil rights/black power movements . . . that presented racial liberation as a struggle to attain manhood." To situate Morrison, Farrell distinguishes between the historical situations of texts produced by white male postmodernists (Pynchon, Heller, Barthelme, Irving, Vonnegut) and "the dozens of works recently written by women from marginalized ethnic groups" who are better called "reconstructive" than deconstructive. Farrell finds the women seeking to do more than destabilize. She finds them able to believe in the possibility of change. She calls on Diana Fuss and Nancy K. Miller to help explain why, unlike the postmodernists, these women writers are not similarly attending the loss of authority, but opposing the loss of the subject. "Ethnic women authors . . . do not characteristically embrace the fragmentation and dispersal of the self that is characteristic of postmodernism, although it is a mistake to assume that these writers substitute a simplistic or romanticized notion of wholeness and community." Rather they see dispersal and fragmentation not as play with a linguistically based (un)reality, but as afflictions to be overcome. Farrell again draws on Morrison's own vocabulary in which "re-membering" is a goal and in which "the trauma of racism is . . . the severe fragmentation of the self, and has always seemed to [her] to be a cause (not a symptom) of psychosis." To this context, Farrell adds others from the sixties and seventies: "the focus on male leadership and needs in the early civil rights movement, the essentialist view of gender evident in the revival of black nationalism, and the masculine bias apparent in academic studies of black male/female relationships." She calls up the voices of Malcolm X, Stokely Carmichael, Eldridge Cleaver, and the Black Panthers on issues of gender and cites the 1965 Moynihan Report, which finds not racism but the "matriarchal structure" of black families a social problem, as well as academic arguments from the 1960s–1970s asserting that black women ought to put aside issues of gender inequality until racial inequality is resolved. In these contexts, Farrell reads *Song of Solomon* as "a feminist novel concerned with the African American 'proto-myth' of achieving 'manhood,'" what Morrison called "her 'giggle'" at that journey, a "novel that evokes both the possibility of flight and the question 'who'd he leave behind.'" It is "a novel about both the sexual and political education of a young man equally concerned with his

formative relationships with several women—mother, aunt,
lovers—and his intersection with the radical militancy of The
Seven Days." Farrell reads Milkman Dead as a protagonist who
"becomes what many black feminists struggle against: the black
patriarch, oppressed himself, yet at the same time oppressor," and
uncovers the issues raised by Macon Dead, Guitar, Ruth, Lena,
Pilate, Hagar, Sweet, Solomon, Sing, and Ryna in a novel recognizing "that communities can both silence members and be sites of
resistance."

Amy Ling in "Maxine Hong Kingston and the Dialogic Dilemma of Asian American Writers" begins with personal reflections on multicultural literary encounters catalyzed by the 1993
national Asian American Studies conference. Her thoughts are
about encounters that can seem to evoke the text as an anthropological "'native informant,'" an evocation laden with the hierarchical binary oppositions of "Same and Other, Normal and Exotic,"
and they lead her naturally to reflect on the experiences and the
misfirings of teaching multiculturalism. "Teaching Asian American literature to white students in the midwest," she writes, "can
be at times comparable to handling nitroglycerine; the material,
the students, and I are all, for different reasons, volatile." Trying
to pin down the differences between an anthropolgist-outsider's
descriptions of cultures and an Asian American writer's descriptions, she points to the issue of tone—to the difference between
"standing aloof" and "standing beside," terms that are complicated when insiders stand aloof, both interpreting a culture and
criticizing it. This very possible complication brings her to the
case of Kingston. Kingston, she argues, is suited to Bakhtinian
analysis. *The Woman Warrior* may be "an extended exploration of
the internal dialogism of three words: *Chinese, American,* and *female.* Each term carries a multitude of meanings in dialogue, if
not open warfare, with each other . . . What does the word *Chinese*
mean from the inside . . . to the people so designated? What
does it mean to the first-generation immigrant, to the second-
generation American born, to the fourth or fifth generation? At
what point does an immigrant Chinese become an American?
What does the term mean from the outside, to the designators,
to the stereotypers, to whites who feel that their places have been
usurped? What's the word's historical, political, and social ramifications, underpinnings and overlays? How does it differ from
other related terms, such as *Japanese* or *Korean?*" Dialogism un-
folds Kingston's text as Ling particularly attends those jarring
moments when "language shifts abruptly" between cultures "and

the disrupture is visible . . . [in] fissures between and overlappings of linguistic plates." Locating Kingston's position in the ambiguities of these shifts is complex—even her pronoun choice shifts between "we" and "they" as she brings "pride of inheritance and a revisionist compulsion" into dialogue. Her location is best identified by the further complexity of recognizing: "The words say one thing; the text does another."

Kristan Sarvé-Gorham in "Power Lines: The Motif of Twins and the Medicine Women of *Tracks* and *Love Medicine*" is also writing about cross-cultural reading encounters. She recenters the outsider reader when she finds a transformation of Anishinabe sacred twin mythology in the structure of Louise Erdrich's novels, attending the two lines of power that flow generationally from Fleur Pillager and Pauline Puyat, two medicine women figures who represent different definitions of power—one traditional Anishinabe and the other Euro-American. In mythology sacred twins are not always actual twins but are often born at different times and to different families (in the Anishinabe mythological pair—Matchikwewis and Oshkikwe—one is older by a year, although both are fathered by Nanabozho.) Twinning in Native American mythology, Sarvé-Gorham points out, is associated with ideas "'of complementarity, of duality that is not the same as opposition.'" This concept of balance emphasizes "the integration of two diversities as creating a whole . . . a balanced bipolarity or twinness . . . reflected in Indian social, political, and ceremonial structures." But it is precisely imbalance that Erdrich uncovers in *Tracks* (as Pauline herself is increasingly "imbalanced"), and it is balance that the descendants will need to restore. To a degree this happens in *Love Medicine* when the power of each medicine woman "survives in traces" in the daughter of each, Marie and Lulu, who eventually reconcile and become respected elders on the reservation, having used "'their inherited powers to ensure the continuance of the nation.'" Sarvé-Gorham's argument draws extensively on ethnography to uncover mythic parallels and to decode cultural contexts in the stories of the two women: Fleur, whose "powers are limited to the traditional Anishinabe world [and] can save neither her land nor her people from the encroachment of Anglo landgrabbers and their commerical values," and Pauline, who finds comfort in Fleur's family but "like a younger sister trying to establish both autonomy and recognition in her older sister's eyes, competes with her in terms of power," a "renegade medicine woman," enhancing her experience as a vision seeker with the power of the Christian religion until she feels prepared to combat Fleur's protecting manitou, Misshepeshu himself.

In "'Chambers of Consciousness': Sandra Cisneros and the Development of the Self in the BIG House on Mango Street" Andrea O'Reilly Herrera elaborates the contexts in which the house is a central signifier in a variety of literary traditions—from "eighteenth- and nineteenth-century 'big house novels'" where houses are "'structures' of economic, political, and social power," to "decaying house" novels of the twentieth century, to architectural metaphors representing literary tradition and the art of fiction itself, to United States fiction emphasizing "'the business of settlement and 'development'"—fiction portraying "the American Dream" as "'the hope of owning a freestanding . . . dwelling'"—to minority fiction in which the house is the "symbol of cultural disenfranchisement," to novels of domestic and gendered spheres in which the house is an emblem of female entrapment. Placing Sandra Cisneros's novel against these traditions, O'Reilly Herrera suggests the house on Mango Street represents "the systems that oppose or challenge her as a woman, a minority, and a writer." Living "'on the border,' the 'fault line,' the 'wound' between two cultures," sharing and yet "dispossessed" from both, the Chicana writer must redesign the "'American house of fiction [which has been dedicated] to defining what is peculiarly American about experience'—in other words, white, male, Anglo-Saxon experience. . . . While Cisneros seeks Virginia Woolf's literary 'room of one's own,'" her Esperanza ("Hope") is not satisfied with "her father's house on Mango Street [which] neither fulfills her needs nor her expectations." Cisneros "uses 'the master's tools' not to disassemble the master's house . . . but to remodel it according to her own aesthetic purpose." Her "adaptation and reinscription of established narrative patterns [rearranges] the furniture in the house of fiction [in] both an act of defiance and, in Adrienne Rich's words, "'an act of survival.'" Cisneros's story of Esperanza's development from child to journal keeper to potential writer is the story of her growth as a young woman unfolding against her own narratives of other women's lives: "a virtual portrait gallery of . . . women who are victimized, or victimize themselves, because of their sexuality." Her tellings of their stories evoke old narratives, plots, and endings, and against these stories of the "wedding-cake house," in the midst of them, Esperanza falls into her own sexuality in the "'monkey garden [where Sally is led by] Tito's 'grinning' buddies," an "unkempt" garden "that her family 'took over,' . . . on one level, a symbol of America as the new Eden" abandoned.

This point of intersection between Esperanza's artistic and sexual development is where O'Reilly Herrera builds.

No selection of ten essays could give full voice to the range of approaches that are current in the study of twentieth-century American women writers. This collection, however, is a gathering of diverse women's voices and approaches and is representative of those currently revisioning the study of literature. In turn, the arguments presented here suggest the diversity of voices and the strategic revisionings represented in the literature itself.

HARRIET POLLACK

BUCKNELL REVIEW

Having Our Way:
Women Rewriting
Tradition
in Twentieth-Century
America

Fooling White Folks, or, How I Stole the Show: The Body Politics of Nella Larsen's *Passing*

Deborah R. Grayson
University of Rochester

POSTSTRUCTURALIST and postmodernist thought has made it increasingly possible for literary theorists and historians alike to scrutinize "race" as a bracketed concept. When we talk about "race" as a bracketed concept, we remind ourselves that "race," like "gender," is a social, political, and cultural construction. It should come as no surprise, then, that at a time when the concepts of race and gender are coming under increasing scrutiny Nella Larsen's *Passing* has resurfaced as an important text of the New Negro Renaissance. Larsen's novel, like some of the tenets of poststructuralist thought, can be characterized as claiming that meaning is inherently unstable and that there is no unity between a stable "sign" and a stable "subject." This essay emphasizes that similarity by using the poststructuralist ideas of Michel Foucault to read these "pre-poststructuralist" elements of Larsen's novel *Passing*.[1]

The poststructuralist ideas of Foucault introduce different methods of formulating how we come to know literary texts and ourselves as (raced and gendered) texts. If we use the critical lens of poststructuralism to read the raced and gendered bodies Larsen presents us with in *Passing,* it would seem that both *Passing,* the novel, and *passing,* the act, force us to question whether we can ever use race or gender as signifiers without simultaneously undermining them. Taking my cue from Foucault, then, I will discuss how the social and discursive construction of the written and physical bodies of black women are inscribed and described. I will do this by extending Foucauldian theories of subjectivity, specifically his notion of "the gaze," to an analysis of *Passing/*passing.

Passing/passing (both the novel and the act) can be read as an example of what happens when we call into question what appears to be neutral and independent—what goes without saying about our bodies and how they are constructed and defined. An analysis of what we take for granted in our constructions of ourselves and of our texts I would suggest, following Foucault, unmasks the political ideologies working obscurely within and upon texts. An examination of how we speak about, or, perhaps, how we go about *not* speaking about race and gender and their effects upon the body, provides some insight into how we are constructed by language.

In *Passing*/passing Larsen invites us to examine how we speak the unspoken legacies of race, gender, and the body in American literature, history, and culture. She does so by (re)presenting the "blackness" of her two central female characters as "whiteness." Through her representations of biracial women, Larsen demonstrates the problem of binary thinking in the context of racial identity and gives us the opportunity to address how our use of language in this context silences a discussion of the complexity of ourselves and of our texts. She also asks us to address how our silence (our failure to use language) implicates us in continuing the legacy of reducing ourselves and our texts to the binary equation of either/or and how this reduction obscures the power dynamics with which this equation is laden. Finally, she asks us to address how our language informs our readings both of texts and of ourselves as texts.

Disciplining Bodies

Passing is often described as the lesser of Larsen's two novels. Since its publication, in fact, *Passing* has often been read as a novel whose primary focus is race with nothing to say about sex or class as the center of identity. Clare Kendry, not Irene Redfield, has often been assumed to be the central character in the novel, and it is often assumed that Clare alone is passing. In addition, Larsen's use of the literary convention of the "tragic mulatta" is often read *not* as a manipulation and a rewriting of this old convention but as a support of and a belief in it. I would suggest that Larsen uses the convention of the tragic mulatta to create a new concept of identity for herself and for African American literary canons.

This new concept of identity takes into account the intersections of race, gender, and class.

The novel takes place over the course of two years when two childhood friends meet again as married women while they are both "passing" in a hotel restaurant in Chicago. The action and later suspense of the novel are set in motion by the competing agendas of these two women. These two competing agendas are important to note because they exemplify how Larsen unmasks the hidden political and ideological functions of language, particularly in the context of racial and gender identity. On the surface, for example, the novel appears to be about Clare Kendry's "passing" and the cultural and psychological costs of her actions. It could also be argued, however, that the novel is about Irene Redfield and her desperate attempts to "keep undisturbed the pleasant routine of her life."[2] Still, these are only two possibilities for reading the novel. A number of contemporary critics—particularly, but not only, black feminists—have begun to reread the novel and to reevaluate its critical response in order to challenge or perhaps extend some of these long-held beliefs about the novel.[3]

Passing invites a different kind of discussion to take place about race and gender—about the exoticized black female body—not only as these issues are problematized in the body of the mulatta but also in situations where it *appears* that race and gender are most physically "precise."[4] In *Passing*/passing, for example, Clare's bod(ies) suggest that when it comes to reading bodies (physical or written) there are no definite either/or answers. Her successful, albeit temporary, usurpation of "whiteness" tells us that we can never assume or accept that what we see is "real" or "true," despite the practice in Western culture "that [equates] knowing with seeing" and understanding.[5] The bodies of Larsen's characters challenge our traditional methods of reading (or seeing) race and gender by emphasizing how our belief in the image, in the hue of skin color or other physical markers of identity, actually blinds us to the possibilities of there being other ways to know, see, or read these same bodies/texts. When the historical situations of black women's bodies in American culture become central to the discussion, we create space for a discussion of their bodies "as a locus of confounded identities."[6] One such identity is the identity of the mulatta figure that I have been describing.

By using what I would call the extreme example of the mulatta figure—extreme because unlike most "visible" bodies the racial demarcations of the mulatta's body are blurred—Larsen's characters invite us to play with the inscriptions and descriptions of "race" upon the body. The existence of the mulatta violates the law and logic of "race" and "race" ideology. In the (re)presentations of the mulatta's bod(ies) as biracial, Larsen contrasts those subjects who are able to suppress the historical (familial) situations of their bodies in invisible abstract bodilessness with those who are not able to suppress their situation because they have been defined as visible and therefore "other" in our culture. In writing the bodies of Clare and Irene, Larsen acknowledges the gaps, contradictions, and parodic potential of the American system's construction of subjectivity. She does so by inserting the supposedly legally inscribed visible bodies of her characters ("black" but not too "black") within this either/or binary equation and then subverting it. Because those of us who have black and/or female bodies have been legally defined as visible in our culture, we usually do not have the option of bodilessness. Larsen's characters, however, can be read as an inversion of this idea because the bodies of her characters look "white" even though they are supposed to be "black."[7]

Foucault's ideas in *Discipline and Punish* provide a way to read *Passing* and the experiences of its central characters in ways that acknowledge their complexity and attests to Larsen's skill not only in portraying psychological ambiguity but also the ambiguities of how raced and gendered bodies are formed and defined. At the heart of Foucault's poststructuralist project is the interrogation of subjectivity itself. Because we are all said to be formed through language, the identity of each one of us can be seen as a kind of text. Some would argue that as individuals we have no control over language or how the textual body is read or written. I join those on the other side of this argument who say that as we are introduced and subject(ed) to other texts of the world (other bodies), we are never entirely at the mercy of what we receive. In fact we rewrite these texts—our bodies. That they indeed can be rewritten is evident in the actions of Clare Kendry and to a lesser degree in the actions of Irene Redfield.

In *Discipline and Punish* Foucault states that "the success of disciplinary power derives . . . from the use of simple instruments: hierarchical observation, normalizing judgment, and their combination in a procedure that is specific to it—the examination."[8] Foucault argues that alongside the construction of major technologies which enhance sight—the telescope, the lens, and the light beam—there are also the minor techniques "of multiple and intersecting observations, of eyes that see without being seen; using techniques of subjection and methods of exploitation, an obscure art of light and the visible . . . secretly preparing a new knowledge of man" (*DP*, 171). In this form of observation, or "the gaze," power is exercised through exact observation. Observation, or the gaze, is used as a tool by those in power to keep those not in power subordinant. The gaze is so powerful because the gazers do not have to be present for their power to be felt. The gaze works by making "the other" always visible as opposed to invisible.

In his discussion of the camp, constructions of working-class estates, hospitals, and asylums, Foucault demonstrates how in an ideal situation "all power would be exercised solely through exact observation"; he argues that "each gaze would form a part of the overall functioning of power" (*DP*, 171). For Foucault a problematic develops: that of an architecture whose purpose is not the passive one of being seen by human beings, but the active one of instituting control over them—"an internal, articulated, and detailed control" (*DP*, 172). In more general terms, this architecture becomes one that "would operate to transform individuals: to act on those shelters, to provide a hold on their conduct, to carry the effects of power right to them, to make it possible to know them, to alter them" (DP, 171). In this instance, the old scheme of architecture functioning as a means of confinement and enclosure that prevents entering and leaving is replaced. Architecture becomes a place of action where one is able to observe individuals carefully, to separate them based on information developed from these observations, and to train these individuals.

In my readings of Larsen's fictional architectonics, Clare and Irene also (re)present the problematic that develops when the architecture no longer exists simply to be seen. If we use the architecture Foucault describes as a metaphor for the skin, or more specifically skin color, then we can say that the hue of skin functions as something more than simply something to be looked upon. Like the old schema of architecture functioning as a means of confinement and enclosure, "race," and to some extent "sex," are also supposed to prevent those inside of it from entering and leaving. Skin, depending on what color it is, is supposed to invite a gaze that is internal, articulated, detailed, and controlled. It is supposed to render those who are inside of it visible and knowable. But Clare's and Irene's skin color inverts the notion of skin color as control. They are able to challenge the idea that once one is inside of a particular body (architecture), one cannot enter and/ or leave this particular "raced" and "gendered" body. Because Clare and Irene look "white," they can and indeed do change their "race" and the particular way "race" causes them to wear their bodies—they enter, leave, and reenter, try on and discard different modes of wearing their bodies. Clare and Irene make the architecture of "race" and "gender" a site (sight) of action. They clearly demonstrate Foucault's point that "although surveillance rests on individuals, its functioning is that of a network of relations from top to bottom, but also to a certain extent from bottom to top" (*DP*, 177). Clare and Irene participate in this "relational power" network by seizing the opportunity to serve as both the observer and the observed, the object and the subject (*DP*, 177). They are not, in other words, totally at the mercy of what they receive but are participatory agents in the use of the simple instrument of hierarchical observation, or "the gaze."

Passing Glances

To a large extent it is Irene, not Clare, who can be considered the central character in the novel, mainly because of the role Larsen gives her as narrator. At no time in her fictional development, for example, do we see Clare without Irene's eyes. Clare, by Irene's description, is always associated with danger and with her desire to have more regardless of the cost to others. In the clever juxtaposition of Clare and Irene, Larsen obscures the fact that it is Irene who is at least just as dangerous as Clare and who, in the end, is really the one who will do anything to protect what is hers regardless of the cost to others.

The first indication that Larsen gives the reader of the power of the gaze occurs at the beginning of the novel when Irene is recognized by Clare while they are both passing for white at a restaurant in Chicago. Lost in thought, Irene suddenly realizes that she is being observed. She begins to wonder how someone she assumes to be a stranger can unabashedly choose to stare at her. Irene grows increasingly uncomfortable under the steady scrutiny of the gazer (Clare). She begins to question herself, begins to feel a range of emotions from anger to fear, from indignation to trepidation. As Clare continues to stare, Irene feels her color heighten under the continued inspection and slides her eyes down. Irene feels discomfort because of Clare's gaze not because "she was ashamed of being a Negro, or even having it declared. It was the idea of being ejected from any place [because she is a Negro] . . . that disturbed her (*P*, 150).

Under the gaze Irene literally becomes more visible and therefore feels more easily detectable and knowable as a black woman. She knows what the discovery of her "blackness" would mean to the gazer who has the power to qualify, classify, and punish. She is aware that if the gazer detects her "race" she can be publicly humiliated, abused, and punished. As a result of Clare's gaze, Irene begins to scrutinize herself; she begins to internalize the gaze in an attempt to dis-cover the reason why she has become a spectacle—the subject of and subjected to steady scrutiny by the gazer (Clare). Irene intuitively knows that the gaze imposes upon her a visibility through which she can be controlled. She also knows, however, and this is an important theme Larsen emphasizes both implicitly and explicitly throughout the text, that because her body is not visible in the way a "black" body is supposed to be, the burden of proof is on the gazer. Irene draws calmness and a brief moment of courage from this knowledge. She reasons to herself that "suppose the woman did know or suspect her race. She couldn't prove it" (*P*, 150).

Gazes crisscross in this opening scene because neither Irene nor Clare realizes the power that each of them has invested in the other's gaze. Though we are never told what Clare sees or what Clare feels as she is gazing on Irene, or the effect Irene's attempts to return Clare's gaze have on Clare, based on Irene's reaction to Clare's gaze we do get the sense that the gaze has a powerful effect on both of them.

In another scene where gazes play a crucial role in the action of the novel, Irene and Gertrude Martin (a childhood friend of Clare and Irene) meet John Bellew, Clare's (white) husband. Once again in this scene the gaze is a site (sight) of crisscrossing meanings where the distinction between what is believed to be true and what is actually true is collapsed. As in the previous scene with Irene in the Drayton Hotel restaurant, Clare is able to cast the gaze, along with the others, on her husband. Clare, Irene, and Gertrude successfully conspire against Bellew by maintaining their silence about their being defined as "black" women. They are able to challenge the rigid color line in American culture that is based on visibility. Because of the rigidness of this racial system, the invisible "visible" bodies of Clare, Irene, and Gertrude are overlooked and they are able to slip through the cracks. Ironically, it is not the "black" women in this scene but Bellew, the "white" man, who is the one visible and therefore knowable. Because he does not know he is sitting in a room surrounded by three "black" women drinking tea (despite Irene's desire to shout this point out to him), the women are not visible to him. Therefore Bellew, unaware of who ("what") he is looking at, does not know he has the power of the gaze. Instead, it is Irene's gaze that is perhaps most penetrating, most visible here. In fact, it could be argued that throughout the novel Irene is the one who best utilizes the power of the gaze. It is through her eyes, after all, that we see almost everything that goes on. Larsen alternately emphasizes and deemphasizes how powerful Irene's gaze is, how it shapes what we, as readers, see, and how we interpret it.

While Irene's eyes are exhibiting the power of the gaze in this scene with Gertrude, Bellew, and Clare, Clare's eyes have become "mysterious and canceling Negro eyes" (*P*, 161). Having to rely once again on Irene's eyes to record the scene (seen), we learn that Clare seems unaffected by what is going on in the room, particularly when her husband, at the beginning of this scene, calls her "Nig." We also learn, based on Irene's powers of observation, what Gertrude's feelings and responses are to this scene. Gertrude, we are told, is startled by Bellew's calling Clare "Nig" and briefly wonders to herself whether Clare has told Bellew about her "race." For his part, Bellew explains to Irene and Gertrude that he calls Clare "Nig" because he believes she has grown progressively darker throughout their marriage. For Bellew, in this instance seeing isn't believing. Even when he is presented with the "evidence" of Clare's dark body, he chooses to reassure himself and Clare that as long as he *knows* she's no "nigger," Clare can be as dark as she wants to be. Through his comments Bellew makes clear what his feelings are about "blacks": though he (thinks he) doesn't know any of them personally, he insists that he "knows them better than they know their own black selves" (*P*, 172). According to Bellew's logic of racial naming, one does not have to know an individual black personally; one must only be able to *identify* them as "black" to know who they are.

The irony occurs in the fact that it is not the "white" man in the scene but the "black" women who have the power of the gaze. Possessing the power of the gaze enables Irene, for instance, to qualify and classify the people and events around her. She records for us the thoughts and feelings of each individual in the room. Unlike Irene's gaze, and to a lesser degree that of the other black women in the scene, Bellew's gaze is made visible to us. In his statements to Clare, Irene, and Gertrude, Bellew not only demonstrates his flawed method of racial naming and the uselessness of ever trying to construct these types of signifiers, he also makes himself visible as a gazer and demonstrates how his gaze functions.

Bellew's gaze is only functional when black bodies are instantly and constantly recognizable. It is this blind spot in his gaze that allows Clare and the others to usurp his power as gazer. In sum, gazes crisscross in this scene in that Bellew's gaze does not detect Clare, Irene, and Gertrude as black, but Clare's, Irene's, and Gertrude's gaze detect Bellew as white—or is he? I ask this question because it seems to me that Larsen forces us to deconstruct our notions of "race" as a biological reality—she forces us to question the possibility of seeing correctly. In so doing, she gives readers the opportunity (power) to challenge what Bellew holds most dear about himself—his apparently "self-evident" whiteness.

When Bellew literally bumps into Irene and her friend Felice Freedland on the street, his gaze and its limitations are again made clear to us. In this scene, once again, Bellew does not recognize that there are multiple ways to read bodies—that is until Irene and Felice force him to see otherwise. It is Felice's "golden" skin and her "curly black Negro hair" that force Bellew to focus his gaze in a way that finally allows him to "accurately" read Irene's, Felice's, and later Clare's bod(ies) (*P*, 226). Though Irene has the opportunity in this scene to deflect Bellew's gaze before he reads her body against Felice's and "recognizes" her, she uses this opportunity instead to make Bellew see her and to let him know that she has seen him all along. This scene is the first instance where Bellew himself is embodied by the gaze.

Another example of where Bellew experiences embodiment by the gaze occurs in the concluding and perhaps most controversial scene in the novel. In this scene Bellew confronts Clare about her racial identity while she is attending a party at the Freedland's (freed-land's) home. Bellew, when he sees Clare in the room with the other "blacks"—when he finally focuses his gaze on their bodies, but most particularly on Clare's body—sees her as "other" too; he sees her as "black," as "nigger," and expresses feelings of "rage and pain" (*P*, 238). In direct contrast to what occurs in the previous scenes, seeing Clare's bod(ies) in the room with other "blacks" this time causes Bellew to reread her body. In the eyes and bod(ies) of the "others" that Bellew is now gazing on, he also sees himself reflected as well. Having been embodied himself by the "others'" eyes acting as mirrors, Bellew must read, must see, must confront the legacy of the unknown and unnamed (white father) and his relationship to his named and known, visible, and embodied "black"/mulatta daughter/wife. In so doing, what comes to the fore is his (white male) participation in making possible bodies like Clare's body (and his daughter's body) to exist—a body whose "race" is not easily detectable.

Reading, "Race," and the Body

That race and gender are considered to be biological facts of the body is based on long-held cultivated beliefs in gender and race ideology in the United States. Even when we are presented with bodies that challenge how we classify and categorize them, we find ways to compensate for their contradiction. Historian Barbara Jeane Fields argues in "Ideology and Race in American History," for instance, that we are able to "refer to physically 'white' people" as "black" because of the "ideological context [of race] that tells people which details to notice, which to ignore, and which to take for granted in translating the world around them into ideas about the world" ("IR," 146). According to Fields, our belief in "race" and race ideology "has long since taught [us] which details to consider significant at classifying people" ("IR," 146). Clearly, what Fields describes here is at work in Larsen's novel, particularly in the way Bellew reads (or perhaps refuses to read) Clare's bod(ies).

Larsen demonstrates in her characters how passing becomes necessary for women who want to claim the multiple meanings of their bodies not only in terms of their appearance but in terms of their historical situations. These women, in other words, want to be free of the oppressive gaze that has historically categorized them as exoticized "other." In her descriptions of Clare and Irene, Larsen demonstrates for us how they attempt to negotiate an existence in a society that does not want to relinquish this gaze and in fact, as Lauren Berlant argues, wants to continue to literally and figuratively polarize their bodies.[9]

Reading the bodies of Clare and Irene shows us how easily our definitions of raced and gendered bodies can be challenged. Clare's and Irene's bodies allow them to pass. Their bodies allow them to tamper with the evidence the law would seek—in this case the evidence of the dark-skinned body—to determine whether "black" bodies have fraudulently usurped the privileges of "white"-skinned bodies. Any attempt to reduce the possibilities for reading their bodies into a mere binary equation demonstrates not only the limitations of our reading strategies but also how we must reshape our views of how we construct and define raced and gendered bodies in American culture.[10]

Notes

1. I use the word "pre-postructuralist" in this context because Larsen's work obviously predates these contemporary theories.

2. Nella Larsen, *Passing* (1929; reprint, New Brunswick, N.J.: Rutgers University Press, 1986), 229. Hereafter cited in the text as *P.*

3. Cheryl Wall, for example, argues that Larsen's work is "among the best written of the time" and that her two novels "comment incisively on issues of marginality and cultural dualism that engaged Larsen's contemporaries such as Jean Toomer and Claude McKay." Claudia Tate argues that though *Passing* does "relate the tragic fate of a mulatta who passes for white, it also centers on jealousy, psychological ambiguity and intrigue." Tate argues that by focusing on these four elements, we can actually achieve a fuller reading of the novel that transforms it "from an anachronistic, melodramatic novel into a skillfully executed and enduring work of art." Both of these critics point to the skill and sophistication Larsen demonstrates in her unfolding of events. They argue that the reason Larsen's skill and sophistication have been "obscured" in the past is because readers have only paid attention to (following Cheryl Wall) "the bourgeois ethos" of the novel. See Claudia Tate, "Nella Larsen's *Passing:* A Problem of Interpretation," *Black American Literature Forum* 14 (1980):142–46; Cheryl Wall, "Passing for What? Aspects of Identity in Nella Larsen's Novels," *Black American Literature Forum* 20 (1986):97–111. See also Charles Larson, *Invisible Darkness: Jean Toomer and Nella Larsen* (Iowa City: University of Iowa Press, 1993) and Missy Dehn Kubitschek, *Claiming the Heritage: African-American Women Novelists and History* (Jackson: University Press of Mississippi, 1991) for more recent reinterpretations of Larsen's work.

4. See Barbara Jeane Fields, "Ideology and Race in American History," in *Region, Race, and Reconstruction: Essays in Honor of C. Vann Woodward* (New York: Oxford University Press, 1982), 143–77. Hereafter cited in the text as "IR."

5. Shari Benstock, *Textualizing the Feminine: On the Limits of Genre* (Norman: University of Oklahoma Press, 1991), xv.

6. Hortense Spillers, "Mama's Baby, Papa's Maybe: An American Grammar Book," *Diacritics* 17 (Summer 1987):65–81.

7. I draw on Lauren Berlant's discussion of embodiment and disembodiment in "National Brands/National Body" in my discussion of the visible and invisible constructions of subjectivity. Berlant points out "how specifically white male privilege has been veiled by the rhetoric of the bodiless citizen, the generic 'person' whose political identity is a priori precisely because it is, in theory, non-corporeal" (112). As Berlant argues, and as I am also attempting to argue here, because of the "implicit whiteness and maleness of the original American citizen," African Americans have obviously not had the "privilege to suppress the body" (113). Their inability to suppress their bodies makes them visible. See Lauren Berlant, "National Brands/National Body: Imitation of Life," in *Comparative American Identities: Race, Sex, and Nationality in the Modern Text,* ed. Hortense J. Spillers (New York: Routledge, 1991), 110–40.

8. Michel Foucault, *Discipline and Punish: The Birth of the Prison* (New York: Vintage Books, 1979), 170. Hereafter cited in the text as *DP.*

9. Berlant, "National Brands/National Body," 111.

10. The character of Hugh Wentworth in the novel is one of the few characters who

looks for multiple ways to read what he sees, but even he falls prey to reductive thinking. In the scene in the novel where Irene and Wentworth are at the Negro Welfare League dance, Wentworth is attempting to focus his gaze on Clare's body and he asks Irene to help him. Until he can get this information he feels he cannot see Clare or know how to read her body. Finding out Clare's race for Wentworth will make her known to him. If he knows what Clare is then he can know whether she is herself one of the gazers or just one of the Negroes to be gazed upon. According to Wentworth, sometimes he will "be as sure as anything that [he's] learned the trick [of racial naming]. And in the next minute [he'll] find [he] couldn't pick one of 'em if [his] life depended on it" (*P*, 206). In response to Wentworth's comment, Irene challenges Wentworth to accept that no one can tell another person's "race" simply by looking. Though it is true that Wentworth recognizes the existence of multiplicity in reading bodies, he still looks for a more unified system. As occurs in Foucault's regime of disciplinary power, Wentworth wants to compose, differentiate, homogenize, and exclude.

5'4" × 2": Zelda Fitzgerald, Anorexia Nervosa, and *Save Me the Waltz*

Michelle Payne
University of New Hampshire

> It would have starved a Gnat—
> To live so small as I—
>
> —Emily Dickinson

> Everything we have done is [mine] . . . I am the professional novelist, and I am supporting you. That is all my material. None of it is your material. . . . [S]he [Zelda] has nothing essentially to say.
>
> —F. Scott Fitzgerald

IN 1933, when Scott Fitzgerald declared ownership and ultimate control over the "text" of his and Zelda's life during a conversation with Zelda and her psychiatrist,[1] he was merely asserting for posterity what he had exercised since around 1919— his right to exploit in his fiction not just his own experiences and emotional anguishes, but also those of the women he knew, particularly Zelda. Many critics have noted the extent to which Scott's female characters are based on Zelda, but it has only been during the last twenty years that feminist critics have begun to question the gender politics involved in such appropriation.

One of the more disturbing ways Scott "enshrined" Zelda in his fiction was using her letters, sometimes lifting whole lines, in delineating a character. But in using the sometimes intimate and emotionally wrenching texts of a living, breathing "character," Scott rather violently molded the identity of his wife for his own personal and literary purposes. To use the language of Sandra Gilbert and Susan Gubar, Scott created in his fiction a reflection of Zelda, a looking-glass in which, as a woman and as an aspiring

39

writer, she gazed at herself, "killed into a 'perfect' image," and saw
"an enraged prisoner."[2] While this image perhaps misleadingly
implies that Zelda is a "stable reality" and does not account for
the historical discourses of power that have produced Zelda's "images," it seems an appropriate metaphor for the Fitzgeralds because they apparently struggled over who could construct and
control the "reflection" of themselves in language. My thoughts
about the rather particular drama of their relationship have been
focused by Michel Foucault's analysis of the more fragmentary,
elusive struggles over the cultural production of meaning articulated in *Discipline and Punish*.[3]

The Fitzgeralds were certainly "masters of invention,"[4] creating
and recreating themselves in their everyday lives and in their fiction, blurring the boundaries traditionally assumed between authors and texts. Zelda in particular lived daily with Scott's
rendition of her "double," an assertive, flamboyant femme fatale,
and she was as committed to upholding that image as she was
resentful of it. This conflict between her complicity with and her
rage at the image inscribed on Scott's literary mirror permeated
her culturally inscribed female body and somewhat unexpectedly
resulted, I will risk arguing, in anorexia nervosa. Her body became a trope in her own life for a larger conflict within the cultural "texts" of femininity. In interpreting the text of Zelda's body
and of her novel *Save Me the Waltz,* I use feminist psychoanalytic
theories of anorexia as well as a Foucauldian analysis of the discipline of "femininity" to reread Zelda's story and go beyond the
usual interpretation of Zelda as primarily a victim of madness.

During the Fitzgeralds' courtship in 1919, Zelda wrote Scott in
New York that she wanted to be "5 ft. 4″ × 2″″" (Z, 46). She was
thinner than she had ever been before, and her concern with her
weight would be a recurring theme in her life. The published
pictures of Zelda from the early 1910s to the 1940s do not reveal
a boyishly slender body of Twiggy or today's models, nor the kind
of emaciated, skeletal body now associated with anorexia. She is
definitely thin, but her photos alone would not be convincing
evidence Zelda suffered from anorexia. Only in turning to Zelda's
written "photos" can we see how dangerously underweight she
became at various points in her life.

Having been thinner as a nineteen-year-old in 1919 than ever
before, Zelda became very sensitive in 1922 about the weight she
gained during her pregnancy that left her looking "matronly and
rather fat" according to Edmund Wilson.[5] She "carefully shaded
her nose, cheeks, and chin with a pencil in an effort to slim her

face" (Z, 87). Within a year she was slender again, but by 1929, after a couple of years studying ballet in Philadelphia and Paris, Zelda was fifteen pounds under her normal weight and would enter Malmaison Hospital in Paris within eight months, suffering her first breakdown (Z, 156–58). It is at this point, I would suggest, that Zelda began to suffer from anorexia. Her weight loss, hours and hours of dancing in front of a mirror, and her own admission that she went for days without eating suggest an intense focus on her body, a disciplining of it uncharacteristic of her prior to this period. In her lifestyle with Scott, the notorious, continual parties and alcohol consumption could hardly be said to suggest a desire to tightly control her body, even if Zelda did swim regularly and "strenuously" during this same period (Z, 136, 141, 184, 107).

It wasn't until the 1930s, the same time Zelda was being treated by psychiatrists for schizophrenia, that the then rare disorder, anorexia nervosa, was recognized not as a physiological but as a psychogenic "disease." Not until the 1950s did Dr. Hilde Bruch, later a leading researcher on eating disorders, encounter female anorexic patients in large numbers; since the 1960s, anorexia has been recognized in epidemic proportions.[6] The cultural conditions many psychiatrists believe have precipitated this current epidemic differ only slightly from those of Zelda's time. In the 1920s they were beginning: changing cultural beliefs about beauty and thinness, and the use of women's bodies in consumerism.[7]

Psychoanalysts and feminist theorists alike have argued that anorexia in its current form is not simply a physiological or psychological "disease," but the consequence of how femininity is constructed in our culture. In her feminist revision of Foucault, Sandra Bartky in particular argues that anorexia is the result of the more subtle and detailed disciplinary practices demanded of women in our culture: dieting, exercising, restricting body movement, and ornamenting the body are "part of the process by which the ideal body of femininity—and hence the feminine body-subject—is constructed," producing a "body on which an inferior status has been inscribed."[8] According to Foucault, the human body has become the target for a new kind of discipline, a "microphysics of power" which operates by breaking down and regulating the body's gestures, space, and time, producing "docile bodies."[9] However, Bartky notes that women's bodies are made to be more "docile" than men's and thus demand a different analysis of the forces that discipline them. Foucault "is blind to those disciplines that produce a modality of embodiment that is peculiarly feminine,"[10] those ritualized practices that induce women to deprive, restrict, or punish their bodies in an effort to attain a more perfected image of femininity. Such practices suggest a woman's body is deficient and in need of constant self-surveillance. The result is that women's identities are produced around not only a "panoptical male connoisseur," but "an oppressive and inegalitarian system of sexual subordination." As an expression of severe and violent punishment of the body, anorexia nervosa, Bartky says, "is to women of the late twentieth century what hysteria was to women of an earlier day: the crystallization in a pathological mode of a widespread cultural obsession."

Feminist psychoanalytic work during this century has generated theories about anorexia remarkably parallel to Bartky's argument. As Bartky says, constructions of femininity demand certain behaviors and appearances, yet those very activities "partake of the general depreciation of everything female." Feminine gestures, rituals, and dress are seen as trivial, just as the bodies women are trying to make more beautiful are seen as already (and always) deficient.[11] This cultural depreciation of everything feminine is what many psychoanalysts argue anorexic women are both participating in and fighting against. Psychoanalysts like Hilde Bruch and Susie Orbach argue that anorexics are "in a desperate fight against feeling enslaved and exploited, not competent to lead a life of their own." They are terrified to choose "wrongly" from the bewildering number of opportunities available to women, including the prospect of sexual freedom.[12] The rigid and rather violent control anorexics exert over their bodies represents an "effort to ward off panic about being completely powerless."[13] Feeling needy and wanting to be safe and protected, anorexics have, nevertheless, internalized and come to fear the "mythology/ideology of the devouring, insatiable female."[14]

When a woman suffers from anorexia, then, her body becomes more than a spectacle of the state's exercise of power, of disciplinary practices gone haywire. An anorexic's body manifests both a cultural devaluation of femininity and a woman's desperate attempt to overcome that devaluation. In psychological terms, anorexia becomes an active attempt at "self-cure,"[15] a form of resistance to the very codes that discipline a woman to choose such self-denial and bodily violence: the "pathologies of female 'protest'" seem to operate "as if in collusion with the cultural conditions that produced them."[16]

Why would women choose to resist their sense of deficiency by using the very means that reinforce those feelings? According to Bartky, the disciplinary practices of femininity become part of a woman's "know how," what she feels skilled to do and therefore that from which she gains a sense of power. Her sense of identity is connected to her sense of mastery of these skills.[17] The better she is able to execute those skills, to exert some control over her seemingly unwilling and rebellious body, the better she may feel about herself. In this way her sense of self can become conflated with her body. At the same time, because she has been taught to deny herself *food,* to prepare food for others as a form of emotional sustenance and yet refuse herself that nurturance, a woman learns to separate her body from her sense of self. Hunger needs become synonymous with a revolt against the discipline she believes she needs to maintain in order to function—her hungry body turns against itself.[18] A young woman may thus begin to see her body as both divorced from her and yet "reflective of the very essence of herself":

> Her body is a statement about her, the world, and her position in the world. Since women live within prescribed boundaries, women's bodies become the vehicle for a whole range of expressions that have no other medium. The body, offered as a woman's ticket into society (i.e., through it she meets a mate, and thus her sexuality and her role are legitimized), becomes her mouthpiece. In her attempts to conform or reject contemporary ideals of femininity, she uses the weapon so often used against her. She speaks with her body.

I quote Orbach at length here because it is important to understand how an anorexic both conflates her body with her "self" (her emotional needs are linked to her body), and yet feels that self alienated from her body (her hunger cues are resisted). Bodily hunger may then become conflated with emotional hunger, with needs and desires that the anorexic has been encouraged to stifle. "Femininity is hunger," Maud Ellmann says in *The Hunger Artists,* and self-starvation is an effort to "release the body from all contexts, even from the context of embodiment itself."[19]

It is quite possible that the state of semi- or complete starvation Zelda imposed on herself between 1927 and 1929 precipitated the anxiety and even the hallucinations that characterized her first breakdown. Having left the Malmaison Hospital within ten days of her first admittance, Zelda entered Valmont, a clinic in Switzerland, twenty days later; during those twenty days she had returned to her ballet lessons with even more drive, and in two weeks she "heard voices that terrified her, and her dreams, both waking and sleeping, were peopled with phantoms of indescribable horror.

She had fainting fits and the menacing nature of her hallucinations drove her into an attempted suicide" (Z, 159). Studies of men on starvation diets have demonstrated that, regardless of one's emotional stability beforehand, "semi-starvation [results] in significant increases in depression, hysteria, and hypochondrias," including binging and purging, "violent emotional outbursts with flights of ideas . . . talks [and threats] of suicide," disorientation, and increased anxiety. In addition, the subjects of a 1950 study became increasingly more isolated and withdrawn, and their interest in sexual activity or sexual fantasy gradually diminished.[20] Biographer James Mellow argues that just prior to Zelda's first breakdown the couple was having sexual problems, due in part to Scott's drinking,[21] but also, I would suggest, due to the rigors Zelda was inflicting on her body, a physical representation of her rejection of hunger and desire. Zelda had also been "easily distracted" and often unable to engage in conversation; she "took refuge in an impenetrable and unnerving silence" (Z, 152).

Zelda's weight stayed seriously below normal from 1929 until at least the late thirties (I have found no references to her weight in the biographies after 1935). In 1933, after Zelda's second breakdown the previous year, Scott's secretary remembers Zelda as "skinny," and in 1934 Malcolm Cowley remarked that her face was "emaciated" (Z, 269, 281). By February of 1934 Zelda was again fifteen pounds underweight when she suffered her third breakdown and reentered the Phipps Clinic in Baltimore, following the appearance of the serialized version of Tender (Z, 284); by the fall of 1935 when she was staying at the Sheppard-Pratt Hospital in Baltimore, one of Zelda's family members came to visit and found her weighing less than a hundred pounds (Z, 307).

At the time, though, Zelda's behavior wasn't viewed as the result of semi-starvation and overexercise. She was diagnosed as schizophrenic, a diagnosis that could explain Zelda's weight loss and "obsessive" dancing as a consequence of a schizoid personality[22] and thus a result of psychological, not cultural/sociological, "pathology." However, the parallels between schizophrenic and anorexic personalities are striking enough that distinctions between the two seem too amorphous to be helpful. Bruch notes that "psychiatrically, the condition appears to be more akin to borderline states—narcissism or schizophrenia—than to neurosis."[23] Schizophrenics and anorexic women often seem asocial and indifferent, introverted, detached from their bodies and the environment, and exhibit contradictory behaviors and feelings (e.g., sometimes they appear docile and submissive, other times rebellious and arrogant).[24] Phyllis Chesler has noted that female schizophrenics are "morbidly concerned with their 'appearance'" but are actually removed from their bodies "in terms of . . . 'satisfaction,' 'confidence,' or 'activity.'"[25] Like anorexics, then, their bodies are both conflated with and separated from their "selves." Given these similarities, the diagnosis of Zelda as a schizophrenic rather than an anorexic may be historical accident. To focus on Zelda's body now in the stories of her writing and her "madness" is to interpret a woman's body culturally constituted and "written on," a docile, disciplined product of the operations of power and language. It is to understand how she experienced her "docile body" as a kind of self-perpetuating prison.

During their courtship, Scott made this link between femininity and imprisonment when he repeatedly said to Zelda that he "used to wonder why they keep princesses in towers" (Z, 50). Alice Hall Petry has argued that Scott kept Zelda in a series of towers throughout her life: he maintained a strict control over what she could and couldn't do, he tried repeatedly to minimize her accomplishments in ballet and writing, and he had the right to have her committed to the various mental institutions she frequented the last twenty years of her life.[26] After her first breakdown, Zelda was given a "somewhat mysterious 're-education' . . . in terms of her role as wife to Scott" that resulted in an increasing dependence on Scott as well as an unwillingness to show him the incredible amount of writing she was doing at this time (Z, 199, 201). Both Scott and her doctors had determined that her ambitions were "self-deceptions" that had contributed to her mental instability (Z, 191). Within Scott's tower, Zelda's desires for autonomy and art made her "mad."

One of the equally significant ways Scott imprisoned Zelda within a "fairy tale" of femininity was using her as a source for his heroines and using her diaries and letters, as well. Beginning with his first novel, *This Side of Paradise,* Scott used Zelda as a model for his female characters, often integrating modified or verbatim chunks of her letters and diaries, prompting Zelda's now famous line from her review of *The Beautiful and the Damned* that Scott must believe "plagiarism begins at home" (Z, 89).[27] This plagiarism extended even to the stories Zelda wrote that were published under Scott's name. When "A Millionaire's Girl" was published in 1930, Scott's name alone appeared in the magazine—in spite of the fact that Zelda had been solely responsible for writing it (Z, 150). Given that this occurred close to her first breakdown and a few months after she turned down her ballet

debut in San Carlo, we need to reconsider, as Petry and Dale
Spender in particular point out, the possible cause/effect relationships between Scott's appropriation of Zelda's writing and her
breakdowns.[28]

Scott himself expressed the emotional impact of their competi-
tion over autobiographical materials when he became angry over
Zelda using material in *Save Me the Waltz* that he planned to use
in *Tender Is the Night*: "Zelda had used him, [Fitzgerald] insisted—
his writing, his life, his material—to her own advantage"; he accused her of building "this dubitable career of hers with morsels
of living matter chipped out of my mind, my belly, my nervous
system and my loins" (Z, 222).[29] He was terrified that the portrait
of him in the guise of David Knight would destroy his reputation,
indicating the extent to which he understood how damaging it
could be to have someone else molding him as a character. Scott's
and Zelda's struggle over who controlled the production of meaning within their own relationship particularizes what Foucault argues is a larger cultural operation of and contention for discursive
power.[30] Scott believed that he had exclusive literary right to the
material of their mutual lives because of his literary superiority.
He demanded that Zelda write nothing about their life or her
psychiatric experience until after his book was finished and that
she then submit all her writing to him first.[31] He wanted, it appears, sole control over himself as a text, but was unwilling to
grant the same to Zelda. In arguing that Zelda was effectively
consuming him ("morsels of living matter") through her writing,
Scott evoked a kind of cannibalism, the death of the artist's model
through the use of words: "her single intention in this somewhat
thin portrait," Scott said, "is to make me a non-entity."[32]

It may be that Zelda had begun to believe that Scott's use of
her was making her a nonentity, or that she had to become one
in order to fulfill her fictional roles. Elizabeth Kasper Aldrich
calls Scott's fictional treatment of real women, Zelda in particular,
vampirish, connecting it to Poe's theory that "the most poetical
topic in the world is, unquestionably, the death of a beautiful
woman." Taking the corollary to Poe's theory that "the dying of
the woman is a prerequisite to the art of which she is subject,"
Aldrich suggests that for Scott in his complex relationship with
Zelda, the fictional representation

> takes a kind of ontological precedence over the model, drains it of its
> own being. Art does not simply copy the life of its subject, it draws *on*

that life, or draws it *out* and into its own. Entity is, like blood, a limited quantity and Art, vampirish.

From this perspective, Zelda as model is "not wife; in so far as she is the subject of art, she is not beloved of the artist, she is cannibalized." Anorexia is one way for Zelda to fulfill her part as model, to drain her body of the substance that feeds Scott's texts, carving up the "beautiful woman" and hence the feminine who is the exploitable/edible substance/flesh of Scott's art.[33] Certainly her anorexia is symbolic of the gradual eating away that occurred of Zelda's emotional and artistic desires. Simultaneously, Zelda's anorexia is her attempt to escape Scott's art, his control over the production of meaning, to produce what she believes is a stronger, impenetrable person who is trying to purge what her culture and seemingly her author-husband have force-fed her—her marginalized status as a female.

Because her body is both written on by her culture and interpreted by it, Zelda's body is analogous to her own writing: out of both she has tried to create an alternative "self," separate from Scott and not subjected to the discourses of femininity. Within Foucauldian analysis, such an alternative is not possible—a person's identity is always already constituted by power, never outside of it.[34] However, as Bartky has noted, this identity is produced from both power and mastery, being subjected to and yet a master of that discipline. In crafting her body as well as her text, Zelda is subjecting herself to and yet mastering the discourses of power that shape her, potentially speaking with the anorexic body/text about her resistance to those discourses. Creating an autobiographical character who turns to and on her body "to bring surcease from [her] tortured mind"[35] and whose sense of identity is always already fragmented and divided, Zelda dramatizes how gender and subjectivity are produced, and potentially resisted, through language.

In 1932 Zelda explained to her husband that *Save Me the Waltz* was her attempt to write the "story of myself versus myself" (*Z*, 221), and in writing the novel, she creates, through the autobiographical Alabama, "a show to join . . . somewhere to enact the story of her life" (*SMTW*, 20) beyond the scripts her husband created. While the novel renders Zelda's reading of her own life and her life with Scott, it also presents a fictional "New Woman" and her struggle for identity amid the conflicting "shows" she might join. Zelda came of age when privileged white women, in particular, had achieved the right to vote, were getting college educations, pursuing careers, marrying later if at all, and having fewer children than their mothers.[36] Elizabeth Ammons contends the women writing during this period wanted to claim a right to the Western, male tradition of art but found that being a woman and an artist seemed incompatible: feeling "emotionally stranded between worlds," they felt comfortable with neither their mother's world nor the world of white male artists.[37] With her husband a part of the male community actively defining the American literary culture in the twenties and thirties, Zelda struggled with these issues quite intimately, and quite tragically.

Recent critics have viewed *Save Me the Waltz* primarily in terms of what it says about women, work, and marriage in the 1920s: Alabama, a "pampered southern Belle,"[38] tries to find a sense of identity and fulfillment first through marriage and motherhood, then secondly, after she is disillusioned, through "meaningful work" as an artist in a man's world.[39] Most critics focus, as well, on the gender issues that help structure the narrative and create the central tensions in the plot: the traditional gender role divisions within the Beggs household and their parallels in Alabama's and David's expectations of each other;[40] beliefs that men's work and art are more significant than women's; and the ways Alabama's experiences reflect being "stranded between the old ideal of feminine subservience to men and the new ideal of equality."[41] For all these reasons, *Save Me the Waltz* is becoming recognized as a novel significant not only for its context in the author's relationship to F. Scott Fitzgerald, but as a modernist novel portraying a woman artist fragmented by her culture's fairy tales.

The ballet section, in fact, has received much critical attention as "one of the finest—and earliest—fictional representations of woman's capacity for wholehearted devotion to work." However, whether it represents a woman finding purpose and a sense of self through that work or realizing the failure of even art to fulfill a woman's life is still in dispute.[42] Is ballet, like marriage, just another fairy tale for Alabama? While Fryer suggests that Alabama's "failure" is "pure chance," Petry suggests that Alabama comes to realize that her ballet, and success, is no longer purposeful but "unfocused" and "obsessive," an activity that demands she subsume her identity to the dance as she did to her husband.[43] While I agree with Petry that Alabama's discipline of her body may have begun as something purposeful and even "beautiful" and that it later becomes obsessive, it is important to explore *why* this shift occurs, why Alabama is "defeated by the very body that was to be her means into the world of art."[44]

Alabama "fails" to continue her ballet because she neglects to attend the bleeding blisters on her heels and finds herself in a hospital bed with blood poisoning, her hands looking like "bird claws," "long and frail and blue over the knuckles like an unfeathered bird" (SMTW, 240).[45] She does not abandon ballet because of "lack of ability or dedication to her efforts;"[46] instead Zelda links Alabama's career end to what seems a passive action on her body but is at the same time an active, self-inflicted abuse. I am arguing, of course, that Alabama has become anorexic, struggling to reconcile and/or resist competing desires. In this novel, ballet becomes a trope for anorexia—torturous, ascetic, bodily rituals concealed by and yet enabling the graceful, seemingly delicate performance of the ballet/body. Alabama's body becomes the "stage" on which she acts out the (culturally inscribed) story of herself versus herself.

Alabama's fragmentary, divided identity is powerfully evoked during her parents' visit to New York after her marriage. In the face of their disappointment, Alabama realizes that "no individual can force other people forever to sustain their own versions of that individual's character—that sooner or later they will stumble across the person's own conception of themselves" (SMTW, 55). Wanting her parents' approval as well as the right to live as she pleases, Alabama is torn: "it's very difficult to be two simple people at once," she tells David, "one who wants to have a law to itself and the other who wants to keep all the nice old things and be loved and safe and protected" (SMTW, 56). Throughout the novel Alabama feels these fragmented parts of herself competing for supremacy:

> Why am I this way, why am I that?
> Why do myself and I constantly spat?
> Which is the reasonable, logical me?
> Which is the one who must will it to be?
>
> (SMTW, 69)

As I have argued earlier, this apparent division between wanting to be a law unto oneself and yet wanting to be protected is particularly characteristic of anorexic women. It is this tension that is developed within the story's larger metaphor of performance and woven throughout the novel.

Images of performances and acting are used to describe much

of the action in the novel as well as the character of Alabama. She is both actively creating herself, describing herself as a "fiction" (*SMTW*, 70), as someone who loves to "give a damned good show" (*SMTW*, 29), as well as passively waiting for herself to be made, to be given "a show to join . . . somewhere to enact the story of her life" (*SMTW*, 20). As a child, she does not know that "what effort she makes will become herself" (*SMTW*, 6); she has "been filled with no interpretation of herself" (*SMTW*, 5) and so believes she is her best self only "when I'm somebody else whom I have endowed with these wonderful qualities from my imagination" (*SMTW*, 70). A "marauder of vagrant enthusiasm," she is trying to create a sense of who she is from the borrowed parts of others, piling "the loot on whatever was at hand, her sisters and their sweethearts, performances and panoplies" (*SMTW*, 12).

Underneath this creative "improvisation," however, is "a strong sense of her own insignificance" (*SMTW*, 31) and ineffectiveness. If Alabama felt insignificant as a child, her relationship with David further compounds it: before they are married, David carves their names on a doorpost, flaunting not only his desire to be "famous" but his discursive power over her when he writes "David . . . David David Knight Knight Knight and Miss Alabama Nobody" (*SMTW*, 37). A princess rescued by a "Knight" from her conservative family, Alabama finds herself fulfilling David's desire to "keep [her] shut forever in an ivory tower for [his] private *delectation*" (*SMTW*, 40, emphasis added). As a result, after playing out the script of wife and mother and ceasing to fulfill David's needs (as well as her own), Alabama finds herself emotionally neglected, her artistic desires openly discouraged. For David, Alabama is significant when she is either his plaything or his domestic servant.

It is important, then, that Alabama decides to become a ballerina at a point when she feels a gulf widening between David and herself and a growing desire for something separate to do. Having been a law unto herself through childhood and early marriage, Alabama begins to "half [hate] the unrest of David, hating that of herself that she found in him" (*SMTW*, 129). She longs for the security and "bed of sureness" (*SMTW*, 120) her father represented to her, and not finding it in David, she turns to her body. During the scene when she decides to become a ballerina, Alabama's reactions to Gabrielle Gibbs and David illustrate the tension she feels between wanting to be safe and protected emotionally within her marriage and wanting to be a law unto herself within her own separate artistic career. At the party she finds herself unusually clumsy and uncomfortable, pitted against the actress/dancer Gabrielle for David's affection, feeling threatened by her, but also wanting to escape her own "neediness": if she did not feel so dependent on David's affection, she would not feel the hurt that confirms her feeling of nothingness. When she tells David she is "going to be as famous a dancer as there are blue veins over the white marble of Miss Gibbs" (SMTW, 118), Alabama is reframing David's earlier assertion of future notoriety that cast her as a nobody; her own fame will result from disciplining her body into a performance that purges the needy, devalued self of their courtship and early marriage.

Because ballet is an art form expressed primarily with the body, it is not surprising that through Alabama's eyes the ballet she later attends is "spare, immaculate legs and a consciousness of rib, the vibrant suspension of lean bodies precipitated on the jolt of reiterant rhythmic shock." But what begins for Alabama as sexual attraction to the dance and the dancers' bodies is simultaneously undermined by "the violins' hysteria" and an image of the dancers in "a tortured abstraction of sex." Something is both attractive and self-annihilating to her in "the poignancy of a human body subject to its physical will to the point of evangelism" (SMTW, 112). Believing that mastery over her body will provide the stability and emotional nurturance she desires, Alabama chooses an art form which magnifies the processes that have constructed her sense of identity and her desires.

"[Y]ield[ing] herself to the slow dignity of the selfless ritual, to the voluptuous flagellation of the Russian minors" (SMTW, 150), Alabama strives to become part of Diaghliev's company. He works his dancers from eight in the morning till the wee hours of one, demanding they weigh less than fifty kilos (SMTW, 144), "insist[ing] they live at so much nervous tension that movement, which meant dancing to them, became a necessity, like a drug" (SMTW, 143). Alabama is attracted to, indeed "obsesse[d]" (SMTW, 154) with the feelings of mastery this discipline gives her. This pleasure induces her to seek to "get rid of some of [her]-self" (SMTW, 141) through her ballet, believing Diaghliev's dancers stand out because of "their obliteration of self to the integral pose of his ballet" (SMTW, 144). Then her body grows "so full of static from the constant whip of work that she [can] get no clear communication with herself" (SMTW, 173). In a passage that could be an anorexic's credo, Alabama explains why she "drove herself mercilessly":

> she would drive the devils that had driven her—. . . in proving herself,
> she would achieve that peace which she imagined went only in surety

of one's self—. . . she would be able, through the medium of the
dance, to command her emotions, to summon love or pity or happiness at will, having provided a channel through which they might flow.
(SMTW, 124)

The discipline of the ballet brings Alabama "a sense of order
and purpose akin to a religious experience,"[47] a self-affirming
"pleasure" in her ability to subdue her unruly, voracious flesh. In
the ballet scenes we see Alabama "flagellating" and "whipping"
herself, working "till she felt like a gored horse in the bull ring,
dragging its entrails" (SMTW, 154), taking "herself for an awful
beating" (SMTW, 125). As Petry asserts, "the anguish of physical
exertion is purposeful and, in its way, beautiful, like the fasting
and even the self-flagellation of the devout."[48] However, this exertion also resembles self-inflicted violence and indicates a tyranny
of state power. For an anorexic, it is a means of authoring herself,
mastering those skills which have come to define her identity
and now promise to provide a sense of control and, to a degree,
autonomy.

A static model of identity, one that assumes a unitary and often
externally oppressed self, would suggest that Alabama's self-
flagellation is a product of repressive, patriarchal forces, forces
she needs to cast off to free her "true" self. Poststructuralist theory, however, has rendered this model less tenable, arguing that
identity is "constituted by the myriad of social relationships and
practices in which the individual is engaged," processes that are
often "contradictory and unstable." The result is a fragmentary,
always fluid identity.[49] Thus Alabama's contradictory identity is
not necessarily pathological, though it is, indeed, a social product.
As an anorexic, Alabama, like Zelda, performs the disciplinary
practices made necessary to maintain sexual inequality and subordination; at the same time, both women are lured by the pleasures
achieved in crafting themselves simultaneously into extremely
feminized and ultimately masculinized female bodies.
Because anorexic bodies are so dissimilar to "normalized" body
images, they demand attention, focusing their audience on the
conflicting, violent discourses/scripts/stories that produce gender
and power relations. The images they create, in fact, reveal the
subjected body and the body as subject, a theme echoed in Save
Me the Waltz in the final scene. Back within the walls of her rented
home, Alabama is once again presiding over dinner parties and
trying to raise her daughter, having given up her desires for art.

David has succeeded in enclosing his princess in his ivory tower and keeping her there, not only in the tower of domestic life but in the "text" of his painting where he has captured the movements of ballerinas for everyone to admire. Her abortive attempt at independent expression enveloped in his canvas, Alabama and her art are frozen in David's artistic looking-glass. David asserts, in fact, that "the waltz picture would actually give you, by leading the eye in pictorial choreography, the same sensation as following the measure with your feet" (*SMTW*, 209). For David, the image is as important as the experience and pleasure of the body's disciplinary performance.

However, after gazing into her husband's mirror, Alabama demonstrates neither pleasure nor disgust. Instead, she goes about emptying ashtrays, while guests are still there, telling David, "It's very expressive of myself. I just lump everything in a great heap which I have labelled 'the past,' and having thus emptied this deep reservoir that was once myself, I am ready to continue" (*SMTW*, 212). This final image, like others in the novel, is paradoxical. Just as she sought selflessness in the ballet and her anorexic body, Alabama is actively purging the ashes of the exploitable/edible self memorialized in David's painting, a self subjected to/structured by the canvas of power relations. Yet, in dumping those ashes of her past, she is also acting as a subject, asserting some control over her identity, her past and her future. Alabama wants to start anew, but she believes she must do so by burning her past, severing herself from the various discourses/stories that have constructed her.

Zelda, on the other hand, does not burn her past but actively revises it in writing *Save Me the Waltz*, crafting a counterreflection of herself to Scott's literary mirrors. She revises, in fact, her own discarded opportunity to dance in Naples when Alabama accepts the position and leaves David and Bonnie in Paris. She does not allow Alabama to have a sustained career in ballet, however, possibly suggesting a fear of her own creativity, as Gilbert and Gubar might suggest, as well as the seductive power of femininity to discipline her into a more docile, more "edible" model for Scott and the androcentric canvases of her culture. It is difficult, indeed, not to see this novel as a failed-artist story, despite the many revisions Zelda made of her own choices, but it is also important to remember that symbolically dumping the ashes of her past is an act of renewal for Alabama, an act of mastery over herself.

Unlike Alabama in the novel's final scene, Zelda did not abandon her desire to be an artist when she was forced to give up ballet, nor did she empty out the "deep reservoir that was once [her]self" by dumping the ashes of her past. During the next several years after *Save Me the Waltz* was published, Zelda continued to write and paint in the midst of being institutionalized, continuing her dream of being an artist distinct from Scott. In addition, while *Save Me the Waltz* gathers Zelda's past together, it is not a past that is burned or purged, but one that is reshaped and preserved, part of the fluid, social process of developing an always fragmentary identity. Written on her anorexic body and the pages of her novel is the story of herself versus herself, testimony to her rage and her resistance to the cultural and quite personal disciplinary discourses which permeated her body and her texts, which shaped and molded her.

Notes

I want to acknowledge a number of people who read various drafts of this essay and offered supportive, challenging, and provocative responses. The ideas presented here are a product of many voices: my thanks to Steve Barrett, Anne Downey, Melody Graulich, Deborah Hodgkins, Harriet Pollack, Patrocinio Schweickart, and Lisa Sisco.

1. The above quotations were brought together by Nancy Milford in *Zelda: A Biography* (New York: Harper & Row, 1970), 273. Hereafter Z, cited in the text.

2. Sandra Gilbert and Susan Gubar, *The Madwoman in the Attic: The Woman Writer and the Nineteenth-Century Literary Imagination* (New Haven: Yale University Press, 1984), 15.

3. Michel Foucault, *Discipline and Punish: The Birth of the Prison* (New York: Vintage Books, 1977).

4. James R. Mellow, *Invented Lives: F. Scott and Zelda Fitzgerald* (New York: Ballantine Books, 1984), xviii.

5. Ibid., 145.

6. In 1941 Dr. Bruch was a resident at the Phipps Clinic in Baltimore, working under Dr. Adolf Meyer, the psychiatrist who treated Zelda after her second breakdown and who was a leading authority on the diagnosis and treatment of schizophrenia. See Hilde Bruch, *Conversations with Anorexics* (New York: Basic Books, 1988), ix. Dr. Bruch was assigned an anorexic young woman while there (she had seen her first case during her internship in the 1930s) and began her research into a disease that actually had been described a hundred years earlier, but had not been seen often enough to warrant further research. See Hilde Bruch, "Four Decades of Eating Disorders," in *Handbook of Psychotherapy for Anorexia Nervosa and Bulimia*, ed. David M. Garner and Paul E. Garfinkel (New York: Guilford Press, 1985), 8–9.

7. Susie Orbach, "Accepting the Symptom: A Feminist Psychoanalytic Treatment of Anorexia Nervosa," in *Handbook of Psychotherapy*, 87–88.

8. Sandra Bartky, "Foucault, Femininity, and the Modernization of Patriarchal Power," in *Feminism and Foucault: Reflections on Resistance*, ed. Irene Diamond and Lee Quinby (Boston: Northeastern University Press, 1988), 71. See also Catherine Belsey, "Constructing the Subject: Deconstructing the Text," in *Feminist Criticism and Social Change*, ed. J. Newton and D. Rosenfelt (London: Methuen, 1985) for a discussion of how women are

interpellated into contradictory discourses and often "retreat" into becoming "sick" as a solution.

9. Foucault, *Discipline and Punish*, 26–27.

10. This and the following quotes and information refer to Bartky, "Foucault, Femininity," 64, 72, 75, and 65.

11. Ibid., 73.

12. Hilde Bruch, *The Golden Cage: The Enigma of Anorexia Nervosa* (Cambridge: Harvard University Press, 1978), x and ix.

13. Bruch, "Four Decades," 10.

14. Susan Bordo, "Anorexia Nervosa: Psychopathology as the Crystallization of Culture," in *Feminism and Foucault*, 106.

15. Bruch, "Four Decades," 11; Orbach, "Visibility," 132.

16. Bordo, "Anorexia Nervosa," 105.

17. Bartky, "Foucault, Femininity," 77.

18. This argument and the following quotes are from Orbach, "Accepting the Symptom," 85–87, and 90.

19. Maud Ellmann, *The Hunger Artists: Starving, Writing, and Imprisonment* (Cambridge: Harvard University Press, 1993), 43 and 14.

20. *Handbook of Psychotherapy*, 525–26.

21. Mellow, *Invented Lives*, 358.

22. Bruch asserts that primary anorexia nervosa is different from its secondary forms, the weight loss often consequent to other psychiatric illnesses like depression, hysteria, or schizophrenia; see "Four Decades," 9–10.

23. Ibid., 10.

24. Louis A. Sass, *Madness and Modernism: Insanity in the Light of Modern Art, Literature, and Thought* (New York: Basic Books, 1992), 76–79.

25. Phyllis Chesler, *Women and Madness* (New York: Harcourt, Brace, Jovanovich, 1989), 55.

26. Alice Hall Petry, "Women's Work: The Case of Zelda Fitzgerald," *LIT: Literature Interpretation Theory* 1 (1989): 69–83.

27. See Milford, *Zelda*, and Mellow, *Invented Lives*, for a more detailed treatment of this issue. See also Dale Spender's argument about this appropriation in *The Writing or the Sex? or, Why You Don't Have to Read Women's Writing to Know It's No Good* (New York: Pergamon Press, 1989), 175–92.

28. Petry, "Women's Work," 69; Spender, *Women's Writing*, 182.

29. For a comparative reading of the two texts, see Sarah Beebe Fryer, "Women on the Threshold of Freedom: Nicole Warren Diver and Alabama Beggs Knight" in *Fitzgerald's New Women: Harbingers of Change* (Ann Arbor: University of Michigan Research Press, 1988), 57–70.

30. Biddy Martin, "Feminism, Criticism, and Foucault," in *Feminism and Foucault*, 6.

31. See Milford, *Zelda*, 272–75; Mellow, *Invented Lives*, 410–13.

32. Quoted in Elizabeth Kaspar Aldrich, "'The most poetical topic in the world': Women in the Novels of F. Scott Fitzgerald," in *Scott Fitzgerald: The Promises of Life*, ed. A. Robert Lee (New York: St. Martin's Press, 1989), 139. Quotes in the following section are from pages 141, 139, and 141 in Aldrich's essay.

33. I thank Patrocinio Schweickart for helping me clarify and elaborate this point.

34. Martin, "Feminism," 9–11, 13.

35. Zelda Fitzgerald, *Save Me the Waltz* (1932; reprint, Carbondale: Southern Illinois University Press, 1967), 199. Hereafter *SMTW*, cited in the text.

36. Carroll Smith-Rosenberg, *Disorderly Conduct: Visions of Gender in Victorian America* (New York: Oxford University Press, 1985), 176–78. Bordo notes that anorexia and other

forms of bodily discipline have peaked in those periods when women were becoming more independent and politically active ("Anorexia Nervosa," 106).

37. Elizabeth Ammons, *Conflicting Stories: American Women Writers at the Turn into the Twentieth Century* (New York: Oxford University Press, 1991), 10, 11, 12.

38. Fryer, "Women on the Threshold," 58.

39. See Fryer, Petry, "Women's Work," and Linda Wagner, "*Save Me the Waltz*: An Assessment in Craft," *The Journal of Narrative Technique* 12 (Fall 1982):201–9.

40. Wagner, "*Save Me the Waltz*," 203. See Wagner also for a more detailed discussion of the novel's elliptical and often fragmentary structure and style.

41. Quotes here and in the next paragraph refer to Fryer, "Women on the Threshold," 70, 67, and 70.

42. Fryer asserts the former; Petry and Wagner suggest the latter.

43. Quotes here and in the following line refer to Petry, "Women's Work," 77, 76.

44. Wagner, "*Save Me the Waltz*," 206.

45. Alabama is evocative of the anorexic characters Gilbert and Gubar discuss, a character whose red shoes (bleeding heels) have been figuratively cut off because she wanted to dance (*Madwoman in the Attic*, 78 and 42).

46. Fryer, "Women on the Threshold," 70.

47. Petry, "Women's Work," 76.

48. Ibid.

49. Jana Sawicki, "Identity Politics and Sexual Freedom: Foucault and Feminism," in *Foucault and Feminism*, 184.

Riding the Dixie Limited: Flannery O'Connor, Southern Literary Culture, and the Problem of Female Authorship

Katherine Hemple Prown
The College of William and Mary

FLANNERY O'Connor enjoyed a level of professional status that was rare among the women of her generation. Recognized as a bold and unique talent by powerful critics like Andrew Lytle, her instructor at the University of Iowa Writer's Workshop, and John Crowe Ransom, the highly influential editor of the *Kenyon Review,* O'Connor rapidly earned a place for herself as among the "top-rate" American writers of the twentieth century.[1] Indeed, if the recent publication of her work in the Library of America series is any indication, then her place in the American literary canon, in the company of such luminaries as Herman Melville, Henry James, T. S. Eliot, and William Faulkner, remains secure.[2] Interestingly, despite her distinction as a woman writer of canonical standing, feminist critics have largely overlooked her work. A number of likely reasons exist for this situation. A devout Catholic and a conservative white southerner, O'Connor embraced the hierarchical politics of her church and region. Her writing reflects this orientation, as it does her belief in the essentially masculine nature of art. Hoping to distinguish herself from "lady" writers in general, O'Connor cultivated a decidedly masculine literary persona. As the manuscripts for her two novels *Wise Blood* (1952) and *The Violent Bear It Away* (1960) suggest, she was on some level aware of the price to be paid for openly identifying herself as a woman writer. Revising her novels to meet the expectations of a critical establishment that considered women writers inferior, O'Connor gradually buried her female identity by emphasizing

masculinist plots, conventions, and characterizations. That her
fiction so successfully conformed to the expectations of the male-
dominated literary establishment of her day accounts, at least in
part, for the relative ease with which she was able to earn a place
in the American literary canon, as well as for the relative neglect
of her work by feminist critics.

Despite O'Connor's refusal to identify herself as a woman
writer, it remains impossible to arrive at a thorough understanding of her work without considering the constraints placed upon
her by gender. But the existing critical response to O'Connor has
been limited by nearly exclusive attention to her status as a Catholic and a southerner. Her allegiances to her religion and her native
region, while strong, were nevertheless profoundly ambivalent.
This ambivalence was largely rooted in gender issues, that is, in
the tensions created by her latent fears regarding the subversive
nature of her professional ambition and her artistic drives. Working within a literary culture built upon the exclusion of women
and blacks, O'Connor played by the rules established by and gov-
erning such influential southern writers and critics as Ransom,
Lytle, Allen Tate, and Robert Penn Warren, whose theories regarding southern and American literary traditions implicitly defined writing in masculine terms. My intention in this essay is to
consider how feminist theory can illuminate O'Connor's personal,
professional, and literary response to the hegemonic discourses
that characterized southern literary culture. In particular, I will
consider how the broader relationship between O'Connor's fiction, both in manuscript and published form, sheds light on the
many tensions created by her status as a white southerner, a
Catholic and, most importantly, as a woman.

Elaine Showalter's "cultural" theory offers perhaps the most
useful feminist approach to O'Connor's work. While Showalter
argues for the existence of a "women's culture," she cautions
against emphasizing common female experience without considering the influence of race, class, ethnicity, religion, and history. At
the same time, her theories concerning "muted" and "dominant"
discourse make it possible to account for the factors that set female experience apart within specific cultures. Drawing on anthropological theory, she contends that women, like other
marginalized groups, occupy two cultural spaces at once. Explains
Showalter, "A black American woman poet, for example, would
have her literary identity formed by the dominant (white male)
tradition, by a muted women's culture, and by a muted black cul-

ture. She would be affected by both sexual and racial politics in a combination unique to her case."[3] Because the knowledge and experience of muted groups is often defined as invalid, those who seek expression through the written word often find themselves in an awkward position, attempting to speak through discourses that would exclude and silence them. Thus women, argues Catherine Belsey, may be free to participate in the dominant "liberal-humanist discourse of freedom, self-determination and rationality," but they are at the same time encouraged to adopt "the specifically feminine discourse offered by society of submission, relative inadequacy and irrational intuition." Female writers, Belsey concludes, often find their attempts to resolve the tensions inherent in such a position overwhelming. "One way of responding to this situation is to retreat from the contradictions and from discourse itself, to become 'sick.' . . . Another is to seek a resolution of the contradictions in the discourses of feminism."[4]

As Showalter's theory suggests, however, there exists another alternative for women writers: embracing masculinist forms and conventions. Indeed, southern women writers, as Anne Goodwyn Jones has demonstrated, have enjoyed a long history of obscuring rebellions—both in life and, for their heroines, in fiction—beneath "the veil of an acceptable formula."[5] O'Connor was no exception. Her career is perhaps best distinguished by the way in which she discreetly managed to mask the subversive potential of her artistic drives, delicately occupying both dominant and muted spheres at once. While she founded her career as a writer in opposition to what critics would term a "female" aesthetic, her very insistence on transcending femininity served in itself as a peculiarly "female" strategy, one designed to obscure a muted voice and self. The literary culture to which O'Connor sought entrée was founded on the exclusion of the muted, marginalized voices of women, blacks, and assorted "others." Yet rather than challenging the exclusionary, and at times misogynist, basis of the literary milieu in which she hoped to succeed, O'Connor undermined all traces of an explicit female identity and aligned herself intellectually, artistically, and professionally with a powerful male literary establishment.

A devout Catholic who worshipped without question or doubt a patriarchal God and adhered to the precepts of a doctrinally conservative and antifeminist church, O'Connor found it easy to disavow "the feminist business" altogether. Attempting to ignore and thereby neutralize her gender as a professional issue, she explained, "I just never think, that is never think of qualities which

are specifically feminine or masculine."[6] This disclaimer notwithstanding, she made a clear decision to distinguish herself from
"ladies," women who cultivated "femininity." As a white southerner from a respectable middle-class family, O'Connor understood that "ladies" remained properly concerned with social
activities and not with intellectual endeavors.[7] In other words, she
understood that to succeed as a professional writer, she must cultivate an unmistakably "unladylike," if not altogether "masculine,"
demeanor in her professional life as well as in her fiction. Indeed,
she admitted to interviewer Richard Gilman that one of the first
moves she made as a professional writer was to drop the name
Mary and assume instead her more ambiguous middle name.
After all, she asked, "Who was likely to buy the stories of an Irish
washerwoman?"[8] Underneath this gender-neutral mask, designed
both to oppose as well as to obscure her female identity, lay the
muted voice that informs her unpublished fiction.

For the most part, however, O'Connor's muted self remained
obscured beneath a veil of conformity. A subversive female voice
does not emerge as a distinctive quality of her published fiction.
Instead, her complicated appropriation of masculinist discourse
was based implicitly on the sexual as well as the racist status quo
of her society. Although she described herself as an "integration-
ist" who believed that King Kong would make a better president
than Richard Nixon, she remained unequivocal in her belief that
integration should proceed slowly, without the direct interference
of politicians and activists (HB, 253, 404). On a personal level, she
took particular care to remain aloof from the politics of the civil
rights movement. In 1959, for instance, she refused to entertain
James Baldwin in Milledgeville on the grounds that "I observe
the traditions of the society I feed on—it's only fair. Might as well
expect a mule to fly as me to see James Baldwin in Georgia" (HB,
329). O'Connor's conservative philosophical and social orientation
manifests itself throughout the body of her fiction, which is more
overtly concerned with questions of orthodox Christian theology
than with the condition of women or other oppressed groups.

Just as she remained uncomfortable identifying herself as a
woman writer, so too did O'Connor remain reluctant to play the
role of lady in her personal life. Argues Margaret Whitt, "Flannery O'Connor, knowing all too well the role of the Southern lady,
was horrified at the prospect of becoming one," understanding
as she did that the "thinking woman does not wish to be a Southern lady because all too often Southern ladies are associated with
the superficial and the banal." Yet refusing to play the role of

lady was not so simple. As a "dutiful daughter," Whitt concludes, O'Connor understood that she must nevertheless try to "conform to the ways of the Southern world, at least in appearance" ("L," 42–43).[9] Her traditional southern upbringing instilled in her a great respect for the customs of her society, which dictated that "ladies," white women of middle- and upper-class origins, devote themselves to husband, family, and household and cultivate such virtues as compliance, sexual "purity," and the ability to remain at all times cheerfully and politely self-effacing.[10] Throughout her life, as Whitt argues, O'Connor maintained a veneer of conventionality and appeared, at least on the surface, to conform to the social role expected of her.

At the same time, O'Connor discreetly managed to violate many of the rules of conduct imposed on young women of her society, class, and race. Like a number of her fellow intellectuals, she considered pursuing a literary career and leaving the South both natural and inevitable ("A," 17). These plans were cut short only after she was forced home by her first episode of lupus erythematosus. By 1953 her health had stabilized and she was able to resume a regular writing schedule. It had nevertheless become clear that she would never be well enough to leave Andalusia, her mother's farm in Georgia. In later years O'Connor often attributed her growth as an artist to this turn of events. The fact remains, however, that her illness forced her to abandon plans to lead an openly unconventional and independent life ("A," 16). Despite these setbacks and her claims to the contrary, she successfully pursued a vocation that took her far beyond the confines of Milledgeville and afforded her the opportunity to disregard many of the demands that her social role might otherwise have entailed. Quietly rejecting the traditional female role, she overcame many of the limitations that might otherwise have prevented her from finding a literary voice.

An incident that occurred early in O'Connor's career, before illness had forced her return to Georgia, reveals the depth of her professional ambition and illustrates the ways in which she managed to ignore southern codes of feminine behavior when she believed her professional integrity was at stake. As her negotiations with the editors at Rinehart testify, she made it clear that she could not always be expected to remain within the bounds of ladylike behavior if it meant sacrificing her broader goals as an artist. Highly insulted by the "Sears Roebuck Straightshooter" criticism *Wise Blood* received in the hands of editor John Selby, O'Connor wrote to her agent complaining that his report on the novel was "addressed to a slightly dim-witted Camp Fire Girl" (*HB*, 9). In a letter to Selby himself, she clarified her position:

> I can only hope that in the finished novel the direction will be clearer, but I can tell you that I would not like at all to work with you as do other writers on your list. I feel that whatever virtues the novel may have are very much connected with the limitations you mention. . . . In short, I am amenable to criticism but only within the sphere of what I am trying to do; I will not be persuaded to do otherwise. (*HB*, 10)

Hardly the polite, self-effacing, and compliant behavior expected of a southern lady, O'Connor had no reservations about sharply asserting control of her work. The published letters and reminiscences of friends and acquaintances offer an intriguing glimpse into these two different personae—the polite and unassuming young lady and the ambitious writer uncomfortable with the customs of life in a provincial town. James Tate and Father Edward J. Romagosa, neither of whom was particularly close to O'Connor, describe her as a thoroughly conventional young woman. "She was," Tate writes, "the most unobtrusive person I've ever known."[11] By contrast, two of O'Connor's most intimate friends, Betty Boyd Love and Maryat Lee, admit that while she was hardly a "rebel," she was nevertheless out of place in Milledgeville. Love, a college friend, attempts to emphasize O'Connor's conventionality, but her recollections suggest that O'Connor was not entirely comfortable in the social milieu in which she lived. "The Southern butterfly," Love writes, "may not have been her type of social creature, but she never exhibited any personal rebellion against the social conventions whose absurdities she portrayed so well."[12] O'Connor's "conventionality" notwithstanding, Love devotes considerable space in her essay to describing the various qualities that distinguished O'Connor from her neighbors. Noting that she "didn't really enjoy" the various social functions that were a part of Milledgeville's social fabric, Love concludes that O'Connor was a "genuinely unusual individual" who was also, perhaps, just a little "eccentric" ("R," 71).

Less guarded in expressing her views on O'Connor's eccentricities, Lee offers an illuminating account of their first meeting. What she had expected to find in O'Connor was simply "another local lady writer, somewhat prim in dress, stockings, and shiney [*sic*] shoes."[13] While O'Connor's physical appearance did not surprise Lee, her candor about coming to terms with life in the South did:

> Then, unforgettably, she mentioned that lupus had necessitated her permanent return from the East to the South. Her voice was more halting now, as she talked about coming home, suggesting to me that she had wrestled mightily with a morass of confusion, conflict, and depression and had developed an intricate plan so that all the personal and professional problems were resolved harmoniously. ("F," 41)

Describing herself as a "rebel" who opposed the provincial ways of her native region, Lee admits that she saw in O'Connor a kindred spirit. For her part, O'Connor admitted to Lee how uncomfortable her living arrangements sometimes made her feel. "She said that being in the house [Andalusia] didn't contribute to her articulateness. . . . Her ambition was to convert the henhouse into a private office, complete with refrigerator" ("F," 42).

O'Connor's occasional frustration with life at Andalusia surfaced in other ways as well. Although largely dependent on her mother's care, she actively pursued friendships with fellow writers, including, besides Lee, Robert Lowell, Elizabeth Hardwick, Caroline Gordon, Allen Tate, Andrew Lytle, Katherine Anne Porter, Eudora Welty, Robert Penn Warren, Robert Giroux, Robert and Sally Fitzgerald, and Elizabeth Bishop. Not only did many of these people prove crucial in advancing O'Connor's career, but most of them were able to visit her periodically for extended stays, bringing the world of letters to her front door. In turn, when her health permitted, O'Connor traveled extensively, visiting friends and delivering lectures at colleges and symposiums. Although she professed to hate the lecture circuit, family finances, despite the grants she received, required it (*HB*, 472). Her travels, in any case, offered her the opportunity to cultivate a circle of friendships that provided her with a sense of intellectual companionship and no doubt made the restrictions entailed by her illness far more bearable. Perhaps more importantly, such friendships, nurtured by a voluminous correspondence, allowed O'Connor to remain a part both of Milledgeville and of the American literary scene of the day. Able to fulfill her obligations to both, she was never forced to renounce her allegiance to either.

Even so, O'Connor's ongoing attempts to mediate between life in Milledgeville and life as a writer were neither simple nor free of obstacles. While she was able to maintain the illusion of social conformity, certain disjunctions inevitably appeared. Chief among these was her status as an unmarried woman. It would be inaccurate to suggest that the society in which she lived did not tolerate unmarried, or even unconventional, women. Indeed, it may have been quite possible for O'Connor to have openly and unapologetically pursued her professional interests and to simply have accepted whatever disapproval might have ensued. What remains particularly interesting about O'Connor is that, whenever presented with the choice, she invariably decided to create the illusion of conformity. Her decision not to marry is a case in point. Her published letters generally remain silent on the subject, which suggests both that she liked to encourage the impression that her refusal to marry was not the result of deliberate choice, but of her illness, and that marriage was a touchy subject she preferred, if possible, to ignore. Nevertheless, in a letter to "A," the anonymous correspondent with whom O'Connor shared the most personal information ("A," 15), she admitted: "There is a great deal that has to either be given up or be taken away from you if you are going to succeed in writing a body of work. There seem to be other conditions in life that demand celibacy besides the priesthood" (*HB*, 176). Like countless other female writers Adrienne Rich has termed "marriage resisters," O'Connor quietly managed to avoid marriage so that she might be able to devote herself entirely to her work.[14] Keeping her motivations for remaining single largely to herself, she was able, once again, to maintain the illusion of social conformity, delicately balancing the needs of her "muted," resisting, female self with the duties that accompanied her allegiance to "dominant" values.

Despite the apparent ease with which she was able to satisfy the demands of her social role and her artistic drives, O'Connor never fully managed to overcome the conflicting pressures created by her professional and personal roles. The conflicts became particularly acute when her work, as it often did, violated southern codes of propriety. O'Connor, as her correspondence suggests, was concerned that her fiction would offend her mother and other "ladies" in the family. Although she could joke about her mother's insistence that she write a "proper" introduction to *Wise Blood*— so as to keep her cousin Katie from being "shocked"—O'Connor was nevertheless relieved to find that the ladies in her family more often than not found her work boring (*HB*, 33). She explained to one of her correspondents the process by which she finally freed herself of anxieties regarding the issue:

> When I first began to write I was much worried about this thing of scandalizing people, as I fancied that what I wrote was highly inflammatory. I was wrong—it wouldn't even have kept anybody awake, but anyway, thinking this was my problem, I talked to a priest about it.

The first thing he said to me was, "You don't have to write for fifteen-year-old girls." . . . When you write a novel, if you have been honest about it and if your conscience is clear, then it seems to me that you have to leave the rest in God's hands. When the book leaves your hands, it belongs to God. (*HB*, 142–43)

Although she claimed to have resolved her fear regarding the scandalous potential of her work by shifting the responsibility for it from herself to God, O'Connor feared causing offense through her "unladylike" fiction. At the same time, the literary standards she sought to achieve dictated that she cultivate "unladylike" qualities. To achieve a reputation as a serious writer, she could not write the kind of fiction that would satisfy an audience represented by the likes of Cousin Katie. Her ability to write fiction that might prove not only incomprehensible, but shocking, to an audience of ladies became, ironically, one of the driving forces behind her artistic vision and a great source of personal pride as well. O'Connor thus negotiated the conflicting demands of both her status as a writer and as a "dutiful" southern daughter in a way that speaks volumes to the crucial role gender played in her artistic development.

Critics, downplaying the significance of gender in O'Connor's work, have largely accepted the claim that her fiction can be understood solely in Catholic and southern terms. However clear the influence of gender on O'Connor's work may be, most critics, following the lead of O'Connor herself, generally emphasize her allegiances to the Catholic church and to the South.[15] More often than not critics judge the merit of her work according to the value they place upon these particular influences. As Frederick Crews has noted, O'Connor scholars frequently use her fiction to further one of two agendas: proving or disproving the value and effectiveness of orthodox Christianity as a subject for literature, or evaluating the extent to which her work was governed by her status as a southerner.[16] In the years since O'Connor's death, critics have reached a broad consensus regarding the centrality of religion and region to her artistic vision; her fiction, most agree, means little unless these influences are acknowledged first.

Little doubt remains that O'Connor's primary influences, on a conscious level at least, were in fact the South and the Catholic church. Although she readily admitted she had, before the onset of her illness, attempted to "escape" her native region under the impression that "the life of my writing depended on my staying away," she eventually realized that her southern background had become inseparable from her broader artistic vision. "The best of my writing," she concluded, "has been done here" (*HB*, 230). Her loyalty to the Catholic church, on the other hand, had always remained constant. "I am a born Catholic, went to Catholic schools in my early years, and have never left or wanted to leave the Church," she wrote (*HB*, 114). Together with her southern heritage, O'Connor's religious beliefs formed the basis of her artistic vision. "The two circumstances that have given character to my own writing," she concluded, "have been those of being Southern and being Catholic."[17]

To take O'Connor at her word, however, is to diminish the complexities inherent in her relationship to the South and the Catholic church, complexities ultimately related to her status as a woman. Just as she maintained an ambivalent relationship to the gender role prescribed by her society, so too did she maintain an ambivalent relationship to both her religion and her native region. Her Catholic faith, for instance, did not serve merely as the mechanism by which she attempted to understand humanity's relationship to God but, more importantly, as the impetus behind her desire and, indeed, her very ability to write. "I write the way I do because and only because I am a Catholic," she explained. "I feel that if I were not a Catholic, I would have no reason to write, no reason to see, no reason ever to feel horrified or even to enjoy anything. . . . I have never had the sense that being a Catholic is a limit to the freedom of the writer, but just the reverse" (*HB*, 114). Her ability to write was, she concluded, "first of all a gift," and it was her responsibility to use it properly (*HB*, 92). In "The Nature and Aim of Fiction" she explained:

> There is no excuse for anyone to write fiction for public consumption unless he has been called to do so by the presence of a gift. It is the nature of fiction not to be good for much unless it is good in itself. A gift of any kind is a considerable responsibility. It is a mystery in itself, something gratuitous, something wholly undeserved, something whose real uses will probably always be hidden from us.

Although she would not have presumed herself to explain exactly the hidden uses behind her own art, she would admit in the same essay that "the reason I write is to make the reader see what I see . . . writing fiction is primarily a missionary activity" (*MM*, 81). By explaining her creative drives in essentially passive terms as impulses that enjoyed the approval of the highest of masculine authorities—God himself—O'Connor could, in part, resolve the dilemma posed by her gender. Catholicism offered her a means of justifying her desire to write, allowing her to conceive of her work not as a frivolous and misguided usurpation of male privilege, but as a responsibility to which she must faithfully "submit" (*HB*, 126).

O'Connor's relationship to the Catholic church was complicated and strengthened by the need to use her faith as a means of justifying her desire to write; her relationship to the South was complicated by the fear that identifying herself as a "Southern writer" would place certain limitations on her work. Although she often credited her southern background as a source that gave her work vibrancy and meaning, she nevertheless felt highly ambivalent about critics' tendency to use the label "Southern" in association with her work. Concerned that this label placed her in an uncomfortable pigeonhole along with writers such as Carson McCullers, Truman Capote, and Tennessee Williams who belonged to what she termed "The School of Southern Degeneracy," O'Connor often denied that she was really a southern writer. The members of this "school," who in her view wrote primarily for shock value and a northern-based mass market, had, O'Connor frequently noted in her private correspondence, done every southern writer a disservice by leading the general public to associate "Southern" with "grotesque," "Gothic," and "degenerate." In her public lectures on the subject she tended to be circumspect and avoid naming those individuals she considered largely responsible for what she thought of as an unfortunate trend. Yet her message was the same:

> If you are a Southern writer, that label, and all the misconceptions that go with it, is pasted on you at once, and you are left to get it off as best you can. I have found that no matter for what purpose peculiar to your special dramatic needs you use the Southern scene, you are still thought by the general reader to be writing about the South and are judged by the fidelity your fiction has to typical Southern life. (*MM*, 37–38)

O'Connor did not entirely blame individual writers for this situation; they were only, she believed, supplying a commodity that northern readers and critics demanded. A good part of the problem lay in the fact that northern audiences were "as incapable now as on the day they were born of interpreting Southern literature." Only when southern writers could begin to rely on southern audiences to interpret *and* purchase their work, would the label "Southern writer" achieve genuine meaning (*MM*, 55).

O'Connor's ambivalence regarding her status as a regional writer, however, was related not only to her fear of being associated with writers whose talents she considered inferior to her own, but to her fear that she did not necessarily deserve being associated with southern writers whose talents she believed were *superior* to her own. William Faulkner loomed particularly large in this scenario. In public she explained that "the presence alone of Faulkner in our midst makes a great difference in what the writer can and cannot permit himself to do. Nobody wants his mule and wagon stalled on the same track the Dixie Limited is roaring down" (*MM*, 45). In private she admitted that "the real reason I don't read him is because he makes me feel that with my one-cylinder syntax I should quit writing and raise chickens altogether" (*HB*, 292). Other southern writers, particularly the Fugitives and Agrarians, inspired the same feelings of inadequacy. Among the few truly "respectable" writers belonging to the popularly conceived "Southern school," O'Connor wrote, are the Agrarians (*MM*, 28). Although she keenly admired Faulkner's talents, she felt a stronger kinship with writers like John Crowe Ransom, Allen Tate, Andrew Lytle, and Robert Penn Warren, who more closely shared her conservative vision of southern culture and the means by which it could best be conveyed through literature (*HB*, 148).[18] That she shared a common artistic vision with these writers, particularly in regard to the importance of the southern past and the traditions it inspired, only intensified her desire to "measure up" to the literary standards they had established throughout the 1920s and 1930s. Indeed, each of these men exerted a strong influence, both directly and indirectly, on O'Connor's development as a writer. She encountered them either as instructors, guest lecturers, or as the authors of her textbooks at the University of Iowa Writer's Workshop. After her graduation from the workshop, she maintained a particularly close professional relationship with Allen Tate, through his wife Caroline Gordon, who served as O'Connor's postgraduate mentor. To O'Connor, writers like Ransom, Tate, Lytle, Warren and to a lesser extent, Gordon, embodied the standards she should strive to meet.

But because O'Connor accepted the view that religion and art were masculine preserves, she remained acutely uncomfortable with her own desire to become a writer. True, she once admitted that women are not *necessarily* fated to "artistic sterility" since art, as she explained, "is a good deal more than a masculine drive— it is, in part, the accurate naming of the things of God" (*HB*, 126).

Thus a patriarchal God might enable women to overcome what amounts to their "artistic sterility" (*HB*, 99). Yet religious faith alone, as her remarks on "Southern literature" suggest, was not enough to ease O'Connor's insecurities regarding her desire to write. Femininity and literature were, she had been taught by her instructors at Iowa and by mentors such as Caroline Gordon, incompatible. The authors she most admired and whom she believed to have most influenced her work were, with the exception of Gordon, all male: Joseph Conrad, Gustave Flaubert, Nathaniel Hawthorne, Henry James, and the Fugitive/Agrarians.[19] Djuna Barnes, Dorothy Richardson, and Virginia Woolf she regarded as "nuts" (*HB*, 98). "Lady journalists" she described as a "tribe" of which she was "deathly afraid," while "penwomen," female writers who claimed professional status, she dismissed as genteel ladies who wrote "true confession stories with one hand and Sunday school stories with the other" (*HB*, 205, 231). And on another occasion she admitted that she was utterly unable to "talk to" the college "girls" in the audiences to which she lectured (*HB*, 254). In short, O'Connor accepted women's intellectual and artistic inferiority as possibly natural and nearly inevitable and was thus forced to find ways to make herself an exception.

The University of Iowa Writer's Workshop proved the ideal setting for just such a task. During her years there O'Connor worked with some of the most prominent southern writers and critics, and through them she absorbed critical and cultural discourses that only confirmed her desire to transcend her gender. As leading figures in both the Fugitive and Agrarian movements, Ransom, Tate, Lytle, and Warren had been instrumental in laying the foundations for what was later to be known as the "Southern Literary Renaissance." By the time O'Connor entered the workshop in the mid-1940s, they were widely acknowledged as authorities not only on southern literature, but on American literature and criticism as well. One of O'Connor's greatest professional fears centered on her concern that this group of writer/critics would not recognize her as a serious talent and would instead label her simply another "lady writer." As a writer with strong ties to the South, O'Connor was particularly influenced by their ideas regarding the nature of the "Southern Tradition" and its meaning to "Southern Literature." Although Fugitive/Agrarian theories concerning the "Southern Tradition" were neither monolithic nor consistent, certain assumptions regarding race and gender were nevertheless unambiguously pervasive: blacks and women rightfully belonged in the margins of southern culture, and it remained imperative for men like Ransom, Tate, and their associates to restore and maintain the purity of the "Southern Tradition." In short, the Fugitive/Agrarians played a crucial role in assuring that evocations of the "Southern Tradition" would replicate and maintain long-standing hierarchies. Although a number of southern writers rejected such a narrow definition of their literary traditions, these ideas nevertheless governed the politics of the "Southern Literary Renaissance" of the 1930s, 1940s, and 1950s.[20] As her correspondence and published work suggest, O'Connor understood that if she was to earn the respect of those critics who determined the nature of "Southern" and, more broadly, American literature, she would have to do more than use her writing as a means of "naming . . . the things of God": she would have to silence the muted, female voice that characterizes her early manuscripts.

Much of O'Connor's published work suggests that she was highly successful in this endeavor. Indeed, the literary landscape that characterizes much of her published fiction is overwhelmingly masculine in orientation. Although women appear in a number of her short stories, they most often serve as comical examples of peculiarly feminine and irrational forms of behavior that invariably leave them vulnerable to attack.[21] Rare is the adult female character who enjoys narrative respect or who survives unharmed. Among the many characters she created, for example, O'Connor admitted that she truly admired just three, Hazel Motes and the Tarwater prophets of *The Violent Bear It Away*; even the cold-blooded Misfit of "A Good Man Is Hard to Find" she preferred to the harmless and well-intentioned Grandmother he shoots (*HB*, 437). Only those female characters too young to have achieved the status of ladyhood—Mary Fortune in "A View of the Woods," Sally Virginia Cope in "A Circle in the Fire," or the daughter in "A Temple of the Holy Ghost," among others—manage to escape the narrator's satirical glare. Interestingly, the narrator often de-sexes young female characters by refusing to offer their names or by referring to them simply as "the child." In stark contrast to women like Mrs. Hopewell of "Good Country People," these androgynous young female characters usually conduct themselves in a highly "unladylike" manner, cursing and disobeying elders, playing practical jokes, and generally acting like rude and uncontrollable tomboys. By claiming the freedom to defy the conventions of ladyhood, they manage to earn the narrator's respect. Consider, for example, "A Temple of the Holy Ghost." Narrated sympathetically through the perspective of the unnamed protagonist, the story concerns the child's epiphanic realization that she, like the hermaphrodite on display at a local fair, must accept God's will. Significantly, this realization is not accompanied by the usual violence that befalls most of O'Connor's adult female protagonists. Instead, her encounter with grace comes quietly, as she sits in church contemplating the words of the hermaphrodite. Later, the child's face does get "mashed" against a crucifix worn by a nun who symbolically and somewhat enthusiastically welcomes her into the church's embrace.[22] This momentary discomfort, however, pales in comparison to the beatings, maimings, maulings, shootings, heart attacks, and strokes that O'Connor's ladies so often suffer. Indeed, by contrasting the girl's quiet insight into her situation with the unthinking, inane, and stereotypically feminine antics of the two teenagers visiting her home, the narrator implies that it is in fact the child's own lack of ladylike traits that ultimately saves her. Linking her epiphany to the fate of the hermaphrodite, the narrator suggests, finally, that by rejecting the trappings of adult femininity the girl might actually attain the genderless state of grace that no lady can ever possibly know. For O'Connor, "ladyhood" was a comical state at best, a perilous and cursed state at worst. Women who embraced it deserved their fate.

That fate most often involved violence. As critics have long noted, O'Connor's fiction is characterized by extreme forms of violence that few of her characters, male or female, escape. Violence became one of the more obvious methods by which she could ensure that her work would be viewed as anything but ladylike, and it manifests itself not only in the numerous murders, assaults, maimings, and untimely deaths, but also in the narrative tone of her work, which can best be described as combative. As she explained in "The Fiction Writer and His Country," O'Connor wrote under the assumption that she was to confront a "hostile" audience: "When you assume that your audience holds the same beliefs you do," she explained, "you can relax a little and use more normal means of talking to it; when you assume that it does not, then you have to make your vision apparent by shock" (*MM*, 34). O'Connor directed this tone at men and women alike, yet numerous letters reveal that she considered female readers more susceptible to the shocking effect of her writing; she took great pleasure in imagining that her work had insulted the genteel sensibilities of "lady" readers. Early in her career, for example, she wrote to Paul Engle concerning the reception *Wise Blood* had received at Rinehart, who then had O'Connor under contract. "I learned indirectly," she wrote, "that nobody at Rinehart liked the 108 pages but Raney (and whether he likes it or not I couldn't really say) [and] that the ladies there particularly had thought it unpleasant. . . . [This] pleased me" (*HB*, 13). O'Connor considered it a mark of her talents as a serious writer that she was able to offend lady readers. Early in 1952 she proudly relayed evidence that this strategy was a success. "Harcourt sent my book to Evelyn Waugh," she wrote to Robert Lowell, "and his comment was: 'If this is really the unaided work of a young lady, it is a remarkable product'" (*HB*, 35). To claim she had produced a work of art that would have proved impossible for most young ladies was for O'Connor the supreme compliment.

To avoid associating herself with the banalities of ladyhood, O'Connor tried to insult the sensibilities of lady readers, subjected her adult female characters to violence and humiliation, and ignored or omitted them altogether whenever she believed they might detract from her larger purpose. While many of O'Connor's short stories take women as the primary focus, her two novels, which she considered her most important works, are concerned almost exclusively with a few male characters. As her correspondence makes clear, O'Connor hoped that her fiction would be distinguished from that of other women by the way in which it grappled with profound theological and philosophical questions. In particular, she sought to claim status as a writer whose concerns reflected the universality of the human condition in its quest for spiritual understanding and fulfillment.[23] Because she associated the feminine with the particular, the mundane, and the trivial, it became difficult for her to allow her female characters, particularly those who were ladies, to represent the universal, the transcendent, or the spiritually profound. Even in short stories, such as "A Good Man Is Hard to Find" or "Good Country People," in which women seem to embody the theological questions with which O'Connor was concerned, she nevertheless managed to redirect the narrative emphasis away from the recipient of grace toward the agent, who is usually male. The Grandmother in "A Good Man Is Hard to Find," for example, appears to serve as the story's protagonist. It is she, after all, who undergoes a profound spiritual crisis and transformation as she faces death at the hands of the Misfit. Yet the Misfit may nevertheless emerge as the true protagonist; violent as he is, he escapes the satire that the narrator directs at the Grandmother. Furthermore, his unfulfilled quest for faith is ultimately more meaningful than the Grandmother's traumatic encounter with grace, which is dismissed altogether when, after wiping her blood from his glasses, the Misfit announces that she "would of been a good woman . . . if it had been somebody there to shoot her ever minute of her life" (*CW*, 153). As O'Connor explained, he in fact speaks for God in pronouncing judgment on the Grandmother, whose own story nearly becomes lost under the profound weight of her killer's crisis of faith (*HB*, 389). Similarly, in "Good Country People" the power of Hulga's awakening is diminished by the banality of the circumstances in which it occurs. While the Grandmother's encounter with grace is traumatic, Hulga's is merely humiliating. Whatever positive or elevating lessons she might have learned from her experience are lost in the indignity of her realization that she, who holds a Ph.D. in philosophy, has been outsmarted by a buffoon of a man. To add insult to injury, the aptly named Manley Pointer—Bible-thumping, leg-stealing con man that he is—arguably emerges as the more admirable character. Hulga's belief in "nothing," like the Grandmother's belief in Christ, is little more than false bravado. But like the Misfit, Manley Pointer has, as he triumphantly explains to Hulga, "been believing in nothing ever since I was born!" (*CW*, 293). Able to recognize and act upon the logic of his beliefs, he becomes the victor. Stealing her leg and appropriating the sense of identity with which she has invested it, Manley leaves Hulga both literally and figuratively paralyzed, herself reduced to nothing.

O'Connor's unpublished manuscripts offer perhaps the most vivid insights into the process by which she gradually redirected the narrative emphasis of her work away from female characters like Hulga and away from female-oriented plots generally. The manuscripts for her two novels serve as an interesting case study.[24] The published version of *Wise Blood*, for instance, centers on three major characters: Hazel Motes, Enoch Emery, and Asa Hawkes. Although women like Leora Watts and Sabbath Hawkes make appearances in a number of scenes, they remain essentially minor characters who serve largely as obstacles in Haze's path toward spiritual awakening. However, in manuscript versions of the novel, which she revised under the direction of Andrew Lytle, her advisor at Iowa,[25] the female characters, who are quite numerous, serve a different purpose. The changes O'Connor eventually made regarding these characters are revealing. In the manuscripts, for example, Haze's mother and three sisters play prominent roles, while in the published version of the novel, he takes on the role of the lone existential hero, utterly bereft of family and friends. Similarly, in the manuscripts Haze's girlfriend Lea actually rivals him as a protagonist, whereas in the published novel she merely serves, in the role of prostitute Leora Watts, as a temporary antidote to his uncontrollable religious impulses. Interestingly, the Lea who appears in the manuscripts is not a prostitute, but an executive secretary in one series and a beautician in another, an independent woman who, unlike Leora, does not exist merely to serve men. The narrator delves into her past, describing how she was lured to the city by a slick con artist who had promised to marry her, and how she aspires to improve her status in life by becoming her own boss. Most revealing, the narrator describes these events exclusively from Lea's point of view, a radical departure from the novels, which rely exclusively on a male angle of vision.

Still other female characters in the *Wise Blood* manuscripts enjoy the luxury of narrative approval and interest as well. Indeed, the bulk of the manuscripts deal with Haze's sister, Ruby, who is pregnant with a child she wants to abort. O'Connor rewrote these chapters as the short story "A Stroke of Good Fortune," one of the few of her published works that focuses specifically on a uniquely female experience. Significantly, O'Connor more than once mentioned this as her weakest and least favorite story, and she attempted to prevent its publication altogether, referring to it as "farcical" (*HB*, 101). The changes she made in the story reflect O'Connor's discomfort with such women's issues as pregnancy and abortion and her fear that writing about such subjects was inappropriate and would leave her open to ridicule.[26] Similarly, the revisions made on her second novel suggest that she also feared the repercussions associated with directing her satirical wit at male protagonists. By the time she started work on *The Violent Bear It Away*, O'Connor had all but abandoned her earlier interest in female characters. However, she had begun to direct at her male protagonists some of the hostility previously reserved for her lady characters. More specifically, she developed an extended critique of traditional male behavior and of the drive toward fraternization and domination that she identified as the impulse behind organizations such as the Ku Klux Klan and the Masonic Order.[27] Yet just as she must have realized that exploring female experience and consciousness would leave her vulnerable to charges that she was not, in the end, a serious artist, O'Connor must have implicitly understood that such a blatant critique of closed male circles might be received as a feminist challenge to the literary culture in which she worked. Not surprisingly, in revision she transformed *The Violent Bear It Away* into a highly masculinist novel in which such challenges are obscured.

In sum, O'Connor built her reputation on a body of fiction that mocked the particularities and banalities of female experience and conformed to the expectations of a male-dominated and androcentric literary and critical tradition. Importantly, however, O'Connor's suppression of her female voice was, despite her extensive efforts to obscure it altogether, never complete. While both *Wise Blood* and *The Violent Bear It Away* are based on the quest narrative and the *Bildungsroman*, traditionally masculinist narrative forms, the novels defy many of the conventions around which these forms have historically centered. Haze's quest, for example, ends not in the achievement of autonomous manhood but in the disturbing realization that he is the passive instrument of God's will. Similarly, Tarwater's journey into mature adulthood takes him not into the future he desires, but into one God has planned for him. Neither character achieves the independence that so often serves as the organizing purpose behind the male quest narrative and *Bildungsroman* forms. Instead, Haze and Tarwater are both forced to conform to the will of a power greater than their own. In accepting passivity and dependence as their lot, they renounce all claims to a traditional masculine identity and become, in effect, "feminized." O'Connor's male characters, mastered by their God, encounter a loss of autonomous selfhood that resembles patterns explored in more traditional women's literature of the early twentieth century.

Only through a reading of her work that remains sensitive to such gender-related dynamics is it possible to uncover the ways in which O'Connor's fiction might, despite appearances, reflect her female identity. Given her persistent use of strategies that oppose and devalue, rather than celebrate, female experience and consciousness, it remains little wonder that feminist critics have for the most part overlooked O'Connor's work. Yet precisely *because* she chose to rely on aesthetic strategies that involved conscious opposition to the "female," her work particularly lends itself to feminist analysis. Although most of the scholarship on O'Connor would suggest otherwise, studies that focus solely on her southern and Catholic heritage are therefore necessarily limited. It remains impossible to account for the complexities inherent in her personal life and in her relationship to her profession, her religion, and her region without making reference to gender: the ambivalence that characterized these various relationships found its origins in her status as a woman. In the end, an analysis of the ways in which gender influenced O'Connor's artistic development not only offers deeper insight into her relationship to the South and the Catholic church, but provides a new perspective on the complexities and multiplicities of female aesthetics. As O'Connor's response to the literary culture in which she worked suggests, female aesthetic strategies do not always involve overt forms of opposition and subversion. Indeed, it is quite possible for women writers to identify against themselves as a means of undermining masculine claims to artistic privilege. At the same time, O'Connor's fiction suggests that it is also possible for women writers to use masculinist narrative forms and male characters as vehicles for exploring female identity and experience. To be sure, O'Connor consciously avoided the path set by such "nuts" as Virginia Woolf and sought instead to identify herself intellectually and artistically with men. But in so doing she was forced, as her manuscripts in particular testify, to alter radically her literary vision. In the process she developed an aesthetic that, while hardly "feminist," was nevertheless peculiarly "female."

Notes

Versions of this paper were presented at the 1991 Southern American Studies Association and the 1992 American Literature Association conferences. I would like to thank the audiences at both sessions for their helpful comments and questions. I also owe many thanks to Susan V. Donaldson, Esther Lanigan, Colleen Kennedy, Anne Goodwyn Jones, and Bruce McConachie for reading and commenting on earlier versions of this essay. Finally, I would like to express my appreciation to Nancy Davis Bray and the Special Collections staff of the Ina and Dillard Russell Library at Georgia College for their assistance and hospitality.

1. John Crowe Ransom to Andrew Lytle, 25 March 1954, *The Selected Letters of John Crowe Ransom*, ed. Thomas Daniel Young and George Core (Baton Rouge: Louisiana State University Press, 1985), 374.

2. O'Connor was only the second twentieth-century author to appear in the series; Faulkner was the first.

3. Elaine Showalter, "Feminist Criticism in the Wilderness," in *The New Feminist Criticism: Essays on Women, Literature and Theory*, ed. Elaine Showalter (New York: Pantheon Books, 1985), 264.

4. Catherine Belsey, "Constructing the Subject, Deconstructing the Text," in *Feminist Criticism and Social Change: Sex, Class and Race in Literature and Culture*, ed. Judith Newton and Deborah Rosenfelt (New York: Methuen, 1985), 50.

5. Anne Goodwyn Jones, *Tomorrow Is Another Day: The Woman Writer in the South, 1859–1936* (Baton Rouge: Louisiana State University Press, 1981), 39.

6. Flannery O'Connor, *The Habit of Being: Letters of Flannery O'Connor*, ed. Sally Fitzgerald (New York: Random House, 1979), 176. Hereafter *HB*, cited in the text.

7. Margaret Whitt, "Flannery O'Connor's Ladies," *Flannery O'Connor Bulletin* 15 (1986): 42. Hereafter "L," cited in the text.

8. Richard Gilman, "On Flannery O'Connor," in *Conversations with Flannery O'Connor*, ed. Rosemary M. Magee (Jackson: University Press of Mississippi, 1987), 52.

9. Also see Louise Westling, "Flannery O'Connor's Revelations to 'A,'" *Southern Humanities Review* 20 (1986): 15. Hereafter "A," cited in the text.

10. For an overview of the scholarship on southern women, see Anne Firor Scott, *The Southern Lady from Pedestal to Politics, 1830–1930* (Chicago: University of Chicago Press, 1970); Dewey W. Grantham, "History, Mythology, and the Southern Lady," *Southern Literary Journal* 3 (1971): 98–108; Irving H. Bartlett and C. Glenn Cambor, "The History and Psychodynamics of Southern Womanhood," *Women's Studies* 2 (1974): 9–24; *Sex, Race, and the Role of Women in the South,* ed. Joanne Hawks and Sheila Skemp (Jackson: University Press of Mississippi, 1983); Kathryn Seidel, *The Southern Belle in the American Novel* (Gainesville: University Presses of Florida, 1985); *The Web of Southern Social Relations: Women, Family, and Education,* ed. Walter J. Fraser, Jr., R. Frank Saunders, Jr., and Jon L. Wakelyn (Athens: University of Georgia Press, 1985); Maxine P. Atkinson and Jacqueline Boles, "The Shaky Pedestal: Southern Ladies Yesterday and Today," *Southern Studies* 24 (1985): 398–406; Jean E. Friedman, *The Enclosed Garden: Women and Community in the Evangelical South, 1830–1900* (Chapel Hill: University of North Carolina Press, 1985); Elizabeth Fox-Genovese, *Within the Plantation Household: Black and White Women of the Old South* (Chapel Hill: University of North Carolina Press, 1988); *Women in the South: An Anthropological Perspective,* ed. Holly F. Mathews (Athens: University of Georgia Press, 1989); *In Joy and Sorrow: Women, Family, and Marriage in the Victorian South, 1830–1900* (New York: Oxford University Press, 1991). As much of this scholarship suggests, many white southern women simply rejected "ladyhood" or, like O'Connor, managed to develop strategies for violating codes of behavior while at the same time maintaining a superficial image of conformity.

11. James Tate, "An O'Connor Remembrance," *Flannery O'Connor Bulletin* 17 (1988): 66. Also see "An Evolving Friendship: Flannery O'Connor's Correspondence with Father Edward J. Romagosa, S.J.," ed. Sura P. Rath, *Flannery O'Connor Bulletin* 17 (1988): 1–10.

12. Betty Boyd Love, "Recollections of Flannery O'Connor," *Flannery O'Connor Bulletin* 14 (1985): 70. Hereafter "R," cited in the text.

13. Maryat Lee, "Flannery, 1957," *Flannery O'Connor Bulletin* 5 (1976): 40. Hereafter "F," cited in the text.

14. Adrienne Rich, "Compulsory Heterosexuality and Lesbian Existence," in *The Signs Reader: Women, Gender and Scholarship,* ed. Elizabeth Abel and Emily K. Abel (Chicago: University of Chicago Press, 1983), 63–164.

15. For an overview, see John Hawkes, "Flannery O'Connor's Devil," *Sewanee Review* 70 (1962): 395–402 and O'Connor to John Hawkes, 5 April 1962, *HB,* 470–71; Martha Stevens, *The Question of Flannery O'Connor* (Baton Rouge: Louisiana State University Press, 1973); Edward Kessler, *Flannery O'Connor and the Language of the Apocalypse* (Princeton: Princeton University Press, 1986); Leon V. Driskell and Joan T. Brittain, *The Eternal Crossroads: The Art of Flannery O'Connor* (Louisville: University Press of Kentucky, 1971); Dorothy Walters, *Flannery O'Connor* (New York: Twayne, 1973); Marshall Bruce Gentry, *Flannery O'Connor's Religion of the Grotesque* (Oxford: University Press of Mississippi, 1986); Jill P. Baumgaertner, *Flannery O'Connor: A Proper Scaring* (Wheaton, Ill.: Shaw, 1988); and Robert H. Brinkmeyer, Jr., *The Art and Vision of Flannery O'Connor* (Baton Rouge: Louisiana State University Press, 1989).

16. Frederick Crews, "The Power of Flannery O'Connor," *The New York Review of Books* 37 (1990): 51.

17. Flannery O'Connor, "The Catholic Novelist in the Protestant South," in *Mystery and Manners,* ed. Sally Fitzgerald and Robert Fitzgerald (New York: Farrar, Straus & Giroux, 1969), 196. Hereafter *MM,* cited in text.

18. James Tate recalls: "We talked about the Fugitives a lot. She liked them. She said all of them had something to contribute. And, of course, she meant the Agrarians, too." Tate, "An O'Connor Remembrance," 68.

19. A close look at Lytle's role in the *Wise Blood* revisions makes it clear that O'Connor's graduate training played an important role in her decision to efface her female literary identity. He began to oversee her work in 1948, and by the following year nearly all of the female characters and female-oriented plot lines had been abandoned. As her advisor, Lytle no doubt played a crucial role in encouraging, or at the very least supporting, O'Connor's decision to omit such material. Both her graduate training and her association with Lytle and the literary establishment he represented would continue to influence O'Connor throughout her career. For more on Gordon's role as O'Connor's mentor, see Veronica Makowsky, *Caroline Gordon: A Biography* (New York: Oxford University Press, 1989) and "A Master Class: From the Correspondence of Caroline Gordon and Flannery O'Connor," ed. Sally Fitzgerald, *Georgia Review* 33 (1979).

20. See Susan V. Donaldson, "Gender and the Profession of Letters in the South," in *Rewriting the South: History and Fiction,* ed. Lothar Honninghausen (Tübingen: Francke, 1993) and "Songs with a Difference: Beatrice Ravenel and the Detritus of Southern History," in *The Female Tradition in Southern Literature,* ed. Carol S. Manning (Urbana: University of Illinois Press, 1993).

21. For more on O'Connor's hostile treatment of female characters, see Louise Westling, *Sacred Groves and Ravaged Gardens: The Fiction of Eudora Welty, Carson McCullers, and Flannery O'Connor* (Athens: University of Georgia Press, 1985) and Martha Chew, "Flannery O'Connor's Double-Edged Satire: The Idiot Daughter vs. the Lady Ph.D.," *Southern Quarterly* 19 (1981): 17–25.

22. Flannery O'Connor, "A Temple of the Holy Ghost," in *Collected Works* (New York: The Library of America, 1988), 209. Subsequent citations of her fiction are from the same volume. Hereafter *CW*, cited in the text.

23. "Plans for Work," undated, The Flannery O'Connor Manuscript Collection, Ina and Russell Dillard Library, Georgia College, Milledgeville, Georgia.

24. The surviving manuscripts for the novels, which are housed at Georgia College in Milledgeville, are not organized into separate, discrete versions, nor are they arranged chronologically. Because O'Connor kept few records, the manuscripts for *Wise Blood* and *The Violent Bear It Away* have instead been catalogued thematically to follow the chapter-by-chapter format of the published novels. The material pertaining to each chapter or thematic section of the manuscripts is arranged in folders: one hundred and twenty-nine for *Wise Blood* and thirty-three for *The Violent Bear It Away.* For a summary of the manuscripts and their contents, see Stephen G. Driggers, Robert J. Dunn, and Sarah Gordon, *The Manuscripts of Flannery O'Connor at Georgia College* (Athens: University of Georgia Press, 1989).

25. Sally Fitzgerald, "Chronology," in *Collected Works,* 1242.

26. Folders 25–134, O'Connor Manuscript Collection.

27. Folders 163–71, O'Connor Manuscript Collection.

"Too Positive a Shape Not to Be Hurt": *Go Down, Moses,* History, and the Woman Artist in Eudora Welty's *The Golden Apples*

Barbara Ladd
Emory University

DESPITE the work of a number of scholars who have shown Eudora Welty's fiction to be deeply grounded in history, there persists a tendency to read Welty as an "ahistorical" writer.[1] In the words of one reader: "Miss Welty is concerned . . . with . . . the interaction of a single consciousness with each unique moment of passing time, . . . not with the historical effect or the social consciousness that evolves from a continuum of time's changes."[2] Reasons for this assessment are complex but, judging from the published reviews and interviews with Welty, one might suggest that the two predominant reasons are gender in general and William Faulkner in particular—and that the general and the particular are intricately connected. One reviewer suggests that Welty made a conscious decision, in order to clear a space for her own voice, to stay out of the Dixie Special's territory, i.e., to avoid History—the assumption being that History belongs to William Faulkner and that Welty knows her place.[3] Ironically, one could ask for no clearer evidence for the profoundly historical nature of the putatively ahistorical than this, particularly where ideologies of gender and history are concerned.

Joan Kelly identifies ideology about women as one of the criteria for determining the status of women in a particular era; certainly the ideology of female authorship is one of the criteria for determining the reception and assigning of place to women artists in a particular era.[4] Leslie Fiedler, for example, writing in the mid-sixties, defines post-Faulkner southern writers as descendants of

Faulkner the father and then divides them into two camps according to gender; one has "the masculine Faulknerians" who are concerned with "complex moral and social problems," and the other has the "distaff Faulknerians" who are defined by the absence of "vigor" (which is "masculine") and by a devotion to the "delicate nuances of sensibility."[5] This is a familiar story which recapitulates patriarchal ideology in familiar ways, and I won't belabor it. The consequence, however, is obvious—women artists were not (and are not) likely to be written into literary History in any more satisfactory way than they are written into official political, economic, or intellectual History. Furthermore, literary history has more often than not been written according to a masculine psychological paradigm (a reality that both Fiedler's and Harold Bloom's work shows very clearly in its appropriation of the Oedipal story as the model within which to define the male writer's "anxiety of influence") and, for that reason, a woman artist, Eudora Welty for example, for whom the male Oedipal paradigm does not work, will not likely be identified as a competitor for the literary status or stature of any male predecessor; she is not likely to be identified even as a player in the same game.[6] More likely, the relationship of a woman artist to the male master will be seen in ways that mirror the expected domestic relationships between men and women in a patriarchal culture—that is, she will be seen as an intellectual or artistic mother, wife, mistress, sister, aunt, or, more tellingly, daughter of the master. She might be given a room of her own (a small one, in the back of the house), but she is likely to be written into literary History in the name of the father. Any analysis of the work of women writers must, I think, take this reality into account.

But the reality of female resistance to this male-centered discourse must also be taken into account. In this specific instance, the woman author, in spite of the reluctance of some interviewers to believe her, has often insisted that she writes from beyond any shadow of Faulkner's influence:

> I'm asked how I could have written a word with William Faulkner living in Mississippi, and this question amazes me. It was like living near a big mountain, something majestic—it made me happy to know it was there, all that work of his life. But it wasn't a helping or hindering presence. Its magnitude, all by itself, made it something remote in my own working life. When I thought of Faulkner it was when I read.[7]

What Welty makes very clear here and in many other interviews is that she assumes, fairly enough, that when she is asked about Faulkner's "influence," she is really being asked about whether she "emulated" him as a literary master. She did not, she says again and again. "Heavens!" she said in 1978, "I would hate to be assigned: 'try to write something influenced by Faulkner.' My pen would drop from my hand."[8]

Apart from "emulation," however, the issue of influence is one that remains of some concern to those of us interested in literary history, in the development—or the directions of movement—of specific literatures. Granting Welty's insistence that she never emulated Faulkner, her work's relationship to his remains of some interest to the extent that it seems to have provided Welty with an occasion for the launching of her own deeply, albeit subtly, historicized literary ventures. Her decision is not so much to avoid History out of deference to Faulkner or to the conventions of gender role as to relocate, to center, the woman's voice with respect to official History, to make the Historically invisible woman visible, to make silence speak—and speak in ways that undermine the ideologies of gender, particularly the ideologies of gender and authorship.[9] Many readers over the years have discussed the ways in which some of Welty's early stories like "The Burning" and "Clytie" echo certain themes and attitudes that someone interested in diminishing Welty might call Faulknerian. More recently, however, Peter Schmidt has made a convincing case for "Asphodel" as parody—which is very different from echo—of *Absalom, Absalom!* The story, he points out, centers upon the return of three unmarried ladies to the decayed mansion formerly held by Mr. Don McInnis, an infamous fellow remarkably like a Thomas Sutpen relieved of the burdens and justifications of History. While there, "they discover to their horror" that Mr. Don is still living in, or about, the house. Soon the renowned proprietor—naked as a jaybird—jumps out at them and chases them off. As Schmidt notes, the comic inversion of Faulkner's tragic plot results in an almost "slapstick" version of *Absalom, Absalom!* and the conclusion he draws is that Welty, at this fairly early stage of her career, "appears to have needed to confront the power of Faulkner as a predecessor before she could invent a new form of comedy for herself."[10]

There are other instances where Welty is confronting—and not being chased off by—the power of this particular predecessor. In "A Worn Path," Welty tells the story of an old woman who undertakes a journey from the Natchez Trace into Jackson, Mississippi, in order to get the "soothing medicine" required by her little grandson, who swallowed lye a few years before and who presents "an obstinate case," his throat closing up every now and then and leaving him unable to talk or to breathe. On her journey, Phoenix, whose eyesight is not good and who carries the shape of a tree etched in wrinkles on her forehead, talks to herself, indulges herself in dreams of servants delivering pastry, does mock heroic battle with imaginary enemies, is threatened (she feels threatened) by the appearance of a hunter with gun and dog, tricks him and steals from him a coin that drops from his pocket when he decides to show off for her. She finally makes it into Jackson and into the doctor's office, but she almost immediately lapses into a kind of stupor, forgetting why she came. She does remember, after awhile. When Phoenix gets the medicine, and a nickel from the nurse, she decides that she is going to put her coins together to buy a gift for her grandson, a little paper windmill. She is going to march right back home carrying that windmill upright in her hand. He won't believe the world contains such wonders. The last reference in the story is to the sound of the old woman's footsteps, "going down."[11]

The evocations of the end of *Absalom, Absalom!* are subtle, but it seems to me that Old Phoenix Jackson enacts a complex, and highly satirical, rewriting of that text. On the one hand, she and her grandson appear to be subversive reprisals of Clytie and Jim Bond at the burning of Sutpen's Hundred. In Welty's text, however, the figure decentered in Faulkner turns out to be the speaker, the storyteller, and her story turns on a derisive, satirical, revisioning of Sutpen's dreams, and on her own survival. For example, Welty's decision to name her protagonist after the phoenix that rises from its death by fire seems to be a variation played upon the attempted destruction of Sutpen's dynasty (transformed here into a treelike pattern of wrinkles on the old woman's forehead)—and the death of Clytie—by fire. The silent and beloved grandson of "A Worn Path" seems no less a subversive comment upon the howling and tragically alienated Jim Bond, the paper windmill that Phoenix imagines carrying to him a devastatingly satiric recapitulation of Sutpen's dreams of power.

For all the intriguing parallels between Welty's "A Worn Path" and Faulkner's *Absalom, Absalom!,* however, "A Worn Path" could never be called "Faulknerian.". The high seriousness and self-conscious historicizing of *Absalom, Absalom!*—all of the insignia of authorial mastery, or transcendence—are simply, and very deliberately, erased by "A Worn Path," the watchful Clytie displaced

by the persistent, but forgetful, figure of Old Phoenix, the longed-
for dynasty displaced by a pattern of wrinkles on an old woman's
face, the tragic ruins of Sutpen's Design displaced by the paper
windmill, the howling Jim Bond displaced by a child silenced by
the swallowing of (a) lye. This pattern of displacement is deeply
functional, for it shifts the perspective to foreground the experiential reality of a black and female figure, the kind of figure who,
in Faulkner's story as in official History, is hardly more than the
decentered guardian of the remains of the male body.

Through such revisions, "A Worn Path" subverts the Faulknerian preoccupation with official cultural memory, or the attempted
reconstruction of the History of the Old South. Unlike Faulkner
Welty is concerned not so much with the construction or reconstruction of the tragic public History of the South—although the
official History of the South is there in every scene—as with the
devotion—and the forgetfulness—of a solitary old woman shaped
by but strategically indifferent to that History.[12] In that way, "A
Worn Path" articulates the resistance of the female—and black—
figure to a male-identified History. Welty makes it very clear indeed that even though the official History of the Old South does
not belong to, or constitute, the likes of Welty's Phoenix, at least
not in the way it belongs to—or constitutes—Faulkner's Clytie
(who is defined according to the economy of official Historical
storytelling in terms of her connections to the Sutpen family),
Phoenix does inhabit that History. The main thing is that her
tenancy in History is a defiant one to the extent that Phoenix's
devotion to the mute grandchild, itself a resistant rewriting of
Clytie's devotion to Henry Sutpen, is a devotion of absolutely no
use to the official cultural History of the South, since the devotion
of most interest to that History has been the devotion (or lack of
it) of the black servant to her white charge.

More importantly, Phoenix Jackson is a representation of the
woman author herself in her own capacity for creative resistance.
In *The Eye of the Story,* Welty suggests that it is important for *authors*
to be "obstructionists," to write as if "they held back their own best
interests—or what would be in *another writer* their best interests"
(emphasis mine), and she associates literary beauty with "reti-
cence" and with "stubbornness."[13] Whereas Ruth Vande Kieft
understands Welty's use of obstruction within the context of those
"mysteries of the inner life" which constitute "what is secret, concealed, inviolable in any human being," I should like to shift perspective just a bit to point out that such obstructionism might also
be seen as a gender-based strategy for resisting the determina-

tions of literary History and of particular—chiefly male—prede-
cessors.[14] Within this context, Old Phoenix may be one of Welty's
first, and most resonant, representations of the woman storyteller
or artist in a patriarchal order, but an interest in female storytellers like this one, women whose attitude toward History (and
histories, stories of all kinds) can be described as resistant—forgetful, indifferent, or "obstructionist"—will remain with Welty.
One might chart a line of descent connecting Phoenix to "Sister"
of "Why I Live at the P. O." to Ellen Fairchild to Virgie Rainey to
Gloria Renfrow to Laurel McKelva Hand as singularly, and crea-
tively, resistant speakers. To say, however, that these characters are
resistant in the face of History is not to suggest that Welty ignores
History. Instead, Welty's strategies for resituating the traditionally
marginalized female figure in the center, or foreground, of a narrative and her use of indifference or forgetfulness or obstructionism with respect to official cultural Histories ought to be read in
relation to those narratives and not as an independent substitute
for them or for the history they construct. Welty's obstructionist
strategies are, in other words, meaningful by virtue of being relational—and they are the perfect means for revealing the hidden
history of women, as well as the mechanisms of that concealment.

In 1942, only seven years before the publication of *The Golden
Apples*, Faulkner had published *Go Down, Moses* and until 1946,
when Malcolm Cowley brought out *The Portable Faulkner*, that was
virtually the only Faulkner in print. It may be partly for this
reason that *Go Down, Moses* forms the largest part of the literary
backdrop or counterpoint for Welty's own most ambitious work
of that decade—the story of Isaac McCaslin's search for himself
through the pursuit of his fathers seems to provide a configuration against which Welty's counternarrative of female development takes shape. It may also be true that a growing sense of the
literary value of obstructionist resistance may be at the bottom of
her insistence that *The Golden Apples* should be read as a cycle of
short stories rather than another novel, for she had been pres-
sured throughout the early 1940s to move from the short story
into the supposedly more capacious (and certainly more lucrative)
form of the novel, and she herself had, in 1941, called attention
to the "gendered" nature of the discourse about novel-writing
when she wrote to Diarmuid Russell that she might be unable to
get beyond her fear of the novel form: "When I only think of a
novel, it scares me. *I never wanted to be contrary*, but it is the natural
thing for me to do what I can within a lesser space. I suspect that

that comes from my being a female, and is permanent."[15] Of course she went on to publish her first novel, *Delta Wedding*, little more than five years later, and by the time she began *The Golden Apples*, Welty seems much more confident but also much more aware of the value of "contrariety," conceptually related, after all, to "obstructiveness." Certainly her growing sense of the uses of obstructionism may also be evidence of her commitment to exploring the development of, and constrictions upon, the female artist within a form that (in her mind, at least) recapitulates, textually, the contextual constrictions of gender. In any event, Welty launches in *The Golden Apples* an intriguing, and powerful, subversion of the patriarchal aesthetic that governs *Go Down, Moses*. She does so by decentering a privileged and masculine version of History and by embracing the possibilities, rather than the horrors, of sexual, domestic, and literary transgressions. Where the characters of *Go Down, Moses* (like the personages in many political, economic, and cultural Histories and in most novels written in the liberal or progressive tradition) are preoccupied with legitimacy, rights of male succession, and redemption from the sins of the fathers, *The Golden Apples* is constructed around illegitimacy or alienation, broken or denied lines of succession, and strategic indifference to the doings of one's ancestors. Such reconstruction signifies upon the manifestation of female desire, often called "vaunting" in Welty's work, in the patriarchal context.

Simone de Beauvoir writes in *The Second Sex* that women "have no past, no history," but women do possess a history, although it is largely hidden, available mainly through circuitous channels of private documents; indirect, tangential, or extraneous references in official History; and the most common records of birth, marriage, and death.[16] Consistent with this realty, Welty's recentering of the female authorial voice in *The Golden Apples*, her resituation of women with respect to official History, and her recovery of women's history are undertaken through circuity, but Welty's reappropriation of women's history and women's voices also signifies at almost every turn upon official History, especially as it is realized in *Go Down, Moses*.

Indicative of Welty's resistance to official or patriarchal historical narrative is the fact that the temporal scope of *The Golden Apples* is considerably more condensed than the scope of *Go Down, Moses*. In other words, Faulkner's work spans more generations than Welty's. In *The Golden Apples*, the youngest generation coexists with the oldest. This difference in temporal scope has a profound effect on the transmission of story. Stories are formal-

ized and contained in *Go Down, Moses,* i.e, stories are deliberately
told and deliberately attended to by the listener. In this sense
History is claimed by the listener who is, in turn, claimed by History. Such is not the case in *The Golden Apples.* For example, when
the children of "The Wanderers" attend the funeral of the character whose voice first introduces us to the world of Morgana, Mrs.
Kate Rainey, they seem wonderfully oblivious to the stories—some
partial, some misrepresentations—that are being told of the dead
woman whose own voice, as narrator/gossip of "Shower of Gold,"
has shaped the fictional community of which they are a part.
Could one imagine Ike McCaslin *not* listening with his whole being
to everything that is being said. It is this indifference, the possibility that at any moment a certain character might fly off in another
direction, not "hear" the rest of the story, escape History if only
for a moment, that constitutes one of the "obstructions" upon
which Welty constructs her, very historical, stories. Of course,
characters never do fly away to disappear entirely, and even children do hear stories of old people and dead ones. At one point,
Virgie Rainey—devoted to what Albert Devlin calls "the work of
historical recovery"[17]—stops a little girl wearing lizard earrings
(real lizards) to ask how she makes the tiny things hold on to her
ears. "Press their heads," the little girl answers "languidly, over
her shoulder."[18] The "over the shoulder" remark, the comic turn,
characterizes Welty's style, but more importantly the transformation of the stories that are circulating around the child into a pair
of earrings that she displays casually, a grotesque adornment, is
essentially Weltian, and a satirical displacing of Faulknerian History from the constitutive to the ornamental.

This tendency to portray official History as something "worn"
upon the body (as Phoenix Jackson and her grandson as well as
the little girl in the above scene "wear" the History of the South
on their bodies) rather than as something that constitutes the
body is, of course, largely shaped by race and gender, the most
Historical of concepts. Faulkner's white and male speakers, Ike
McCaslin for example, politically and economically empowered,
own—and are owned by—the political and economic History of
the South. Legitimacy and entitlement by law are, of consequence,
central to Faulkner's discourse in *Go Down, Moses* and most of his
other major works. On the other hand, Welty's most important
female characters are hardly so central as agents for the political
and economic institutions that have dressed them and others with
respect to power and money. Consistent with this realty, many
of the most important of Welty's young female characters are

unfathered in one sense or another—some are orphans, some are working-class girls like Virgie Rainey, but even the respectable "town girls" like Nina Carmichael, Cassie Morrison, and Jinny Love Stark are in no position to lay claim to a paternally derived inheritance that might empower them as agents of History. Nevertheless, although Welty populates Morgana with strong female characters of all classes, a close look at those characters who are the most autonomous, the most imaginative, the most central to Welty's narrative of female "vaunting," or female desire—Mattie Will Sojourner, Miss Eckhart, Easter/Esther, Virgie Rainey herself—reveals that they are not so often the daughters of Morgana's prominent families as "outsiders" like Phoenix Jackson, representatives of the rural "folk," of the working class, or "de-classed" in some sense (as Miss Eckhart is by having no husband and by teaching music, an occupation that earns her the name "Miss Do-Daddle," no doubt to signify that she has no real business). They are, in other words, women whose own cultural "legitimacy," ensured in a patriarchal culture through a woman's identification as property of the father or husband, i.e., member of a male-headed family, is problematic. Whereas Faulkner is preoccupied with the burdens of legitimacy and inheritance, alienation and disinheritance—chiefly of women—are more to the point of Welty's discourse, and in focusing on the desire of those women who are the most alienated and the most deeply disinherited by patriarchy, she opens a window onto the social order that marginalizes them and on the mechanisms of that marginalization.

Perhaps the story in *The Golden Apples* that most clearly rewrites Faulkner is "Moon Lake," an account of the visit of a group of town girls and a group of orphans to a summer camp not far from Morgana and a story that recapitulates, with some very significant differences, the story of Ike's coming of age at Major De Spain's hunting camp. In a sense, Welty's summer camp for girls is a kind of ironic reprisal of that hunting camp, the base from which Ike, the most direct male descendant of the male "original," can explore the boundaries of his all-male community and his ties to History. It is here that he acquires the skills necessary to becoming the best hunter in Yoknapatawpha. In *Go Down, Moses*, this legitimate son takes his gun and goes hunting for his paternal origins, and he might be said to find these origins through the mediation of certain totemic animals, particularly Old Ben, the renowned bear who carries within himself more wounds than seem consistent with his continued life and health. The trouble with Ike is that he refuses, or is unable, to own his inheritance once he finds it. When faced with a clear shot at Old Ben, he falters and does not shoot. There is admittedly a difference of opinion as to the meaning of this scene, but it would seem to establish itself—along with Ike's discovery, in the summer before, of information about his grandfather's incestuous relationship with his slave daughter— as the determining moment in Ike's life, a metaphor for the necessary repudiation of inheritance that he hopes will begin to redeem him, and the land, of the curse left upon it by the originating pater familias.

Welty's heroines, of course, have no comparable inheritance to claim or to repudiate. But Welty has situated "Moon Lake" at the time of the increasing popularity of girls' summer camps, where they would (said the rhetoric) learn to follow a trail, to cook over open fires, to paddle canoes—but above all to swim, a skill that was promoted as a "survival technique." The irony of the summer camp at Moon Lake, of course, is that "the camp ideal" and the camp reality do not mesh. The girls go through the forms of entering the water, singing "Good morning, Mr. Dup, Dup, Dup" with Miss Gruenwald, their counselor and a Yankee, but no one takes the lessons very seriously.[19] Surrounding the sex-segregated camp, there are men and boys to do the things that girls "can't" do—to swim, to play the bugle, to save drowned orphans. But Welty makes it very clear that the presence of men and boys is not entirely benevolent—there is, after all, "On fine days . . . the danger of some sad meeting, the positive danger of it" ("ML," 107). A black fisherwoman, Twosie, tries to warn the girl campers in "Moon Lake" of the presence in the woods surrounding the camp of a man "with great big gun" ("ML," 107), but it is not until much later in the story that the girls develop some sense that a figurative gun might be aimed at them. When Easter, the head orphan, attempts to dive into the lake, her heel is given "the tenderest, obscurist little brush" by Exum, the young son of the camp cook, and Easter, or Esther (as she herself writes her name), a female Goliath, "dropped like one hit in the head by a stone from a sling" ("ML," 125). Easter doesn't resurface, and it is only through the efforts of Loch Morrison, the Boy Scout, that she is rescued from the water. The girl campers, however, are not entirely committed to the rescue of Easter; they seem to sense some violation of her (and of themselves) in the efforts to save her life. "I'm so tired!" one girl says after awhile; "My arms are about to break, you all," says another (a girl who had helped to carry Easter's arms in her own to the picnic table where Loch would perform mouth-to-mouth resuscitation); "Wish she'd go ahead and die and get it over with," says Little Sister Spights; "I give up," says Jinny Love Stark ("ML," 134). The girls' wish for, or concurrence in, Easter's death as she lies unconscious under the life-saving efforts of the Boy Scout is less an expression of childish cruelty or thoughtlessness, I think, than an indication of their own very clear sense of shared violation. It is more than anything else an expression of ego-protectiveness, their disparagement of Loch Morrison's pride after he brings Easter around understandable as jealousy, and their denigration of the "minnowy thing that matched his candle flame" as they watch him stand later that night naked in the door of his tent a testament to their new realization that to be female is to be the victim and not the hero ("ML," 138).[20] In a text that privileges the "vaunting" of any figure, they, too, want badly to "shine forth" as Loch Morrison does after his rescue of the orphan, but Welty makes it very clear that the conventions of their community are not going to permit them to do so. In "Moon Lake," the girls' summer camp offers no real challenge for the testing of one's survival abilities, but is only a theater for the dramatic presentation of a girl's growing up within a patriarchal order as loss, a stage upon which is shown the girl's fall into a deathlike passivity from which she is "resurrected" into womanhood by a "life-saving" effort that looks a lot like rape.

But if "Moon Lake" is a dramatization of the way the patriarchal order requires, as a necessary stage in the ascent of the son to the status of the father, the reduction of the female subject to object, it is also a protest. Many have observed that *The Golden Apples* is thematically an exploration of the development (in some cases) and constriction (in others) of the woman artist, particularly as she functions as a representation of woman desiring. In addition to Easter/Esther who insists upon writing her own name in her own way and whose "fall" is an allegory of the reduction of the female writer to the body which is written upon, there is Miss Eckhart, transformed by the playing of Beethoven, but finally abandoned and mad; Cassie Morrison, so fascinated by art and so frightened at the same time; her mother who "could have *sung!*" but commits suicide instead;[21] and finally Virgie Rainey— the most talented of these women—who seems to attain, by the end of "The Wanderers," an autonomy that so many of the others seek and fail to find. (Not only can Virgie swim, she swims naked.) But it is important to add that throughout *The Golden Apples*, the female aspirants seek "author"-ity in a culture that defines authorship in terms of paternity rather than maternity, that situates literary and cultural "authority" chiefly in male bodies, that defines "female" chiefly as the object of male desire or loathing. Furthermore, as "Moon Lake" shows so clearly, the impact of patriarchal desire and of the male body upon these female aspirants is inescapable (as the impact of *Go Down, Moses* on Welty's text is inescapable), although each character comes to terms with patriarchal power in different ways and some survive to reappear in the text while others are sacrificed to History. From Mrs. Kate Rainey and Mattie Will Sojourner, who are early manifestations of the restive female imagination, to Virgie Rainey, the final manifestation of female "vaunting" in this text, female questers in *The Golden Apples* seek out "author"-ity in different ways and with different degrees of complicity with and rebellion against their appropriation by the patriarch.[22]

The nature of this appropriation of the female aspirant, its costs for her, and her opportunities for resistance are again represented in "Music from Spain." Although I do recognize that "Music from Spain" is, on the most obvious level, the story of a male protagonist, Eugene MacLain, and his pursuit of the guitarist Bartolome Montalbano through the streets of San Francisco as part of his own pursuit of the imagined autonomy of the father, the story contains an equal if very different relevance for the story of female vaunting as it is developed in the stories of Mattie Will Sojourner, Easter/Esther, Miss Eckhart, and finally Virgie Rainey. To the extent that one consents to read this story solely as Eugene MacLain's story, i.e,. as the story of the male child's unresolved Oedipal conflict, one might argue—as Schmidt does— that Montalbano becomes a fitting object for Eugene's chaotically intermingled emotions of love and rage, a representation of both maternal and paternal power, and a manifestation of Eugene's desire for both possession and repudiation of parental authority (*HS*, 73). But the relevance of this story, and of the figure of the Spanish guitarist, is not solely for the legitimate son of King MacLain; Montalbano is equally, if more indirectly, significant to the story of female aspiration in *The Golden Apples*, and within *that* story his role is somewhat different. Whereas for the male child, Montalbano is "the perfect being to catch up with," a powerful recapitulation of the absent King MacLain in comfortable and unchallenged possession of the insignia of maternal authority (the hair, the fingernails, the wide mouth), for the female child he represents devastation.[23] It is significant to Welty's exploration of the impact of the patriarchal ethos upon female desire in *The*

Golden Apples that Eugene MacLain, the legitimate son of King MacLain in search of his own power, leaves in his wake the scattered appurtenances and apportionments of female authority. At one point he notes a tramp watching beefs being unloaded into a butcher's "leering like a dandy at each one of the carcasses as it went by; it could have been some haughty and spurning woman he kept catching like that" ("MS," 165); at another shop "filets of sole [are] fixed this way and that . . . as in a plait, like cut-off golden hair" ("MS," 167); at a sideshow a hawker intones "'Have-you-seen-Em-ma?' in a voice so tired it gave the effect of down-right menace" ("MS," 175); at another moment, Eugene recalls a freak he had paid Sunday school money to see as a child, but "Thelma was an optical illusion, a woman's head on top of a step-ladder; and she had been golden-haired and young, and had smiled invitingly" ("MS," 175); later, a "dumpy little woman tripped forward on high heels into the street" and right into the path of a streetcar ("MS," 181). A psychoanalyst might point out that it is consistent with male Oedipal experience that in struggling for, and attaining, an identification with the father and the father's power in a patriarchal culture, in becoming the patriarch, the male child does attempt to do some violence to the power of the mother, render her unimportant, contemptible, or monstrous. In a sense he, like Eugene, builds his fine day upon that violent displacement of her authority.

There is no more effective evocation of this psychological reality, particularly as it is relevant to the woman artist, than the text's pairing, for the briefest of moments, of a patriarchal "male body"—i.e., the Spanish artist's—with the vision of an exotic woman dressed in "humble brown," but who seems to Eugene to have been "marked as a butterfly is, over all her visible skin. . . . [with] [c]urves, scrolls, dark brown areas over light brown . . . as if by design." Not only is the oddly marked woman a stranger, "a Negro or a Polynesian" and someone who "would be considered disfigured by most people," she has called attention to herself by wearing an "exotic" hat, "with curving bright feathers about her head." Her audacity inspires in Eugene the thought of

> a disgrace or sadness that had to be as ever-present as the skin is, of hiding and flaunting together. It was so strong an aura that by softly whistling Eugene pretended to people around that the woman was not there, and tried to keep the Spaniard from seeing her. For he might pounce upon her; something made him afraid of the Spaniard at that moment. ("MS," 174)

This is a remarkable moment in *The Golden Apples*. That Eugene MacLain, whose imagination is preoccupied with scenes of violence against women and whose own liberating excursion is begun by slapping his wife's face, should be so "protective" at this moment toward this particular woman would seem to be out of character—except for the fact that Eugene's situation as a male character in search of his own enabling father may have made him particularly sensible of the violence done to women in that transaction through which the male child becomes the father. Of chiefest significance, however, is that his impulse is to "hide" her in what amounts to an acknowledgment of his own complicity in and need for the violence. In other words, if the transgression into visibility of that which has been camouflaged or displaced by a patriarchal power strikes Eugene MacLain as "disgraceful," that return and its repression is nevertheless necessary to his agenda of resuscitating the patriarchal discourse which legitimizes him. But in the light of Welty's interest in exploring women's resistance within patriarchal discourse, the transformation of what should be (if we pay attention to the butterfly analogy) the camouflaging "design" or inscription into an attention-getting display calls the reader's attention once again to the trope of "invisibility-made-visible" or "silence-made-to-speak" not only as it concerns the return of the displaced within Eugene's text but as it concerns the manifestations of female desire in a patriarchal context.

Welty is not simply trying to incorporate "Woman" as an enabling horizon within a hermeneutic space marked as male property, to explore "the feminine" as resource, but to configure female creative agency, to explore the female creative agent, for the text is more and more devoted as one story follows another to the tracking of those female wanderers "terribly at large . . . roaming, like lost beasts," would-be artists like Miss Eckhart, Virgie Rainey, and the strangely marked woman of "Music from Spain" ("JR," 85). It is through her pursuit of these wanderers that Welty displaces the story of the legitimate son's accession to the father's place with the story of the daughter's alienation from History and recenters the woman's voice with respect to History, for these wanderers function as representations of the woman author herself in various modes of complicity or creative resistance. On the most local level, of course, these stories may be dramatizations of Welty herself in those various modes of complicity with or creative resistance to Faulkner, but finally the import is more sweeping: Welty and Faulkner function as actors in a drama which is more about gender per se. In other words, Welty's text underscores the fact that for the many female aspirants in (or outside of) *The Golden Apples,* for all those women camouflaged or disfigured, made silent or anonymous by patriarchy, Montalbano (like Faulkner) would be in no sense "the perfect being to catch up with" for the simple reason that he is a representation of the patriarch whose authority, whose freedom and visibility, is to some extent dependent upon the expropriation of her own.

No doubt acting out of a tendency that may be the inevitable result of reading Welty's gynocentric story in terms established by androcentric narratives of the son's pursuit of the insignia of adulthood in his pursuit of the variously represented patriarch, many readers have attempted to identify those "dragon's teeth" of *The Golden Apples,* those children who might be in some sense descended from King MacLain. As relevant as suggestions of such relationships might be, one must note that aside from the legitimate—and male—twins Ran and Eugene, no children are ever really acknowledged in the text. This is, I believe, an instance of one of those enabling obstructionist tactics that Welty valued. As if to construct a purposeful silence around the very issue that generates the coherence of so many novels in the patriarchal tradition, and *Go Down, Moses* in particular, Welty allows the dragon's teeth to remain unclaimed. Whereas Ike McCaslin searches the old ledgers to trace his own family genealogy, no character in *The Golden Apples* seems to care whether or not King MacLain might be the father of this or that unclaimed child. In fact, the unclaimed child—especially if the child is female—might be better left unclaimed in the sense that knowledge of, or acknowledgment by, the father would appear to be something to be avoided, resisted, or "obstructed" as dangerous to the girl's ability to realize her own power as female subject.

Welty's obstruction of the patriarchal plot (i.e., the search for the father) lays a foundation for a female aesthetic of history—an aesthetic of subtly broken silences, strategically dropped stitches, and powerfully authorizing undertows—analogous to those private documents; indirect, tangential, or extraneous references; and records of birth, marriage, and death wherein the stories of women are archived in official History. In other words, resistance to the patriarchal narrative provides Welty with a strategy for making female experience visible, and audible, once again. But what is that experience in *The Golden Apples?* On the surface it remains somewhat hard to get to. Much of it is *either* ensconced in a male mythology that naturalizes Historical experience as part of an essential and amoral order (i.e., recontextualizes it as part of the natural rather than the social world) *or* related to the reader through fleeting memories rather than being a part of the realized action of the story. On the one hand, Mattie Will's sexual encounter with King MacLain in "Sir Rabbit" seems to play directly into the familiar modernist mythologizing of sexual violence, as do Easter/Esther's "resurrection" by the heroic young Boy Scout and Miss Eckhart's identification with the Medusa who turns men to stone. But the other way of dealing with female experience in this text, of reclaiming it and transforming it, is through fleeting, and strongly contextualized, memory. The casual revelations of "The Wanderers" are often surprising—and important for their use of the silencing of women as a means to claim the stories of those women. We learn in this final story that Snowdie MacLain did in fact hunt for her wandering husband, that she hired a detective and "never told anyone." We learn that Cassie's beautiful mother, who "could have *sung*," committed suicide instead. We learn that Jinny Love did not leave Ran MacLain after the suicide of Maideen Sumrall and the scandal. We learn in fact that the death of that innocent—whose parrotlike talk was so comforting to Ran MacLain in his trouble—has made for him a successful political career. And we learn that Virgie Rainey, Welty's most powerful representative of female desire in *The Golden Apples,* may have been pregnant at the age of seventeen by Bucky Moffitt—while we do not learn what has become of the child:

> At seventeen, coming back, she'd jumped the high step from the Y. and M. V. train. . . . Having just jumped from the endless, grinding interior of the slow train from Memphis, she had come back to something—and she began to run toward it, with her suitcase as light as a shoebox, so little had she had to go away with and now to bring back—the lightness made it easier.
>
> "You're back at the right time to milk for me," her mother said when she got there, and untied her bonnet and dashed it to the floor between them, looking up at her daughter. Nobody was allowed weeping over hurts at her house, unless it was Mrs. Rainey herself first, for son and husband, both her men, were gone.
>
> For Virgie, there were practical changes to begin at once with the coming back—no music, no picture show job any more, no piano. ("TW," 233–34)

This is a particularly rich moment in the text of "The Wanderers," a kind of parable in the larger history of female experience. It is hardly surprising that any suggestions of Virgie's pregnancy at the end of the summer of "June Recital" when she is sixteen years old and playing the piano at the picture show are muted, even though the mysterious trip to Memphis (where else?), the "grinding interior," the light suitcase (as light as a shoebox), and the daughter's return by "the back way"—even her subsequent personal history on the margins of respectability—do point to the possibility of a hidden or denied or aborted pregnancy. Such submergence of relevant detail in context has been precisely the point of Welty's method in so many instances. This has been, after all, the fate of female experience through the ages, and a more eloquent evocation of the silencing and invisibility of women, costs as well as comforts, is hardly imaginable.

The most immediate consequence of Virgie's transgression in the above-remembered scene is her subordination to what Elizabeth Evans calls the patriarchal mother, i.e., the mother whose authority is dependent upon and whose voice is complicitous with patriarchy. Virgie is not even allowed to cry for her own loss; Kate Rainey claims that right, "for son and husband, both her men, were gone." But even more seriously, Virgie's music—her voice—is denied to her as is her visibility at the "picture show." What is left to Virgie is, apparently, service, subordination, anonymity. In the eyes of her community, her life has been ruined. Virgie's supposed understanding of that community assumption may be behind the rage she feels so many years later at the grave of Maideen Sumrall, who did very literally take that conclusion to heart when she committed suicide after having been "ruined" by Ran MacLain.

But Virgie is unlike Maideen Sumrall in one very important respect; she is contrary. Virgie is too powerful a representation of Welty's female aspirant in her capacity for creative obstructionism to permit herself to be reduced from subject to object: "In that interim between train and home, she walked and ran looking about her in a kind of glory, by the back way" ("TW," 234). It is this time and this path that Welty has gone to such lengths in *The Golden Apples* to recenter, and it may well be that in the above scene Welty is granting to her strongest protagonist that inheritance, suggesting that Virgie's "glory" is going to reside in her capacity to conjure with that inheritance.

If, unlike Faulkner's male questers, female aspirants in *The Golden Apples* do not choose to pursue identity through the means of a hunt for a legitimating father, the funeral of Mrs. Kate Rainey does appear to inaugurate Virgie's search for a mother who can empower. Mrs. Rainey, so deeply compromised by her complicity with the patriarchal order, is clearly not that mother. One might even argue, as Evans does, that Mrs. Rainey's death is necessary to Virgie's liberation.[24] One effect of that death is to bring Virgie face-to-face with King MacLain, who some readers have suggested may be the "real" father of Virgie Rainey (and various other girls in Morgana). He is certainly the most talked-about of fathers, the most mysterious, and the most omnipresent. At Mrs. Rainey's funeral, he "lifted his wobbly head and looked arrogantly at Virgie through the two open doors of her mother's bedroom . . . Then he made a hideous face at Virgie, like a silent yell. . . . He did not mind taking his present animosity out on Virgie Rainey; indeed he chose her" ("TW," 27). The self-assertion of the unsought father—his own "animosity" toward the daughter and in the face of death (itself one of the distinguishing features of the originating ancestor in so many of Faulkner's works and the source of his heroic transgressions)—is displaced in this scene, distanced from the newly focused Virgie by the intercession of the "open doors of her mother's bedroom." Significantly the displacement of paternal "animosity" is effected by the (erased) body of the mother—the open doors lead into the bedroom where the mother does not lie (having been moved into the front parlor)—as if to underscore the interrelatedness of the patriarchal mother Kate Rainey (i.e., the mother defined by her relationship to her men) and the father himself. Virgie's response to King MacLain's assertion of rage through the open doors of the vacated bedroom is to sit "up straight" and touch "her hair" (a badge of female power in this text), to wonder if the kinship she feels is with father or son, King or Ran.[25] Kinship is reenvisioned in the gynocentric text; it is not (as it is in Faulkner) a tracking of the Spirit Buck, the Bear, the Man from whom one inherits, but more a matter of triangulation, of charting one's position with reference to two fixed points a known distance apart. No doubt the difference is at least partly the result of the difference between male and female Oedipal experience in a patriarchal culture, but the most important consequence for our reading of the gynocentric text is to note that one way of genealogical plotting (whether one is thinking of the plotting of domestic, political, or literary history) is preoccupied with sameness, the transfer of authority from father to son, the transformation of son into father, redemption from the sins of the past; the other way of genealogical plotting is preoccupied with difference, distances, displacements, decentering, and acceptance of loss.[26] Virgie's questioning of kinship when confronted by the patriarch is central to Welty's obstructionist agenda, for it underscores the empowering nature of a woman's resistance to filling a "place" allotted to her within a patrilineal order. Welty's work—in *The Golden Apples* and elsewhere —tends not toward the destruction of an old order or the establishment of a new one, but to a liberating alienation or distance which makes possible movement, change, a journey.

Despite the clear suggestions of Virgie's empowerment here, it has been suggested that Welty's heroines in *The Golden Apples* are "wanderers" who are "blocked not only by social restrictions but also by . . . their view of themselves as monstrous," which Schmidt terms the "Medusa's gaze" (*HS*, 52). Yet one might point out that the real problem is not so much that the heroines see themselves as monstrous but that the patriarchal narrative constructs them in such terms, leaving them with only two choices—to concur in their own objectification and appropriation by the patriarchy or to resist, to embrace their "contrariety." In the above scene, Virgie takes the second choice—by refusing to see herself as the monstrous object of that horror, by turning King's expression of horror and rage back upon him (it is *his* "hideous face" after all that she sees)—and becomes the most successful of Welty's female aspirants in *The Golden Apples*. The death of the patriarchal mother and King's "choosing" of Virgie as the object of his animosity prompts Virgie to remember Miss Eckhart and her picture of Perseus and the Medusa, Siegfried and the Dragon, and to redefine her own identity in terms of the Medusa and the Perseus together.

> Miss Eckhart had had among the pictures from Europe on her walls a certain threatening one. It hung over the dictionary, dark as that book. It showed Perseus with the head of the Medusa. . . . Around the picture—which sometimes blindly reflected the window by its darkness—was a frame enameled with flowers, which was always self-evident—Miss Eckhart's pride. In that moment Virgie had shorn it of its frame.
>
> The vaunting was what she remembered, that lifted arm.
>
> Cutting off the Medusa's head was the heroic act, perhaps, that made visible a horror in life. . . . She might have seen heroism prophetically when she was young and afraid of Miss Eckhart. She might be able to see it now prophetically, but she was never a prophet. Because Virgie saw things in their time, like hearing them—and perhaps because she must believe in the Medusa equally with Perseus—she saw the stroke of the sword in three moments, not one. In the three was the damnation—no, only the secret, unhurting because not caring in itself—beyond the beauty and the sword's stroke and the terror lay

their existence in time—far out and endless, a constellation which the heart could read over many a night. ("TW," 242–43)

What Virgie manages to accomplish in the final pages of "The Wanderers" is a revisioning, or rereading, of the fixed constellation which frames the woman as Medusa already defeated and the Perseus as hero. She shears the "threatening" picture of Perseus with the head of the Medusa of its flowered frame in order to bring back into the light the repressed violence of the act. Schmidt argues that in Welty's work she transforms "the nightmare of the [woman] artist-as-Medusa into a vision of artist-as-sibyl" and he pursues a reading of the sibyl in women's texts as a subversive figure whose "prophecies represent the power to open all texts, to make a 'space' in them for revisions and supplementary revelations" (*HS*, 49, 248). In so claiming, Schmidt follows Gilbert's and Gubar's analysis of the sibyl as a representative of female power, "the primordial prophetess who mythically conceived all women artists."[27] But what Welty tells us about Virgie Rainey in the above passage is that she has *not* been transformed into a prophetic sibyl, for good reasons. In classical mythology the sibyl—unlike Virgie Rainey—does see "heroism prophetically"; her role is often to announce a coming catastrophe and the heroism of a male redeemer; sometimes she sets the riddle that he must solve or sends him on a heroic quest. In this sense, the sibyl is hardly more than a patriarchal alternative to the Medusa, an instance of what Alice Jardine, in her study of women and postmodernism, refers to as the unexpected return to discourse of the silenced woman.[28] Finally, the story of the sibyl is the story of the woman artist's appropriation by the patriarchal narrative which removes her from History and from her own power of agency—in the sense that the sibyl can tell only what is foreordained in some authorized narrative and is unable to intervene in human affairs. Virgie's development is more radical; she has learned to see "things in their time, like hearing them"; she has learned that she "must believe in the Medusa equally with Perseus" and to see the sword's stroke that destroys the Medusa as one part of a three-part narrative—the lifted arm, the stroke, and then the Medusa's head held aloft by Perseus ("TW," 243). In other words, she sees the violence as well as the glory of heroism. And in reclaiming her capacity to see the violence, to see what amounts to the history of her own repression, Virgie, like Welty, resists—although she does not deny—the alienation from History of female creative power. She resists the reification of her own creative desire as *either* a dragon to be slain *or* a male-identified sibyl who must underwrite (or prophesize) the slaying. In other words, she resists the traditional gender differentiation which victimizes womanhood and unsexes the female artist, making her complicitous with the removal of *female* authority from its place in time and History. Virgie resists the mythology, the history, and the ideology of the patriarchy.

At the end of this text, Virgie

> smiled once, seeing before her, screenlike, the hideous and delectable face Mr. King MacLain had made at the funeral, and when they all knew he was next—even he. Then she and the old beggar woman, the old black thief, were there alone and together in the shelter of the big public tree, listening to the magical percussion, the world beating in their ears. They heard through the falling rain the running of the horse and bear, the stroke of the leopard, the dragon's crusty slither, and the glimmer and the trumpet of the swan. ("TW," 244)

Although the final pages of "The wanderers" and particularly the lines excerpted above have struck some readers as mere sound, an indulgence in the lyrical that is excessive and finally irrelevant to the story, it seems to me that Welty's decision to depict the "horse," the "bear," "the dragon," and the "swan"—all important as fixed constellations, stable figures in classical (patriarchal) mythology—in terms of movement and sound underscores Virgie's capacity to imagine King's death, to subvert the fixed and silent gender configurations of patriarchal ideology. The final lyrical presentation of what Virgie *hears* in the falling of the rain recapitulates what Virgie *sees* earlier in the story when she sees the "stroke of the sword in three moments, not one." In other words, this final lyrical song voices the sounds of violence that patriarchal narrative silences—the running, the striking, the slithering away, and the fabled trumpeting of the dying swan. And it is precisely in Virgie's capacity to "hear" between the lines of the patriarchal narrative that we find a key to Welty's own method of storytelling, which is a rehistoricizing of classical mythology.

Although one might hesitate to assign names to characters an author chooses not to name, it is intriguing to speculate that Welty might have chosen to emphasize Virgie's kinship with another earlier manifestation of the resistant female storyteller by bringing Phoenix Jackson—both beggar and thief in "A Worn Path"—very quietly into Virgie's story at the end. In any event, the insinuation of the anonymous black woman under the "big public tree" with Virgie may provide a clue to Virgie's future. Do we expect her, now that her mother had died, to "be heard from in the world," as Miss Eckhart predicted? Or has History been too much for her? It does seem likely that at the age of forty-something Virgie Rainey is not likely to pick up her music where she left it at sixteen. It is another instance of Welty's understanding of the power of History that she makes it very clear indeed that Virgie's future—whatever she does with her new consciousness—will take account of her past, of the time she has lost. Patricia Yaeger argues convincingly that Virgie, in the last pages of "The Wanderers," "achieves a freedom she has always sought—not by enacting the violent stories that have been thrust on heroic men like Siegfried or Perseus but by achieving a dialectical vision of the rhythms of victim and victimizer that are the pulse of every heroic and gender-specific text."[29] But the fact remains that if Virgie has attained a certain kind of freedom, she is more alienated than ever. Not even Mr. Mabry, who believes that eventually Virgie is coming to him, recognizes her as she sits in the shadow of the "big public tree." In a text so concerned with the "vaunting" of any character, Welty seems to claim invisibility for Virgie at the end of "The Wanderers."

The final irony, of course, is that if Virgie is invisible to Morgana, to Mr. Mabry, she is anything but invisible to the reader, having been placed very deliberately at center stage in the final scene of the story. Maybe, in so placing a figure usually marginalized, usually invisible or anonymous, Welty is claiming that it is possible for Virgie to be "heard from in the world," provided the world learns how to listen, by contraries.

The upshot, of course, is that Welty's work is very much engaged with the "historical effect" and the "social consciousness that evolves from a continuum of time's changes." Her difference from Faulkner and many other male writers is that she focuses on the social and historical consciousness of women as women in a patriarchal order—although she never constructs that order as natural or inevitable. In fact she "obstructs" it at every turn. The various kinds of relationships that her female aspirants establish with the patriarchal community in *The Golden Apples* constitute Welty's exploration of the options available to women within a patriarchal culture, and particularly to the woman author, in her attempt to define her own relationship to patriarchal literary history. The woman writer might, in short, celebrate the shenanigans of the patriarch like Mrs. Katie Rainey, or she might function like Mattie

Will Sojourner as a kind of echo, or she might even fall into complete silence and invisibility like Easter/Esther, or she might suc-
cumb to madness like Miss Eckhart, or she might commit suicide
like Maideen Sumrall and Mrs. Morrison. But there is always the
possibility that she might play the piano at the Bijou, sometimes
letting "a whole forest fire burn in dead silence on the screen"
or, "when the sweethearts had found each other," she might
"switch on [her] light with a loud click and start up with creeping,
minor runs" ("JR," 52).

Notes

The quotation "Too positive a shape not to be hurt" is from Welty's story "The Whole
World Knows."

1. See Albert Devlin's *Eudora Welty's Chronicle: A Story of Mississippi Life* (Jackson: University Press of Mississippi, 1983); Michael Kreyling, *Author and Agent: Eudora Welty and
Diarmuid Russell* (New York: Farrar, Straus, & Giroux, 1991); Peter Schmidt, *The Heart of
the Story: Eudora Welty's Short Fiction* (Jackson: University Press of Mississippi, 1991). Essays
and chapters of books which treat Welty in this way are too numerous to mention here.

2. D. James Neault, "Time in the Fiction of Eudora Welty," in *A Still Moment: Essays on
the Art of Eudora Welty*, ed. John F. Desmond (Metuchen, N.J.: Scarecrow Press, 1978), 35.

3. Robert Daniel, "The World of Eudora Welty," *Hopkins Review* 6 (Winter 1953): 50.
I am capitalizing the word as "History" when I refer to official cultural, intellectual, or
literary history as it has been written by the majority of historians. I do so to distinguish
such recorded history from the obscured or hidden histories of women and other marginalized populations.

4. Joan Kelly, "Did Women Have a Renaissance?" in *Women, History and Theory* (Chicago: University of Chicago Press, 1984), 20, 47.

5. Leslie Fiedler, *Love and Death in the American Novel* (New York: Criterion Books,
1960), 449–50.

6. Harold Bloom, *The Anxiety of Influence* (New York: Oxford University Press, 1973),
37. See Sandra M. Gilbert's and Susan Gubar's *The Madwoman in the Attic: The Woman
Writer and the Nineteenth-Century Literary Imagination* (New Haven: Yale University Press,
1984), 46–53 for an analysis of the implications of Bloom's Oedipal model for feminist
scholarship.

7. Linda Kuehl, "The Art of Fiction XLVII: Eudora Welty," in *Conversations with Eudora
Welty*, ed. Peggy Prenshaw (Jackson: University Press of Mississippi, 1984), 80.

8. Jan Nordby Gretlund, "An Interview with Eudora Welty," *Conversations with Eudora
Welty*, 221.

9. For a different approach to Welty's attempt to recenter the woman's voice, see Patricia Yaeger, "'Because a Fire Was in My Head': Eudora Welty and the Dialogic Imagination," *PMLA* 99 (October 1984): 955–73. Although I have found Yaeger's groundbreaking
study of Welty's expropriation and transformation of W. B. Yeats's poems, "The Song of
the Wandering Aengus" and "Leda and the Swan," invaluable, my own analysis diverges
from hers on the question of the implications of Welty's strategies of subversion. Yaeger
rejects the possibility that Welty's appropriations of male texts might "come under the
auspices of Harold Bloom's theory of the 'anxiety of influence' or Gilbert and Gubar's
theory of the 'anxiety of authorship'" chiefly because Welty "does not deny, repress, or

disguise her obligation to Yeats"; instead she borrows her own collection's title, *The Golden Apples*, from a line in "The Song of the Wandering Aengus," "as if to signal Yeat's complicity in her story. . . . Neither a strong misreading nor a simple repetition, Welty's use of the 'Song of the Wandering Aengus' is dialogic" (964). One cannot, of course, make an identical claim for the way Welty expropriates Faulkner's *Go Down, Moses* (or *Absalom, Absalom!*). In this case, Welty does pursue, for reasons having to do with her own efforts to establish a voice of her own within a literary terrain supposedly "claimed" by Faulkner, a "strong misreading."

10. Schmidt, *The Heart of the Story*, 133, 131. Hereafter *HS*, cited in the text. Although I disagree with Schmidt on several points, his excellent study has been useful to me in my own attempts to come to terms with issues of gender and authorship in Welty's work.

11. Eudora Welty, "A Worn Path," in *Collected Stories of Eudora Welty* (New York: Harcourt, Brace, Jovanovich, 1980), 148–49.

12. Of Faulkner Welty said: "You know his work encompassed so much and so many books and so many generations and so much history, that that was an integral part of it. I don't write historically or anything. Most of the things I write about can be translated into personal relationships"; see Jo Brans, "Struggling Against the Plaid: An Interview with Eudora Welty [November 1980]" in *Conversations with Eudora Welty*, 299. Writing historically, of course, is not the same thing as writing about history. What is so striking about "A Worn Path" and so much of Welty's fiction is her ability to situate her work within history to such a deep degree that the "personal relationship" is often a manifestation of or comment upon a historical relationship, like her "literary historical" relationship with Faulkner.

13. Eudora Welty, "Looking at Short Stories," in *The Eye of the Story* (New York: Random House, 1979), 105.

14. Ruth Vande Kieft, *Eudora Welty*, rev. ed. (Boston: Hall, 1987), 13–14.

15. Kreyling, *Author and Agent*, 49, emphasis mine.

16. Simone de Beauvoir, *The Second Sex* (1953; reprint, New York: Vintage Books, 1974), xxii.

17. Devlin, *Eudora Welty's Chronicle*, 131.

18. Eudora Welty, "The Wanderers," *The Golden Apples* (New York: Harcourt, Brace, 1949), 228. All subsequent citations to stories are from this edition of *The Golden Apples*. "The Wanderers" is hereafter "TW," cited in the text.

19. Eudora Welty, "Moon Lake," 101. Hereafter "ML," cited in the text.

20. For an alternative reading of the meaning of this "dangling signifier," see Patricia Yaeger's "The Case of the Dangling Signifier: Phallic Imagery in Eudora Welty's 'Moon Lake,'" *Twentieth-Century Literature* 28 (Winter 1982): 431–53.

21. Eudora Welty, "June Recital," 41. Hereafter "JR," cited in the text.

22. At this point I should like to clarify that I am speaking about the male body in a special sense—in the sense that the male physical body as it appears in this text is a representation of the patriarchal cultural (or textual) body. In *The Golden Apples*, the two are nearly inseparable. For example, in "Sir Rabbit," when Mattie Will Sojourner reflects that in experiencing King MacLain's body (through a powerful fantasy that has struck some readers as an imagined rape) she has also been unfortunate enough to have to "put on what he knew with what he did," she points very deliberately not only to the analogical relationship between the physical and the literary bodies for the female storyteller, but to the appropriation of her own voice by the patriarchal aesthetic: "Like submitting to another way to talk, she could answer to his burden now" ("Sir Rabbit," 95). That Mattie Will's encounter with MacLain is most likely the product of her own powerful imagination only strengthens the thematic ties between the male physical and literary bodies and underscores Mattie Will's own complicity with the patriarchal.

23. Eudora Welty, "Music from Spain," 171. Hereafter "MS," cited in the text.

24. Elizabeth Evans, "Eudora Welty and the Dutiful Daughter," in *Eudora Welty: The Eye of the Storyteller*, ed. Dawn Trouard (Kent, Ohio: Kent State University Press, 1989), 57–68.

25. In this as in so many other texts, hair functions as a badge of female creativity and power. See Elisabeth G. Gitter's "The Power of Women's Hair in the Victorian Imagination," *PMLA* 99 (October 1984): 936–54.

26. See discussions of the female Oedipal experience and the girl's development of autonomy in Nancy Chodorow's *The Reproduction of Mothering: Psychoanalysis and the Sociology of Gender* (Berkeley: University of California Press, 1978) and Juliet Mitchell's classic *Psychoanalysis and Feminism: Freud, Reich, Laing and Women* (New York: Pantheon Books, 1974).

27. Gilbert and Gubar, *The Madwoman in the Attic*, 97.

28. Alice Jardine, *Gynesis: Configurations of Women and Modernity* (Ithaca: Cornell University Press, 1985), 25.

29. Yaeger, "'Because a Fire Was in My Head,'" 963.

"This Holocaust I Walk In": Consuming Violence in Sylvia Plath's Poetry

Jacqueline Shea Murphy
University of California, Berkeley

BODIES melt, voices shriek; hooks pierce; human flesh is chopped, like meat, wrapped and unwrapped. People eat and get eaten:

> My night sweats grease his breakfast plate
> . . . .
> My ribs show. What have I eaten?
>
> ("The Jailer," 185)[1]

People wait to be eaten:

> I am red meat. His beak
> Claps sidewise: I am not his yet.
>
> ("Death & Co.," 205)

Mothers beg for their babies to be saved from becoming food for others' cravings:

> And my baby a nail
> Driven, driven in.
> He shrieks in his grease
>
> . . . .
> O You who eat
>
> People like light rays, leave
> This one
> Mirror safe, unredeemed. . . .
>
> ("Brasilia," 210)

But these mothers plea in vain to exempt their children from the violent oppression of the world:

> It is a heart,
> This holocaust I walk in,
> O golden child the world will kill and eat.
>
> ("Mary's Song," 208)

Images of tortured, cut-up, oppressed, and consumed bodies can be heard echoing throughout the poetry Sylvia Plath wrote during the last months of her life. These final lines to "Mary's Song," in particular, with its singled-out body part (the heart), its reference to the atrocities of the Second World War, its speaker's sense of complicity in the war's horrors, and the ultimate inescapability of violence shown in its future tense (the world will kill and eat, regardless), becomes a coda to Plath's work. Taken together, these images show the acute awareness of violence that anguished Plath and gave her work its off-noted intensity.

Less established (though hotly debated in Plath criticism) is the source of this violence and the intense horror it evoked in Plath's poetry. Lawrence R. Ries argues in his study of violence in contemporary British poetry, *Wolf Masks,* that the violence haunting Plath came from the intensified violence of the world around her, most explicitly from the Second World War. She and other poets writing in the late 1950s and early 1960s, Ries claims, were responding to a world littered with the ideological and physical debris of the war. These effects included "the destruction of millions of human beings, the ruins of a desecrated Europe, and . . . the distorted sensibility born in those who witnessed the death and violence of the war."[2] The war itself, combined with the political tensions following it—the cold war—and the potential for nuclear annihilation of the planet that the bombings of Hiroshima and Nagasaki made vivid, produced a world where violence in poetry was accurate, appropriate, and even called-for.

But Plath's use of holocaust imagery—the Jew, the Nazi, the concentration camp body which haunt her later poems—seems to come from more than a desire to translate the violence of the world that she saw around her. It was not, after all, the immediacy of the concentration camps and their horrors that compelled Plath to use these images and metaphors in her work; she wrote the bulk of these poems almost two decades after the war, and after a decade of writing poetry without a proliferation of Nazi images. The most often advanced competing interpretation of

Plath's violent and fascistic images argues that while these are undeniably connected to her keen sensitivity to political horrors (not explicitly gendered), they are also inextricably tied to the immediate personal struggles she faced as a woman. Numerous critics and biographers have traced the split she apparently felt between the need to be the perfect 1950s housewife dutifully supporting her poet husband and her own desire to write herself successful—in her life and in her work.[3] Some have argued that the political references in her poems are analogies to her own relation to patriarchy—that when, for example, she refers to Jews and Nazis, she is writing about her position as a woman in a male-dominated world.[4] At second glance, even the Ted Hughes quote that Ries calls on to prove that "the violence of her poetry was a reaction to the violence of the world" hints at a gendered violence at the root of Plath's horror. Ries quotes Hughes as saying:

> Her reactions to hurts in other people and animals, and even tiny desecrations of plant-life were extremely violent. The chemical poisoning of nature, the pile-up of atomic waste, were horrors that persecuted her like an illness—as her latest poems record. Auschwitz and the rest were merely the open wounds, in her idea of the great civilized crime of intelligence that like the half-imbecile, omnipotent, spoiled brat Nero has turned on its mother. (*WM*, 36)

The concentration camps, in his simile, become "merely the open wounds" of an already-established murderous mutilation of a female body, the despot Nero's flexing of his political muscle by demanding that his mother be cut up so he can see her womb.

Reading patriarchy at the base of Plath's violence, however, poses some problems, as Jacqueline Rose notes in a piece on Plath and sexuality. Rose suggests that feminist readings of literature might circumscribe them, leaving out "the specific question of culture and history which seem to be raised by a writer like Plath." She writes:

> The paradox of a concept like patriarchy in this context, and Plath's work has of course been read as a protest against a patriarchal world, is that its very exhaustiveness can operate in the form of an exclusion of the immediate, albeit monumental, political history, even if that history could finally be explained within its terms.[5]

Rose's comments suggest that Plath's violence and intensity do not come solely from a sensitivity to Nazi violence and the horrors of a post–World War II world; but neither do they come solely from

Plath's literal and metaphoric problems with her dead father, her poet-husband, and (as critic Steven Gould Axelrod has recently suggested) the patriarchal literary and poetic traditions in which she was immersed.[6] "In relation to Plath," Rose writes, "the line dividing sexuality and history simply cannot be drawn" ("SP," 19). This interconnection seems accurate and also central to the poems Plath wrote toward the end of her life.[7] Plath, I think, intertwined images of Nazi brutality with feminist protest not only as a way of registering the horrors of the death camps, and/or the oppression and circumscription of women's lives; her point was not even, as Axelrod posits, to show the "Holocaust and the patriarchy's silencing of women [as] linked outcomes of the masculinist interpretation of the world" (SP, 55)—a reading which subordinates anguish at political history to patriarchal protest, as Rose cautions against. Rather, in these poems, quests for power—a Fuhrer's or race's or a father's attempts to dominate—were and are so shockingly brutal not only to show a connection between fascism and patriarchy, but also and more strikingly, I think, to highlight the violence and disempowerment that quests for power and domination, in themselves, produce.

The profusion of bodies and body parts in Plath's late poems, and the violence that they register, works to articulate this position. One striking commonality between Nazi power and patriarchy is the emphasis both place on controlling bodies.[8] Patriarchy has functioned historically, as various critics have demonstrated, by controlling and containing the female body.[9] The fascism of World War II likewise reinforced the centrality of bodies, of actual physical flesh, in attempts to garner power. Nazism required the physical destruction of people's bodies, a destruction that was designed to lead ultimately to the eradication of an entire culture; Hitler's power was to be gained by destroying and mutilating human bodies so as systematically to remove an entire body of people from existence. Some have argued that this system was itself gendered; Klaus Theweleit's *Male Fantasies,* a compelling study of the imagery and rhetoric surrounding the Nazi *Freikorpsmen,* for example, argues that these fascists operated out of a fear of female bodies and desire to escape women. (Theweleit traces in numerous *Freikorpsmen* posters, pamphlets, and writings a dread of being swallowed and engulfed, where women's bodies are, as Barbara Ehrenreich writes in her introduction to the study, "the holes, swamps, pits of muck that can engulf.")[10] But even without Theweleit's explicit equation of Nazi desire for power with the desire to control *women's* bodies, the Nazi desire to control bodies seems to suggest a gendered subtext, given the proverbial mind/body split in which women have become associated with the bodily and men with the loftier, philosophical mind. These two forms of oppression—fascism and patriarchy—then, converge in their insistent awareness of real, physical flesh and the power it wields. Nazism, because of its blatant, horrific, dramatic call for power and because of the violence (six million and more dead bodies) that this call required—becomes a fitting metaphor for the violence that patriarchal power demands; at the same time, images of patriarchal power enacted through careful control of women's bodies help to articulate the political horror of Nazism. Bodies violated and controlled in encounters with authority recur in Plath's late work: the gendered complaint of the Applicant's anatomized body, her glass eye and rubber breasts, echo in Lady Lazarus's lampshade skin, Jew linen face, and right foot paperweight. The common ground—the common horror—here, is authority expressed violently on oppressed bodies.

Sylvia Plath, though, wanted authority. She wanted to be an influential, respected, famous, successful, artist; she wanted the power wielded by successful artists, even while she recognized the violence that having power can entail. What her later poems chronicle, I think, is her attempt to grapple with the doubleness of her desire. Her "bee poems," for example, present a painful awareness of this doubleness; the speaker's fascination with the control she can wield over the bees alternates with her terror at the harm they can do her. "Mary's Song" (208) illustrates the anguished complicity the speaker feels in a world where oppression has been carried on for thousand of years. "Lady Lazarus" (198) shows the bodily violence of her move into the oppressor position. The poems show authority expressed on others' bodies—cut up, made to crackle, killed; they show a poet grappling with authority in a world where to achieve power, as Hitler writes, "one is either the hammer or the anvil," where "if men wish to live, then they are forced to kill others,"[11]—and struggling, too, with the gendered, theoretical, implications behind these claims.

Bodies, then, in the later Plath poems, matter immensely. Open at random her collected poems from 1962 on and almost invariably a body or body part will appear on the page. A horrific fascination with the body's physical vulnerability becomes the subject of several poems: "Cut" (191) luxuriates in the image of a sliced finger: "What a thrill— / My thumb instead of an onion," the poet writes. "Fever 103°" (188) anatomizes a burning, feverish body: "I am a lantern— / My head a moon / Of Japanese paper,

my gold beaten skin / Infinitely delicate and infinitely expensive."
In "Paralytic" (217), the speaker imagines existence from inside
an arrested body frame:

> It happens. Will it go on?—
> My mind a rock,
> No fingers to grip, no tongue,
> My god the iron lung
>
> That loves me, . . .

In other poems, a heightened awareness of appearance and
beauty emphasizes the physical. In "The Applicant" (182), the
speaker inquires about the body of a "perfect" wife:

> Do you wear
> A glass eye, false teeth or a crutch,
> A brace or a hook,
> Rubber breasts or a rubber crotch,
>
> . . . .
> A living doll, everywhere you look.

In "A Birthday Present" (173), a similar attention to beauty and
female anatomy clothes a death wish:

> What is this, behind this veil, is it ugly, is it beautiful?
> It is shimmering, has it breasts, has it edges?

Other poems highlight bodies by illustrating the potential for
their mutilation or dismemberment. In "The Rabbit Catcher"
(164), snares constrict the rabbit and the poet; in "Berck-Plage"
(167), body parts are washed ashore; in "The Detective" (174), the
body is explicitly absent, its removal chronicled piece by piece;
and in "The Jailer" (185), "Lady Lazarus" (198), and "Daddy"
(183), power struggles are played out on someone's flesh. This
insistence on the bodily continues throughout Plath's work in
other ways as well—including the prevalence of wombs and babies,
and the images of the crucifixion and of Jesus' body in it. All in
all, a remarkable number of very different issues get worked out
on bodies, both the speaker's own and others', all the way up to
Plath's final published poem, "Edge" (224), where

> The woman is perfected.
> Her dead
>
> Body wears the smile of accomplishment, . . .

Most of these bodies are featured in explicit or implicit struggles for control, for dominance, for authority. The Applicant's body, for example, needs to fit superior requirements. The speaker in "The Rabbit Catcher" becomes ensnared—constricted and strangled—by the hands encircling a tea mug. In a number of these power poems, images of bodily control merge with images of warfare and struggle for political control. "Cut" (191), for example, moves from the speaker's slicing of her thumb and the thrill it gives her to a struggle between a pilgrim and an Indian:

> Little pilgrim,
> The Indian's axed your scalp.

From this one-on-one melee, the thumb becomes an army, the bodily mutilation of a lead-in to the specific warfare of the American Revolution:

> Out of a gap
> A million soldiers run,
> Redcoats, every one.

The cut then becomes, moving chronologically even, a reference to racial violence and the attempts white supremacists make for dominance in the United States:

> The stain on your
> Gauze Ku Klux Klan . . . .

Cutting her own body, in other words—exercising a maiming control over it—spreads in the poem to increasingly diffuse violent struggles for power and dominance, struggles that have, in different forms, existed for centuries.

In "Fever 103°" (188), a similar collapse occurs between what happens to the poet's body and what happens during historical, political struggles for control, although here the violence of the world moves not from her thumb to the world but instead from the outside world into her body. Here, the poet refers specifically to the nuclear horrors that resulted from the struggle for political control of World War II: the "yellow sullen smokes" from the fever ravishing the speaker's body will, she is afraid, "trundle round the globe / Choking the aged and the meek" and turning orchids ghastly white with radiation. The fever then becomes "Like Hiroshima ash" and her head "a moon / Of Japanese paper, . . . Glowing and coming and going." The poet's feverish head, then, comes to contain the infinitely incredible violence of Hiroshima.

The most arresting—and certainly the most well-known—occurrences of a desire for power and control spreading violently between one body and the world, though, happen in the poems where Plath makes explicit references to the holocaust. In "Mary's Song" (208), violence to an individual body (here, Jesus, Mary's son) escalates into "This holocaust I walk in"; the poem makes explicit the escalation and proliferation of violence caused by subjugating a body. "The Sunday lamb cracks in its fat," the poem opens, and then the fire that broils this Christ image becomes "The same fire / Melting the tallow heretics, / Ousting the Jews." In this world where dominance and authority come to those who control others, in other words, the same violent force spreads over centuries, outward from one body: the Roman desire for power which required that Christ, the Sunday lamb, be crucified, then moves to melt Christians, the "tallow heretics" who insist on their belief in him; when authority has shifted to these Christians, the same fire—that which controls by cracking, melting, burning—then spreads to oust the Jews, to gas in ovens that "glowed like heavens" those who do not believe in Christ and who instead are blamed for killing him. This fire feeds on whatever bodies—signaled by the central, fleshy image of a lamb roast cracking in its fat, reinforced by the reference to the holocaust's glowing ovens—it can find. The poet returns to the scene, complicit in the burning oppression of these bodies over centuries, in the poem's final lines. "It is a heart, / This holocaust I walk in," she writes, making the holocaust a body part, and a vital one, and showing herself to be walking in it. The poem's final line then circles back to the same horror that opened the poem, the Sunday lamb being consumed, "O golden child the world will kill and eat," signaling the never-ending horror of this cycle of oppression.

In "Daddy" and "Lady Lazarus," a collapse between violent control of the poet's body, and violent control of bodies in history, becomes even more dramatic. These poems not only hint that the poet glows like Hiroshima, or walks in the heart of the holocaust, but enact a transformation of that body into an explicit agent of oppression. In them, the speaker moves from the position of the oppressed—the Jew, the mutilated concentration camp victim—to that of the oppressor, capable of killing and consuming others' flesh. "Daddy, I have had to kill you" says the speaker who "may be a bit of a Jew" in "Daddy"; "Beware / Beware / . . . I eat men like air" says the dead and dismembered—unwrapped hand and foot—Lady Lazarus, whose skin has glowed "Bright as a Nazi lampshade" and whose face is "a featureless, fine Jew linen" when she returns from the dead. This violent dichotomy—be oppressed or oppress, be controlled or control, be mutilated or mutilate—seems evident. The prevalence of this dynamic supports the idea that not only survival but power per se, in its many different forms, is a large part of what these poems embody and address.

In suggesting that the thrust of these poems has to do not only with patriarchal protest but also with the ways that power and authority are obtainable, I do not mean to gloss over the ways that the power struggles Plath writes about are explicitly gendered. The speakers, first, are nearly all female and speak to expose or get back at men: Lazarus has returned from the dead a "lady" who is ready to eat men. "Daddy"'s little girl wants to kill her fascist father. Mary, the mother, sings of the violence that men will do to her child. Plath also chooses particularly gendered metaphors of oppression to describe power struggle. As the poems quoted throughout suggest, oppression gets figured, in her dichotomies, as cooking or eating others; being oppressed means being eaten. Those in control are those who can eat or who can keep others from eating: in "Mary's Song," the world will kill and eat Jesus, figured as a lamb roast. Lady Lazarus will return from being dismembered not to rip men to bits, but to eat them. The speaker in "The Arrival of the Bee Box" (177) contemplates the control she has over the bees: "They can die, I need feed them nothing, I am the owner." The vampire who said he was Daddy drank the poet's blood for a year. "The Jailer" (185) has his break-fast plate greased by the sweat of the one he has imprisoned; his prisoner starves until his or her ribs show. In "Death & Co." (205), the speaker is red meat. In "Brasilia" (210), a mother pleads that her baby be saved from oppression by begging that he not be eaten:

O You who eat

People like light rays, leave
This one
Mirror safe, . . .

Self-assertion, too, gets expressed in terms of this particular di-chotomy of eating or being eaten. In "Ariel," the speaker ex-presses her electrified, almost gleeful, suicidal drive by exclaiming she will fly into a cauldron—will assert herself by placing her own self in a cooking pot. Perhaps she will become food for others, but she will do it to herself. This eating, cooking, feeding, and food imagery abounds in Plath's poetry; women's cultural connection with food make it, I think, a particularly gendered way of expressing a desire for power and a fear of being overpowered. At the same time, though, describing power in terms of food and eating reinforces the centrality of the body in struggles for dominance. Food is the literal mainstay of the body, without which the body will shrivel and die. Still, then, what Plath ends up with is a structure where people—including women—can either oppress or be oppressed, and where either position gets marked on bodies. The move she makes in her later poetry, given this, seems entirely understandable. In one move she seeks to imagine women in the place of power, mutilating others' bodies; Lady Lazarus eats men, daughter kills Daddy. The power structure stays intact; she just imagines being the one in control mutilating others. In another move, she emphasizes the power of the oppressed, mutilated body. As she recognizes, the oppressor is entirely dependent on the oppressed. The torturer's power depends on the prisoner's body:

> What would the dark
> Do without fevers to eat?
> What would the light
> Do without eyes to knife, what would he
> Do, do, do without me?
>
> ("The Jailer," 185)

The Nazi's power depends on the Jew:

> So, so, Herr Doktor.
> So, Herr Enemy
>
> I am your opus,
> I am your valuable,
> The pure gold baby
>
> That melts to a shriek.
> I turn and burn.
>
> ("Lady Lazarus," 198)

The mutilated, oppressed body, in this formulation, is recognized as important: cut bodies, perfect dead bodies, feverish bodies, are authoritative texts to be read. This configuration flips the dichotomy of oppressor/oppressed, so the oppressed body ends up on the top. As a poet creating texts from pain, her mutilated body becomes a source and manifestation of her power. A. Alvarez, commenting on "Daddy," notes how this dynamic works: "This is the strategy of the concentration camps. When suffering is there whatever you do, by inflicting it upon yourself, you achieve your identity, you set yourself free."[12] As everyone knows, this is precisely what happens next: Sylvia Plath converts her kitchen oven into a gas chamber. Plath asserts herself by recreating fascist history and turning it against her own body; in both her poetry and her life, she adopts the fascist model of power.

I have been assuming that this system—power expressed through control of the body—is completely undesirable, especially for women, whose bodies are metaphorically and often literally the ones oppressed under it. But it is possible, I know, to see a system that makes bodies the locus of power as liberating for women. Promoting and empowering the (female and female-identified) body—the maternal, the sexual—is hardly a new feminist move; it has been the goal behind much of the so-called "French" feminist project of the 1980s.[13] Neither, for that matter, is promoting the *oppressed* female body as a way of claiming authority for women particularly novel. Christine de Pizan's *Book of the City of Ladies,* written in 1405, presents women's experiences of torture and self-mutilation as proof that they (and because of them, women in general) deserve respect. Saint Catherine has her breasts torn off, and milk pours from them; the virgin Marina has her body stretched out and her flesh ripped off with iron hooks; the blessed Blandina is placed on a grill, roasted, and sliced.[14] The women endure triumphantly, without flinching. By exercising control of their violently violated bodies, these women serve as examples of the authority of women's lived experience.

What interests me, finally, then, is Plath's inability to imagine any way out of this bodily bind, any way of asserting herself without reverting ultimately to a fascist—a violent, dichotimized—model for obtaining power, a model that, as Hannah Arendt notes, itself enables totalitarianism:

> What totalitarian rule needs to guide the behavior of its subjects is a preparation to fit each of them equally well for the role of executioner and the role of victim.[15]

The nagging discomfort that tempers the awe that readers—including this one—sometimes feel in response to Plath's poetry may be in part the product of her (and our) failure to conceive a power and authority not based on a dichotomy, not requiring an overpowered body. Stunningly articulating this disease is, I think, as far as Plath got.

I wanted to look at this double bind, not to judge Plath and what she did, but to examine what I think she was saying and to wonder (and of course only speculate) why she—who was, according to Ted Hughes, so repulsed and horrified by violence and fascism—ended up writing the poems she did and dying the way she did. The difficulties that Plath embodied seem telling in ways that extend beyond the particulars of her poems and her life and death. Her attempt to figure and claim authority for herself, in the shadow—or at least the intense awareness—of fascism and the model for claiming authority it made vivid, parallels, in some ways, the solutions of other women writers and thinkers of this century, such as Virginia Woolf and Simone Weil; they too confronted fascism's threatened and actual disempowerment by killing themselves, although their conflicts with fascism were, to be sure, more immediate. Weil, especially, turned the very terms of the war against her own body. This brilliant French philosopher-scholar-mystic pleaded to join the underground in 1942, but her request to be parachuted behind Nazi lines was denied.[16] Hitler's horrors had led her to turn from the ideological pacifism she had previously believed in; she was then denied the opportunity to become, in a sense, the oppressor—to fight Nazis and Nazism directly, to overpower them (to become, in Plath's poems, "Daddy"'s killer). Her move from there was to make herself *into* the oppressed and use her own oppression to combat the war. Weil starved herself to death when, diagnosed with tuberculosis and told by her doctors to eat well, she refused more nourishment (and took in even less) than what was allowed French troops at the front. In striving to confront the increasingly powerful fascism before her, she moved through the dialectic of options available to her (be the oppressed; be the oppressor; be the oppressed but claim it as powerful), and ended up subjugating her own body to death. Weil and Plath, confronted with fascism (for Weil, actual Nazi threat; for Plath, more metaphorically, the violence of gaining authority), turned its terms against themselves. The disturbing similarities between these responses point all the more urgently to the fact that Plath, and we, have yet to think of a notion of power, or of not-power, of something other than power, some way of existing together without requiring the overpowered, some notion of shifting, fluctuating self-assertions; of nonheirarchies, of something other than being on top, or validating the bottom, a space where bodies can move in and out of formation, and where, (say . . .), the movement itself is what keeps it together.

Notes

1. All Plath citations are taken from Sylvia Plath, *The Collected Poems,* ed. Ted Hughes (New York: Harper & Row, 1981). The title, followed by the number of each poem rather than the page number, will be cited parenthetically after each quotation.

2. Lawrence R. Ries, *Wolf Masks* (New York: Kennikat Press, 1977), 8. Hereafter *WM,* cited in the text. Ries focuses on Thom Gunn, Ted Hughes, and John Wain, as well as Plath.

3. See, for example, Sandra M. Gilbert, "A Fine, White Flying Myth: The Life/Work of Sylvia Plath," in *Shakespeare's Sisters: Feminist Essays on Women Poets,* ed. Sandra M. Gilbert and Susan Gubar (Bloomington: Indiana University Press, 1979), 245–60; Paula Bennett, *My Life a Loaded Gun: Female Creativity and Feminist Poetics* (Boston: Beacon Press, 1986); Mary Lynn Broe, *Protean Poetic: The Poetry of Sylvia Plath* (Columbia: University Press of Missouri, 1980); Lynda Bundtzen, *Plath's Incarnations: Woman and the Creative Process* (Ann Arbor: University of Michigan Press, 1983); and Steven Gould Axelrod, *Sylvia Plath: The Wound and the Cure of Words* (Baltimore: Johns Hopkins University Press, 1990).

4. See, for example, Carole Ferrier's "The Beekeeper's Apprentice," in Gary Lane, ed., *Sylvia Plath: New Views on the Poetry* (Baltimore: Johns Hopkins University Press, 1979).

5. Jacqueline Rose, "Sylvia Plath and the Obscenity of Literary Criticism," 20; an essay written for the Oxford English Limited Conference, "Prohibited Pleasures," May 1987. Hereafter "SP," cited in the text.

6. Axelrod's recent *Sylvia Plath: The Wound and the Cure of Words* sees Plath's struggle with the patriarchy of poetic form and tradition at the core of her voice and vision. Further references to this work will be cited in the text as *SP.*

7. I have focused here on the poems Plath wrote from 1962 on, where I think these issues come together most dramatically and with an accelerated frequency that makes me think they were vital to Plath and what she was trying to express and to where she finally ended up. A number of her earlier poems also address these issues and use the images and metaphors I am talking about.

8. For a compelling discussion of ways the body figured, similarly, at the base of theoretical conceptions of both race and gender in America, see Karen Sanchez-Eppler, "Bodily Bonds: The Intersecting Rhetorics of Feminism and Abolition," *Representations* 24 (1988): 28–59.

9. See, for example, Peter Stallybrass, "Patriarchal Territories: The Body Enclosed," in Margaret W. Ferguson et al., eds., *Rewriting the Renaissance* (Chicago: University of Chicago Press, 1986). Stallybrass genders Bakhtin's analysis (see Mikhail Bakhtin, *Rabelais and His World* [Bloomington: Indiana University Press, 1984]) of the way unruly bodies in the Renaissance disrupted or subverted class structures, suggesting that a "female grotesque" could interrogate class and gender hierarchies alike. See also Barbara Ehrenreich and Deirdre English, *Complaints and Disorders: The Sexual Politics of Sickness* (New York: Feminist Press, 1973).

10. See Klaus Theweleit, *Male Fantasies* (Minneapolis: University of Minnesota Press, 1987), 1:xiii.

11. Gordan W. Prange, ed., *Hitler's Words* (Washington, D.C.: American Council on Public Affairs, 1944).

12. A. Alvarez,

13. I do not, however, think that the overall tenor of Plath's late poetry describes joyous

female bodies, although one might well find flickers of this kind of joy in her poems; she was writing before that position had been clearly and loudly voiced and did not voice it herself.

14. Christine de Pizan, *The Book of the City of Ladies,* trans. Earl Jeffrey Richards (New York: Persea Books, 1982), 222, 226, 241.

15. Hannah Arendt, *The Origins of Totalitarianism* (New York: Harcourt, Brace & World, 1966), 468.

16. According to Anna Freud, Weil's request was denied in part because she looked "so obviously Jewish," as quoted in Robert Coles, *Simone Weil: A Modern Pilgrimage* (Reading, Mass.: Addison-Wesley, 1987), 58, and in part, Coles suggests, because she was a woman (33).

The Dream in Flames:
Hisaye Yamamoto, Multiculturalism, and the Los Angeles Uprising

King-Kok Cheung

University of California, Los Angeles

THE 1992 Los Angeles riot broke out three months before I was to give a paper in a panel entitled "The American Dream" at the Japanese American National Museum in Los Angeles. I chose to speak on Hisaye Yamamoto's "A Fire in Fontana," not only because this memoir casts sobering reflections on the American Dream, but also because it speaks directly to current events. As in so many of Yamamoto's short stories, "Fire" has a double structure. The external plot, which juxtaposes the ruthless killing of a black family and the 1965 Watts rebellion, yields provocative parallels with the incidents surrounding the acquittal of four police officers accused of brutally beating Rodney King. The internal plot, which traces the narrator's evolving racial consciousness and her deepening black allegiance, offers insights into the meaning and possibility of what is now called "multiculturalism"—a challenge faced today by teachers and community leaders alike.[1]

Yamamoto, author of *Seventeen Syllables and Other Stories* (1988), is a *nisei* (second-generation Japanese American) born in 1921 in Redondo Beach, California. During World War II she was interned in a detention camp in Poston, Arizona. After the war she worked from 1945 to 1948 as a columnist and rewrite person for the *Los Angeles Tribune,* a black weekly. She volunteered in 1953 to work for a Catholic Worker community farm on Staten Island, and returned to Los Angeles after her marriage in 1955. In 1986 she received the American Book Award for Lifetime Achievement from the Before Columbus Foundation. Yamamoto was one of the first Japanese American writers to gain national recognition after the war—a time when anti-Japanese sentiment was still rampant. Several of her stories appeared in Martha Foley's lists of "Distinctive Short Stories" and one was included in *Best American Short Stories*. Her reputation has been especially strong in Asian American literary circles. The editors of *Aiiieeeee! An Anthology of Asian-American Writers* consider her to be "Asian-America's most accomplished short story writer"; Elaine H. Kim describes her fiction as "consummately women's stories."[2] What distinguishes Yamamoto's writing is not merely her craft of storytelling and her feminist consciousness, which are justly celebrated, but also her ability to include, empathize with, and give voice to people of different racial backgrounds long before the civil rights movement.

"Fire" is an autobiographical essay about Yamamoto's experience as a staffwriter with the *Los Angeles Tribune,* a job that "colored the rest of [her] life."[3] The narrator was reminded of that experience, and specifically of an incident that she had to "report" for the *Tribune* shortly after World War II, when she watched the Watts riot on television. She begins her recollection by describing the milieu of the newspaper office, which was on the mezzanine of the Dunbar Hotel.[4] People who stayed in the hotel included celebrities like Billy Eckstine, Ossie Davis, and Ruby Dee. Those who visited the newspaper office were less spectacular, though one character seemed timeless: "A tall young police lieutenant, later to become mayor of the city, came by to protest the newspaper's editorial on police brutality" ("F," 369).

The episode that gives the memoir its title concerns a young black man named Short, who showed up in the editorial office one day and informed the staff that ever since he had bought a house in a white neighborhood in Fontana he had been getting threatening notes from his neighbors asking him to "get-out-or-else" ("F," 370). He hoped to enlist the help of three black newspapers, the *Los Angeles Tribune* included, to publicize his situation and to muster support for his right to live in Fontana. Later that week his house went up in flames. Short, his wife, and his two children were killed in the blaze.

Though the fire "appeared to have started with gasoline poured all around the house and outbuildings," the police's "official conclusion was that probably the man had set the gasoline fire himself, and the case was closed" ("F," 370). Among those who doubted this conclusion was a white priest who wrote a play called *Trial by Fire;* after it was presented on the stage the priest was "suddenly transferred to a parish somewhere in the boondocks of Arizona" ("F," 370).

The television coverage of the Watts riot brought back to the narrator the memory of the fire, which had left her with "something like an itch [she] couldn't locate, or like food not being cooked enough, or something undone which should have been done, or something forgotten which should have been remembered" ("F," 370). The scenes she saw on television, horrible as they were, also offered her a sense of resolution:

> Appalled, inwardly cowering, I watched the burning and looting on the screen and heard the reports of the dead and wounded. But beneath all my distress, I felt something else. . . . To me, the tumult in the city was the long-awaited, gratifying next chapter of an old movie that had flickered about in the back of my mind for years. In the film . . . there was this modest house out in the country. Suddenly the house was in flames. . . . Then there could be heard the voices of a man and woman screaming, and the voices of two small children as well. ("F," 373)

It appears that another family of four—just like the black family in Fontana—was burned to death during the Watts riot. But this time the skin color of the perpetrators and the victims might have been reversed.

I will discuss the implications of this chilling ending later. For now I would like to show how this external or surface plot of the memoir—through its juxtaposition of individual abuse and civil disorder, its revelation of the elusiveness of the American Dream, and its interrogation of the police and the media—resonates with the events surrounding the Rodney King beating. With King, the connection between the first "not guilty" verdict given the four officers and the subsequent L.A. riot in 1992 was hard to miss, though the media played down the connection.[5] In "Fire," the connection between the fire in Fontana and the burning that occurred during the Watts riot is made in the narrator's mind. The juxtaposition of the two fires suggests that mass insurrection has roots in the quotidian violation of individual rights. Short and King were both victims of violence who had allegedly brought injury on themselves (though King admittedly was not guiltless). These cycles of individual abuse and group rebellion support Robert Gooding-Williams's contention that the beating of King, the verdict and its aftermath should not be treated simply as news, "as transient curiosities that have accidently supervened on the circumstances of day-to-day life."[6]

Anger at injustice can spawn further injustice, however. Like Short and King, the victims of the Watts riot and the L.A. riot got what they did not deserve. Just as the fire in Fontana destroyed Short's "American Dream," the dreams of many immigrants who had believed in succeeding in America through hard work were also reduced to ashes during the 1992 fire. Apparently the American Dream is not equally accessible to all Americans; even individual lives seem to differ in value. Short's right to own a house in Fontana was violently revoked; the murder of his family was whitewashed as suicide. Elaine H. Kim has noted how many Americans of color cried in vain for help during the 1992 upheaval:

> When the Korean Americans in South Central and Koreatown dialed 911, nothing happened. When their stores and homes were being looted and burned to the ground, they were left completely alone for three horrifying days. How betrayed they must have felt by what they believed was a democratic system that protects its people from violence. . . . What they had to learn was that . . . protection in the U. S. is by and large for the rich and powerful. If there were a choice between Westwood and Koreatown, it is clear that Koreatown would have to be sacrificed.[7]

Unlike the fire in Fontana and the Watts riot, in which the conflict was largely between blacks and whites, the recent uprising revealed friction between racial minorities as well. Yamamoto, uncovering interethnic cleavages in "Fire," is ahead of her time. She shows how people of color may discriminate against one another, either out of ethnocentrism or because they have internalized the attitudes of the dominant culture. The narrator recalls a Korean real estate agent who put her children into Catholic schools because the public schools were "integrated." Yet this same woman did not hesitate to urge local real estate onto her black clients because the resulting profits made possible "her upward mobility into less integrated areas" ("F," 373). Mutual disdain and stereotyping between African Americans and Korean Americans loomed large in the 1992 riot. As Sumi K. Cho points out, "many Korean shopowners had accepted widespread stereotypes about African Americans as lazy, complaining criminals. . . . On the other hand, many African Americans also internalize stereotypes of Korean Americans [as] callous unfair competitors."[8] Cho argues that this mode of thinking is often reinforced by the media: "the media [were] eager to sensationalize the events by excluding Korean perspectives from coverage and stereotyping the immigrant community. . . . Stereotypic media portrayals of Koreans as smiling, gun-toting vigilantes and African Americans as vandals and hoodlums trivialize complex social and economic problems.[9]

The media also played a problematic role in "Fire." The brutal murder of Short's family was presented by both the police and the press as suicide. The narrator, a reporter herself, though sickened by the event, was unable to vent her outrage through divulging the bigotry of Short's white neighbors: "Given the responsibility by the busy editor, I had written up from my notes a calm, impartial story, using 'alleged' and 'claimed' and other cautious journalese" ("F," 371). She deplores the journalistic ethics that forced her to present a partial story in the guise of impartiality, that obliged her to cite dubious "official" sources, and that prevented her from offering her own analysis of the fire in Fontana. The media coverage of the recent L. A. riot, in zeroing in on the conflict among racial minorities, similarly deflected blame from the dominant culture. Kim compares the coverage to the Chinese film *Raise the Red Lantern,* in which three concubines and wife plot endlessly against each other while the husband who controls and exploits them all remains very much out of the picture and outside the fray: "We only hear his mellifluous voice as he benignly admonishes his four wives not to fight among themselves."[10]

My intention in reading Yamamoto's memoir against the recent upheaval is not, however, simply to furnish parallels but also to draw instructive examples from the internal plot about the narrator's political evolution. The civic awareness and interracial empathy exemplified by the narrator run counter to the group-oriented politics that threaten to splinter our multicultural society today. While I welcome the present curricular emphasis on ethnic history and cultural knowledge, I believe a more interactive approach is needed to discourage insularity and to promote understanding among different groups. As scholars and teachers we must do more than simply focus on the history and concerns of a particular ethnic group. Merely adopting what Ronald Takaki calls the "add-on" approach is not enough: "[Educators]. . . add a week on African-Americans and another on Hispanics. . . . Meanwhile, inter-group relationships remain invisible, and the big picture is missing."[11]

Such an approach cannot remedy the social fragmentation demonstrated in the 1992 upheaval. To me one of the most troubling revelations emerging from the occurrences that preceded and followed the "not guilty" verdict was the seeming inability of people to relate to and stand up for those of another race. Such an inability, as Cho argues, was responsible in part for allowing the hostility between African Americans and Korean Americans that had been building up long before the Rodney King beating to go unchecked: "Because Korean- and Asian-American academics failed to speak up and condemn the light sentence that Judge Karlin rendered in the Du [the female shopkeeper who killed a black teenager suspected of shoplifting] case *before* the riots forced this reckoning, we were complicit in the sentencing as well. Likewise, African-American scholars could have taken a position on the blatant promotion of hate violence against Korean Americans in Ice Cube's lyrics but failed to do so."[12]

While it is understandable that people identify most readily with and therefore are more defensive or protective of those of the same extraction, it would promote the search for justice by all concerned, juries included, if more Caucasians and Asians could speak with moral indignation about the double standard of justice in America that is often stacked against African Americans, and if more African Americans could unequivocally condemn actions such as the battering of Reginald Denny and the burning of Korean stores. The media was perhaps again to blame in often selecting black spokespersons to defend blacks, white spokespersons to denounce them, and so forth (as in the coverage of the Denny trial). Yet this kind of media coverage can well turn into a self-fulfilling prophecy, reinforcing in the public mind that only people of the same color could and should stick together.

The alternative attitude of the narrator in "Fire" offers an effective antidote to colorfast ideology. She not only crosses racial barriers but also combats prejudice without resorting to the rhetoric of opposition, and addresses interracial conflict rationally and feelingly. Her memoir opens as follows:

> Something weird happened to me not long after the end of the Second World War. I wouldn't go so far as to say that I, a Japanese American, became Black. . . . But some kind of transformation did take place. . . . Sometimes I see it as my inward self being burnt black in a certain fire. ("F," 366–67)

The narrator felt so incensed by the fire in Fontana that she began to identify viscerally with African Americans, grappling with both white and Asian prejudice against blacks. The "blackening" of her inward self occurred, however, even before that fire. Interned for being a Japanese American during World War II, she could readily connect the injustices she herself had encountered with the

discrimination against blacks she witnessed in the fifties and sixties. On her way back to the internment camp in Arizona during
World War II, she was sitting next to a blond woman on a bus
out of Chicago who, upon seeing an African American man being
denied a drink at a restaurant south of Springfield, "was filled
with glee." The narrator instinctively linked her "seatmate's joy
and [her] having been put in that hot and windblown place of
barracks" ("F," 367).

Recognizing common oppression and forging alliances with
other marginalized groups can prevent people of color from being caught in the "Red Lantern" trap Kim describes. Yet, like the
polarization of black and white spokespersons by the media, a
rhetoric of opposition based on skin color—specifically the generic whites versus nonwhites—may exacerbate divisions along
racial lines and homogenize important differences within each
group. The narrator indicates that "more than once [she] was
easily put down with a casual, 'That's mightly White of you,' the
connotations of which were devastating" ("F," 369). But outward
pigmentation cannot encode political sensibility, as the narrator's
black allegiance attests.

Her gravitation toward African Americans notwithstanding,
the narrator refrains from writing all white people off. While she
gives ample glaring examples of white prejudice, she also fur-
nishes counterexamples. Unlike Miss Moten, the African American secretary at the *Tribune* office who, upon hearing Short's story,
"spat out the words 'I hate White people! They're all the same!'"
("F," 370), she begins her memoir with exceptions to this rule:

> I remember reading a book . . . based on the life of Bix Beiderbecke,
> in which the narrator early wonders if his musician friend would
> have come to the same tragic end if he hadn't become involved with
> Negroes. . . . In real life, there happened to be a young White musi-
> cian in an otherwise Black band. . . . His name was Johnny Otis. . . .
> In more recent years he has become the pastor of a church in Watts.
> I suppose he, too, arrived at a place in his life from which there
> was no turning back. But his life, as I see it, represents a triumph.
> ("F," 366–67)

The narrator, as indicated earlier, also makes a point of remembering the white priest who was relocated after his play cast
doubts on the police theory about the fire in Fontana. These
anecdotes suggest that regardless of one's skin color it is possible
to reach out to people of a different race.

To conclude on this sanguine note alone, however, is to ignore

Yamamoto's trenchant testimony, implicit in her account of the narrator's inner transformation, about the depth and magnitude of racism (often aggravated by the reluctance of the dominant culture to confront or even admit the problem) and its profound emotional impact on the afflicted minorities. Isolated cases of whites who ally with blacks socially or politically are insufficient, Yamamoto implies, to allay the anger of those subject to persistent abuse or to prevent them from seeing all white people as the enemy.

The narrator demonstrates the cumulative and erosive effects of racism by tracking her own mounting indignation and diminishing self-assurance. During the early stages of her apprenticeship with the *Tribune,* she was puzzled by her co-workers' preoccupation with race: "The inexhaustible topic was Race, always Race. . . . Sometimes I got to wondering whether Negroes talked about anything else" ("F," 369). However, after protracted exposure to hate crimes in the course of doing her job, which included "[toting] up the number of alleged lynchings across the country and [combining] them into one story" ("F," 368), she found herself becoming more and more like her black colleagues, to the extent of losing several correspondents because of her own obsession with race: "When one fellow dared to imply that I was really unreasonable on the subject of race relations, saying that he believed it sufficient to make one's stand known only when the subject happened to come up, the exchange of letters did not continue much longer" ("F," 371). Her initiation at the newspaper office was compounded by lessons on the street, as when she heard a white driver insult the driver of her bus, "Why, you Black bastard!" The black driver kept going, but the narrator "was sick, cringing from the blow of those words." She who had been shocked earlier by Miss Moten's wholesale denunciation of whites at this point "knew Miss Moten's fury for [her] very own" ("F," 372).

The most telling indication of the narrator's transformation appears at the end of the memoir, quoted earlier, when she describes the rampage she saw on the screen during the Watts riot as "the long-awaited, *gratifying* next chapter of an old movie that had flickered about in the back of my mind for years" (my emphasis). Throughout the memoir, the narrator, while revealing her growing affiliation with black Americans, has shown unusual sensitivity in chronicling race relations and remarkable restraint in expressing her own sentiment. Her use of the adjective "gratifying" (albeit qualified by mention of her "cowering" and "distress" at the spectacle) to describe the destruction on the screen stands out as a grim reminder of the pernicious effect of racism on the afflicted psyche. In admitting to feeling "a tiny trickle of warmth which [she] finally recognized as an undercurrent of exultation" while watching the burning of another family of four (who were likely to be as innocent as the Short family), the narrator makes us aware that those who constantly suffer from racist abuse or bear witness to it cannot be expected to always think and feel rationally, that no amount of reasoning and individual good will can check the anger and hatred of those incapable of obtaining justice from law enforcement officials (who may, in the event, actually persecute the victims or turn a deaf ear to their grievances), that inequity will provoke retaliation, if only vicariously and even at the expense of other innocent people.

While this haunting ending concludes the external plot, the internal plot of the narrative offers a different form of vengeance and provides a resolution which I believe is more promising and gratifying to the writer and reader alike. At the beginning of the memoir, the narrator, after judging the life of Johnny Otis to be a "triumph" because of his commitment to blacks, wonders: "But I don't know whether mine is or not" ("F," 367). She doubts whether her life amounts to a similar triumph (despite her own unquestionable loyalty to blacks) presumably because the "burning" of her inward self has left considerable scars. She has suffered the impotent rage and gnawing frustration of being unable to speak up on behalf of African Americans. Empathy alone cannot take away her sense of guilt for what she has *not* done.

The narrator repeatedly evokes this feeling of paralysis and futility. She regrets her inability to articulate the true cause of the fire in Fontana. She reflects on the way she could have reported and the way she actually reported the news by recalling two characters often seen in Little Tokyo. One was a Japanese evangelist who, before the war, "used to shout on the northeast corner of First and San Pedro in Little Tokyo" ("F," 370). His call to salvation could be heard from a distance and, closer up, one could see "his face awry and purple with the passion of his message" ("F," 371). The other was a boy in a wheelchair, pushed by a little girl or another boy. Dependent as a baby, this boy, who appeared regularly on the sidewalks, "always wore a clean white handkerchief round his neck to catch the bit of saliva which occasionally trickled from a corner of his mouth" ("F," 371). The narrator sees herself mirrored in the disabled boy rather than in the ardent evangelist, though she wishes it were otherwise:

It seems to me that my kinship . . . was with the large boy in the wheelchair, not with the admirable evangelist. . . . For, what had I gone and done?. . . I should have been an evangelist . . . shouting out the name of the Short family and their predicament in Fontana. But I had been as handicapped as the boy in the wheelchair, as helpless. ("F," 371)

She felt similarly choked after hearing the racial slurs against the black driver: "I wanted to yell out the window at the other driver, but what could I have said? I thought of reporting him to management, but what could I have said?" ("F," 372). On another occasion, she objected to some guests' obnoxious remarks about "edgeacated niggers," but she "knew nothing had been accomplished" ("F," 372).

The narrator's recurrent failure to defend black people through speech or writing had been so debilitating and demoralizing that she quit her job with the *Tribune*:

Not long after [the incident on the bus], going to work one morning, I found myself wishing that the streetcar would rattle on and on and never stop. I'd felt the sensation before, on the way to my mother's funeral. If I could somehow manage to stay on the automobile forever, I thought, I would never have to face the fact of my mother's death. A few weeks [later] I mumbled some excuse about planning to go back to school and left the paper.

I didn't go back to school, but . . . I got on trains and buses that carried me several thousand miles across the country and back. . . . I was realizing my dream of travelling forever (escaping responsibility forever) . . . and most of the time I didn't argue with anyone. ("F," 372)

The passage, particularly the analogy to the mother's funeral, intimates the narrator's anguish at her lack of agency and, more specifically, her loss of faith in the efficacy of her own words. Yet stopping writing altogether and escaping responsibility forever can hardly assuage the curdling inside.

It is in the context of the narrator's deepening silence that the memoir represents, knowingly or not, her ultimate triumph. In the very act of writing it, the narrator has effectively exposed a long-forgotten crime. Like the play of the white priest (and like the video of the Rodney King beating), this memoir disputes the police version of what happened and opens the audience's eyes to a flagrant violation of civil rights. Though the criminals remain unidentified, the readers decidedly can tell that the black family in Fontana was murdered, can perhaps even know Miss Moten's fury as their very own. One is reminded of an analogy in Maxine Hong Kingston's *The Woman Warrior:* "The [Chinese] idioms for *revenge* are "report a crime."[13] Yamamoto, through her memoir, has figuratively avenged the Short family by reporting the hate crime, writing/righting the wrong. She has implicated the white neighbor(s), the conniving police and, to some extent, the press and journalism, as she finds she can only articulate truth and voice her protest in another medium. She has written the story that may make up for the "lame" report she wrote earlier for the *Tribune;* she has vindicated and reclaimed her own voice. Finally, by committing the fire in Fontana to an eponymous memoir, she has ensured that this disturbing event will never be forgotten as mere "news."

The American Dream seems to have narrowed with time, from a dream—albeit never realized—of freedom and democracy for all to one of personal and often material success. Because this nation celebrates individualism almost without reservation, the American Dream has become increasingly self-centered. Individuals no longer look beyond their own welfare, and an oppressed group cannot look beyond its own oppression. Worse still, people may fulfill their dreams at others' expense. Without the bigger dream, however, individual prosperity may come to naught. Short's dream of living in a house of his own was snuffed out along with his life. The Korean real estate agent realized her dream of upward mobility by exploiting her black clients. The dreams of many new immigrants went up in the flames of the 1992 L.A. riot. To prevent the American Dream from turning into a national nightmare, we need a multicultural education that will not only provide us with knowledge about different ethnic groups but will also foster a sense of accountability across racial lines.

Yamamoto's memoir, through its double structure, offers two scenarios of what can happen in our multiracial society. The external plot forewarns that injustices such as the live incineration of the Short family (or, more recently the police brutality again Rodney King) seed civil unrest that can lead to irreparable breach among peoples, that can culminate in uncontrollable social explosions not unlike the one we experienced in 1992. The internal plot, by contrast, evinces the possibility of reciprocal solicitude and personal agency. It suggests that we can take someone else's dream

and grievance as our own, that even though we cannot alter the
color of our skins, our inner selves can take on different shades.

Notes

1. Hisaye Yamamoto, "A Fire in Fontana," in *Rereading America: Cultural Contexts for
Critical Thinking and Writing,* ed. Gary Columbo et al., 2d ed. (Boston: Bedford Books,
1992), 366–73. Hereafter "Fire," cited in the text. An earlier version of the present essay
was presented at the Japanese American National Museum and was excerpted in *Humanities Network* 15 (1993):2–3, 10. I have also discussed Yamamoto's technique of "double-
telling" at length in my book *Articulate Silences: Hisaye Yamamoto, Maxine Hong Kingston, Joy
Kogawa* (Ithaca: Cornell University Press, 1993), 27–73.
Opinions differ on whether to characterize the postverdict upheaval in Los Angeles as
a riot or a rebellion. I believe elements of both were present and hence use terms such as
"riot," "civil disorder," "rebellion," "uprising," and "insurrection" interchangeably.
2. *Aiiieeeee! An Anthology of Asian-American Writers,* ed. Frank Chin et al. (1974; reprint,
Washington, D. C.: Howard University Press, 1983), xxxiv. Elaine H. Kim, *Asian-American
Literature: An Introduction to the Writings and Their Social Context* (Philadelphia: Temple
University Press, 1982), 160.
3. Hisaye Yamamoto, "Writing," in *"Seventeen Syllables"/Hisaye Yamamoto,* ed. King-Kok
Cheung (New Brunswick, N.J.: Rutgers University Press, 1994), 64.
4. The Dunbar Hotel, located at 4225 S. Central Avenue, was the first hotel in America
built specifically for blacks in 1928 "because prejudice made it impossible for blacks to
find adequate lodging while traveling. During its heyday in the 1930s, almost every prominent black who visited Los Angeles stayed at the Dunbar." See Richard Saul Wurman, *LA/
Access* (Los Angeles: Access Press, 1982), 90.
5. Robert Gooding-Williams observes that views presented on television after the L. A.
riot suggested that the commotion had little to do with the verdict: "the conservative view
saw the 'rioters' [as] embodying an uncivilized chaos. . . . The liberal view . . . emphasized
the social causes of the 'riots'. . . . It strains credulity to deny . . . that the uprising in Los
Angeles was not for many an act of political protest." See "Look, A Negro!" in *Reading
Rodney King: Reading Urban Uprising,* ed. Robert Gooding-Williams (New York: Routledge,
1993), 169, 170.
6. Gooding-Williams, "Introduction: On Being Stuck," *Reading Rodney King,* 1.
Gooding-Williams states that his book on Rodney King deliberately "contests the representation of the Rodney King incidents as *news,* viz., as new and dramatic news events, no less
than it contests the remembrance of these incidents as old news. By stripping these incidents of the aura of the extraordinary, this book attempts to recover and to explicate their
connections to the uneventful and ordinary realities which, while ignored by the news,
persistently affect life in urban America" (2).
7. Elain H. Kim, "Home Is Where the *Han* Is: A Korean-American Perspective on the
Los Angeles Upheavals," *Reading Rodney King,* 219.
8. Sumi K. Cho, "Korean Americans vs. African Americans: Conflict and Construction," *Reading Rodney King,* 199.
9. Ibid., 197, 203.
10. Kim, "Home is Where the *Han* Is," 217.
11. Ronald Takaki, "Are the Multicultural Experiments Working?" *Washington Post,* 1

August 1993, 36. See also Ronald Takaki, *A Different Mirror: A History of Multicultural America* (Boston: Little, Brown, 1993).

12. Cho, "Korean Americans vs. African Americans," 209.

13. Maxine Hong Kingston, *The Woman Warrior: Memoirs of a Girlhood among Ghosts* (1976; reprint, New York: Vintage Books, 189), 53.

"Who'd He Leave Behind?":
Gender and History in
Toni Morrison's *Song of Solomon*

Susan Farrell

College of Charleston

WRITING about her first novel, *The Bluest Eye*, Toni Morrison advocates historical contextualizing. "In order to fully comprehend" the notion of "a secret between us and a secret that is being kept from us" implied in the novel's opening sentence, Morrison writes that "one needs to think of the immediate political climate in which the writing took place."[1] The immediate political and historical context surrounding Morrison's third novel, *Song of Solomon*, however, has not yet been closely and critically analyzed. Most of the criticism has been concerned with the mythic dimension of the book, whether traditional Western mythic structures or particularly African American myths and folktales. Jacqueline de Weever's "Toni Morrison's Use of Fairy Tale, Folk Tale, and Myth in *Song of Solomon*" (1980) was followed by A. Leslie Harris's "Myth as Structure in Toni Morrison's *Song of Solomon*" and Dorothy H. Lee's well-known piece, "*Song of Solomon: To Ride the Air*" (1982). Later, Genevieve Fabre argued that, by moving "away from sociology" into the realm of "mystery, poetry and prophecy," *Song of Solomon* followed "guidelines" which Alice Walker established for black women writers (1988). Marilyn Sanders Mobley, in her 1991 book, *Folk Roots and Mythic Wings in Sarah Orne Jewett and Toni Morrison*, explained *Song of Solomon* as "a nexus of myth and folklore, magic and realism that at once draws on narratives from Greek mythology, African myth, African-American folklore, and fairy tales." And Trudier Harris, in *Fiction and Folklore: The Novels of Toni Morrison* (1991) refocused critical attention on specifically African American myth and folklore in the novel. Unlike criticism directed at Morrison's first two novels, *The Bluest Eye* and *Sula,* early criticisms of *Song of Solomon* seldom raised the issue of feminism. And when this issue was addressed, scholars usually limited their comments to descriptions and evaluations of Pilate's role in the novel. For instance, Carolyn Denard, in her article "The Convergence of Feminism and Ethnicity in the Fiction of Toni Morrison," devotes only one paragraph, focusing solely on Pilate, to a discussion of *Song of Solomon.*[2]

Perhaps the first comprehensive attempt to address Morrison's feminism in relation to *Song of Solomon* was Gerry Brenner's 1987 "*Song of Solomon*: Rejecting Rank's Monomyth and Feminism." In this article, Brenner perceptively and convincingly shows how Morrison sets Milkman up as a hero, only to undermine and reject the sexism of traditional Western notions of the heroic. However, in the second half of the essay, Brenner claims that Morrison rejects feminism as well, largely through her portrayal of "pathetic" female characters. In a startlingly insensitive and unpersuasive reading, Brenner asserts that Hagar, when she "overreacts" to her desertion by Milkman, is the "most pathetic" of these female characters:

> She is utterly resourceless in a crisis. Forsaken by Milkman, she becomes obsessively jealous, impotently vindictive, and most pathetic of all, deluded with the notion that the acquisition of allegedly beautifying commodities will magically repossess Milkman.[3]

Not only does he resort to masculine metaphors in his description of Hagar (she is "impotent"), Brenner seems to have forgotten the lesson taught us by *The Bluest Eye,* that racist and sexist social forces underly constructions of female beauty in the U. S. Is Hagar really to blame for seeking these "beautifying commodities" when the world around her tells her, and has told her since birth, that women *must* be beautiful, and further, that "true" beauty equals whiteness? Is she to blame when these values are reinforced by Milkman's attraction to "light-skinned" women? However, Brenner reserves his most caustic remarks for his descriptions of Lena who, he asserts, is "doomed to spinsterhood" and whose speech denouncing Milkman is "forceful and partly gratuitous" and "certainly signal[s] some personal anger in Morrison's own life" ("RR," 120). Failing to read the struggles of Morrison's black women characters as indicative of the historical, very real position of black women in America, Brenner dismisses feminist anger and social analysis as the author's "personal" problems.

In addition, Brenner misreads the end of the novel when he

overlooks the significant change and growth that Milkman has experienced in the course of his journey. Brenner tells us that

> when Milkman leaps at the novel's end into Guitar's arms and certain death, his act is but one more gesture of irresponsibility; he flies, indeed, from the burdens of doing something meaningful in life, preferring the sumptuous illusion that he will ride the air. ("RR," 119)

Brenner cautions against using Milkman as a role model. For Brenner, Milkman ends up only as "someone silly enough to thrill to the notion that the capacity to fly is important" ("RR," 119). The capacity to fly, however, is indeed important in the novel; Milkman's leap is not to "certain death," but, I will argue, toward life and change.

More recent critical analyses of *Song of Solomon* have tended to focus on gender issues in greater detail than the earlier pieces did. Barbara Hill Rigney, for instance, places Morrison's works in the context of French feminist theorists in order to explore Morrison's use of a "feminine language," arguing that "Morrison does write what the French call *différence*, that feminine style that opens the closure of binary oppositions and thus subverts many of the basic assumptions of Western humanistic thought."[4] As a result of her largely psychoanalytical focus, though, Rigney tends to ignore the specifically African American historical context of the novel. Although she recognizes that women suffer as a result of the male desire for flight, she never reads this suffering as growing out of a particular time and place. In her 1993 book, Denise Heinze fruitfully explores patriarchal family dynamics in the novel, even arguing that "for families to survive, they must include men who—and this is most important—are feminized." Yet, Heinze never explores how this "feminizing" takes place in *Song of Solomon*, rather choosing to immediately switch the discussion to Morrison's fourth novel, *Tar Baby*, where "Milkman, Pilate's convert, will appear again in a more symbolic, feminine role in the form of Son."[5]

Perhaps the most insightful piece to date on the topic of gender in *Song of Solomon* is Michael Awkward's 1990 *Callaloo* article, "'Unruly and let loose': Myth, Ideology and Gender in *Song of Solomon*." In this article, Awkward argues convincingly that *Song of Solomon* should be read as both critiquing the "sometimes virulently phallocentric nature of traditional Western myths, including Afro-American ones" while at the same time affirming "the ideological perspectives of these narratives where they involve the

nature of black survival."[6] Unlike Brenner, who argues that, in
Song of Solomon, Morrison rejects *both* a traditional monomyth *and*
feminism, Awkward recognizes that Morrison affirms aspects of
both. Her position as a black female writer affords the novel a
complex ideology of "afrocentric and feminist politics." However,
like Rigney and Heinze, Awkward fails to place the novel into
its immediate historical context. He focuses on a universalized,
nebulous sense of myth—on the *"general* failure" (emphasis
added) of Western (including African American) myths to allow
full female participation. In contrast, this essay proposes that
Morrison's third novel be read as a response not only to general
Western mythic structures, not only to general feminist attacks
on patriarchy, but to quite particular and specific historical contexts: the developing dominant American literary background of
postmodernism, as well as the racial and gender liberation movements of the 1960s and 1970s in America, especially the strain
within the civil rights/black power movements of the 1960s that
presented racial liberation as a struggle to attain manhood.

When literary critics attempt to characterize American literature written since 1960, they use the term "postmodernism" more
than any other. The label "postmodern," however, while perhaps
suited to the work of authors such as Thomas Pynchon, Joseph
Heller, Donald Barthelme, John Irving, and Kurt Vonnegut, is
inadequate for describing other significant contributions to contemporary American literature, in particular, the dozens of works
recently written by women from marginalized ethnic groups.
These ethnic women writers respond to very different cultural
and historical contexts than the postmodern authors. The American postmodernists, heavily influenced by the experience of
World War II, saw cultural authority carried to its extreme in
Nazism. They often created characters who were paralyzed by
vast impersonal systems that could not be meaningfully changed
by human action. Thus, the postmodernists typically rejected both
collective (cultural) and individual authority. Their texts often
turn inward in obsessive self-reflection as their authors grapple
with a linguistically based reality. But Morrison and a group of
other ethnic women writers, whose work is largely informed by
the protest movements of the 1960s and 1970s, tend to focus
outward; they believe real political change is possible. Consequently, the literature produced by these women writers does not
stop at deconstruction, as the postmodernists often do. While an
author like Cherríe Moraga, in *Loving in the War Years,* dismantles

traditional notions of *la familia* and *machismo*, she nevertheless wishes to retain the benefits she believes close-knit Chicano family structures have provided. Thus, rather than merely destabilizing the notion of family, Moraga reconstructs it in terms of "suffering and celebrations shared" among friends.[7] For contemporary ethnic American women writers, this rebuilding gesture—what Ihab Hassan calls the (re)constructive force of postmodernism—is as much a necessary step as the destabilizing or deconstruction of a Western cultural authority that is traditionally both white and male.[8] Ramon Saldívar, in his discussion of Chicano authors, insists on this same point: "The subversive edge of each of the texts I examine effects deconstruction. But this deconstruction always implies the reconstruction of what has been undone at the site of its former presence."[9] And Maxine Hong Kingston, while calling for a "global novel" that "brings chaos to the established order," nevertheless does not want to leave things chaotic. Her urging of authors to write "happy endings to struggle," her idea that a place of sanctuary or refuge grows out of chaos, is the reconstructive part of her literary project.[10] Place, home, and community become the materials for suggesting both problems and possibilities. These books, then, with their reconstructive impulses, are not only more overtly political than the books in the main current of postmodernism, they are more likely to sanction a cultural ethics.

These women authors are not willing to accept the complete loss of self or of legitimate cultural authority that might result from a solely deconstructive, ironizing strategy. While Western authority might be viewed as something which needs to be challenged, whose loss is not to be lamented, the absence or loss of the subject *is* lamentable and not a psychologically and linguistically inevitable human condition. Slavery, colonization, and oppression are what produce the loss of personal ego and clear morality in these texts. Critic Diana Fuss, following the lead of Nancy K. Miller, argues that "like the female subject, the African American subject (who may also be female) *begins* fragmented and dispersed, begins with a 'double-consciousness' as Du Bois would say" so that "the condition of dispersal and fragmentation . . . is not to be achieved but to be overcome."[11] Similarly, Patricia Waugh argues that, for marginalized groups, the notion of identity as *constructed* was recognized long before postmodernism and post structuralism. Those defined as "other" by the dominant culture may never have experienced the sense of selfhood and personal autonomy granted the white male postmodernists. Thus, they do not have the luxury to proclaim the death of the self, having no historically recognized and valorized, if illusory, selves to proclaim dead.[12]

Or, as Toni Morrison quite forcefully puts it: "the trauma of racism is, for the racist and the victim, the severe fragmentation of the self, and has always seemed to me a cause (not a symptom) of psychosis" ("U," 16). Morrison makes this idea explicit in *Beloved* by associating the institution of slavery with a literal fragmentation of the self—dismemberment. Re-membering, then, is a way of becoming whole again, of putting one's self back together. In *Beloved*, Denver's mind is "opened" by Nelson Lord's advice to take care of herself: "It was a new thought, having a self to look out for and preserve."[13] Similarly, Paul D. helps Sethe to value her subjectivity when, in the last few pages of the book he tells her, "You your best thing, Sethe. You are" (*B*, 273). And in *Sula*, we see the inherent tragedy of a character who learns not only that there is no "other" to count on, but that there is "no self to count on either."[14] While Sula is "completely free of ambition, with no affection for money, property or things, no greed, no desire to command attention or compliments—*no ego*" (*S*, 119, emphasis added), she also feels no compunction about causing pain to others, and she lives out her life as a social pariah, finally dying alone, taken to the mortuary by the white people, who take hours to discover her first name. Ethnic women authors, including Morrison, do not characteristically embrace the fragmentation and dispersal of the self that is characteristic of postmodernism, although it is a mistake to assume that these writers substitute a simplistic or romanticized notion of wholeness and community.

We must remember, however, the political commitments of these women writers are various, complex, and historically contingent. If it is true that these works constitute a movement in contemporary American literature largely because of their identification with historically marginalized groups, the particulars of history are absolutely essential to any understanding of individual texts. Certainly this is the case with *Song of Solomon*, a novel about both the sexual and political education of a young man equally concerned with his formative relationships with several women— mother, aunt, lovers—and his intersection with the radical militancy of The Seven Days. The black power movement of the sixties and the story of women's place in it, along with assumptions about black women present throughout American culture (and readily apparent in government studies, academic reports, and sociological conclusions), are pieces of the historical context to which Morrison's novel responds. Read in this context, *Song of Solomon* is a feminist novel concerned with the African American "proto-myth" of achieving "manhood," a novel that evokes both the possibility of flight and the question "who'd he leave behind?"

One strain within the civil rights/black power movements of the 1960s—perhaps best represented by Stokely Carmichael's infamous remark that "the only position for women in SNCC (Student Nonviolent Coordinating Committee) is prone"—presented the movement as a struggle to attain manhood, but a manhood that African American feminists such as Michele Wallace have argued was based largely on the standards embraced by middle-class American whites.[15] Focusing primarily on racial oppression, many male leaders in the movement failed to recognize the specificity of female oppression, what has been called the "double bind" faced by women of color. Along with this failure came a related problem—a refusal to interrogate gender roles as they were played out in the movement, a blindness some of these leaders maintained to their own oppressive tendencies. The problem only seemed to worsen as the decade progressed. A masculine focus intensified as attention shifted from issues of civil rights and integration to black nationalism and black economic autonomy—black power. A more radical approach to black liberation emphasizing separatism over integration and the use of violence for self-defense was espoused by Elijah Muhammad and his Nation of Islam, whose main spokesperson became Malcolm X. Extremely influential in the thought and teachings of later black power advocates such as Stokely Carmichael, Eldridge Cleaver, the Black Panthers, Amiri Baraka, and others, Malcolm X overcame racial oppression, extreme poverty, and a life of crime and drugs to become a charismatic and influential leader of the black liberation struggle. But his attitude toward women never really escaped the streets of his youth or the patriarchal dogma of the Nation of Islam. In his autobiography, Malcolm not only asserts that "some women love to be exploited," but, moreover, that "*all* women, by their nature, are fragile and weak: they are attracted to the male in whom they see strength."[16] Further, reiterating the common "Sapphire" stereotype of black women popularized by the radio show *Amos 'n' Andy*, Malcolm apparently believed that if a woman *was* strong, she was castrating, disagreeable, and unfeminine.[17]

The Sapphire image—explicit in the notorious 1965 Moynihan Report, a government-sponsored examination of black family structure—was frequently evoked by the dominant white culture to justify sexual exploitation and oppression of black women.[18]

The Moynihan Report argued that problems within black communities were due not to racism, but to the deterioration of the black family, which, in turn, was due to the "matriarchal structure" of these families. Although immediately challenged by African American intellectuals, both male and female, for such things as skewed statistics, for ignoring the real discrepancy in the earning power of working black women and other jobholders in the U. S., and for underlying racist and sexist assumptions, the report reinforced the increasingly masculine focus of the movement itself. The link between the attitudes of some black men within the movement and the basic gender attitudes of patriarchal America was further demonstrated in the work of African American sociologists Calvin Hernton and Robert Staples. In his 1970 article, "The Myth of the Black Matriarchy," Staples, while ostensibly refuting Moynihan's conclusions, echoed the basic proposal of the Moynihan Report—that black women sublimate their needs and their ambitions to the desires of black men. In this piece, Staples argued that any discussion of "sex-role antagonisms extant in the black community will only sow the seed of disunity and hinder the liberation struggle."[19] In other words, black women must tolerate sexism until racial liberation has first been achieved: "black women cannot be free *qua* women until all blacks attain their liberation" ("M,"16). Hernton, in his influential 1965 book, *Sex and Racism in America,* reduced the problem of sex and race in America to the incident of the biracial couple, labeling as "feminist" only those women who question the validity of the black man's "attraction" to the white woman. And, according to Hernton, black women who question this attraction are most likely sexually dissatisfied and unattractive themselves.[20] Thus, in a view which Brenner echoes in his article on Morrison and feminism, Hernton dismisses "feminism" as "psychosexually" and "personally" motivated rather than "political, ideological, or economic."

These three main strands—the focus on male leadership and needs in the early civil rights movement, the essentialist view of gender evident in the revival of black nationalism, and the masculine bias apparent in academic studies of black male/female relationships—were the primary sources of what has been called the most sexist period in African American history: the black power movement of the late 1960s. And nowhere are these views so evident as in the thought and writing of Black Panther activist Eldridge Cleaver who, according to cultural critic Manning Marable, viewed the black liberation movement "first and last as the effort to assert one's manhood, in the sense of patriarchal hegemony

exhibited by the old planter class."[21] In *Soul on Ice,* written from
prison while incarcerated for rape, which, at one time, he considered an "insurrectionary act," Cleaver presents his view of gender
differentiation. Cleaver posits male and female as eternal comple-
ments; each has an essential, biologically based "true" nature, con-
stituting two separate parts of a whole. The basis of heterosexual
attraction, for Cleaver, is the "primeval Urge" or the "magnetism
of opposites" which will "fuse male and female back together in
. . . the lost unity of the Primeval Sphere." Straying from "unitary"
gender roles will not only result in the "sickness" of homosexuality,
but will disrupt history as well—preventing the eventual playing
out and resolution of the class struggle.[22] Although his attempts to
explore the social and historical dimensions of black male/female
antagonism and to set the stage for a revaluing of the black woman
should be applauded, Cleaver's ideas about gender are confusing
at best, and at worse, seem not much different from the views of
the white patriarchy he critiques.

While some black women ascribed to traditional Western views
of complementary, dominant/submissive gender roles, others
were more critical about the interplay between racial and sexual
oppression. A female-authored SNCC position paper, for instance, critiqued the treatment of women in the movement as
early as November 1964. Nevertheless, early black feminists recognized that, for them, the white women's movement was not a
viable alternative. Linda LaRue argued in 1970, for example, that
sexual exploitation was qualitatively different and "secondary in
nature" to the workings of white racism, that blacks were "oppressed" while white women were only "suppressed." LaRue also
cautioned that white women would attempt to capitalize on gains
achieved by the black movement without going through the same
struggles and groundwork that went into the earlier movement.[23]
Morrison herself, in an essay titled "What the Black Woman
Thinks About Women's Lib," asserted that suspicion was the answer to the question implied by her title: "too many movements
and organizations have made deliberate overtures to enroll Blacks
and have ended up by rolling them. They [black women] don't
want to be used again to help somebody gain power—a power
that is carefully kept out of their hands."[24] In addition, the predominantly white women's movement was found lacking for myopically viewing "male chauvinism" as the root of all oppression in
society, when racial prejudice seemed like a much more pressing
concern to many black women. Thus, black women hoping to
correct the shortsightedness of their men did not find much relief

in the women's liberation movement of the late sixties and early seventies. Addressing primarily the needs of white middle-class women, the women's movement in that period was often insensitive to the particular problems confronting women of color, and sometimes, in fact, operated on blatantly racist assumptions. Dissatisfied with both the black power movement and the women's liberation movement, African American feminists became increasingly vocal through the 1970s, viewing racism and sexism (and often class oppression as well as heterosexism) as inextricably intertwined within the American system. The sexism/racism debate raged fiercely throughout the seventies, eventually leading to the creation of a specifically black female movement which, by the eighties, established ties with oppressed women of other ethnic backgrounds in the U. S. and around the world.

Toni Morrison's *Song of Solomon,* written in the mid-seventies and published in 1977, can then be read as a black woman's response to the African American political situation in the U. S. of the mid-seventies, particularly to the aftermath of the civil rights/ black power movements. In such a reading, Milkman Dead, the novel's protagonist, becomes what many black feminists struggle against: the black patriarch, oppressed himself, yet at the same time oppressor. In *Song of Solomon,* Morrison not only criticizes racist structures that have emotionally crippled an urban black family in the 1960s, but she also condemns black sexism of the same era, describing the novel as her "giggle" at the "proto-myth of the journey to manhood." While celebrating a classic African American folktale about slaves flying to freedom, *Song of Solomon* also asks who gets left behind when the dream of flight becomes an exclusively male fantasy of escape.

Milkman's sexism, his refusal to validate the female, is asserted from the early pages of the novel, beginning with his relationship to his mother, Ruth Dead. Morrison writes that Milkman "had never loved his mother, but had always believed that she had loved him. And that had always seemed right to him, the way it should be."[25] Later, Milkman tells Guitar his dream in which Ruth is smothered by tulips. When asked why he didn't help her, Milkman replies that "she was having fun. She liked it." Described as long thin tubes "getting taller and taller," then "pressing up against . . . his mother's dress" (105), the tulips become phallic representations. Ruth is being smothered by the tulips much as she is stifled in ordinary life by her domineering husband, Macon Dead. And Milkman sees Ruth as complicitous in her oppression. Milkman's disdain for and distrust of black women is further demonstrated in his relationship with his own cousin, Hagar.[26] Abandoning his relationship with Hagar to date a red-headed, light-skinned woman, Milkman seems to be motivated by the standards of beauty offered by white America. His choice echoes those that, according to Michele Wallace among others, caused dissatisfaction among black women in the movement—the all too frequent choice of liberation leadership to become involved sexually with white women.

Implied as well in Milkman's rejection of Hagar is a rejection of his own blackness. Raised in a middle-class family, exposed to the bourgeois acquisitiveness of his father, Macon Dead, Milkman is in danger of denying his history, his particularly African American heritage. Although Milkman is confronted with stories of his family's past told to him by the older generation of characters— Macon, Ruth, and Pilate—he at first rejects this historical grounding, seeing it as a burden rather than as a means to liberation: "'Goddam,' Milkman said aloud, 'What the fuck did he tell me all that shit for?" (76). Further, Milkman's relationships with members of his family are just as tenuous and burdensome as his relationship to the past, to family history. When Macon explains his violence toward Ruth, Milkman feels "curiously disassociated from all that he had heard":

> As though a stranger that he'd sat down next to on a park bench had turned to him and begun to relate some intimacy. He was entirely sympathetic to the stranger's problems . . . but part of his sympathy was the fact that he himself was not involved or in any way threatened by the stranger's story. (74–75)

Although he describes his father as a stranger, as a completely separate and therefore unknowable person, Milkman can't even imagine his mother as a distinct individual: "Never had he thought of his mother as a person, a separate individual, with a life apart from allowing or interfering with his own" (75). Both views place Milkman's parents in stereotypical Western gender roles—his father's individuality impenetrable while his mother's identity remains diffuse and indistinct, blurred with that of other family members. Milkman, in fact, ignores his particular family history, as well as his particular African American heritage, when he plots a universalized narrative to explain his actions: "He was a man who saw another man hit a helpless person. And he had interfered. Wasn't that the history of the world? Isn't that what men did?" (75). It is not until part two of the novel, when Milkman is made to question his own patriarchal assumptions, that he begins to form a new script for what men—and women—do in this world.

If Milkman desires to become the black patriarch in this historicized reading of Morrison's novel, the position of Milkman's sister Magdalene (Lena) Dead, a minor character who has only marginally entered the story up until the very end of part one, parallels that of many African American women in the early seventies. She is the quintessential "other," doubly silenced, in terms of both race and gender, finally making her voice heard to her more vocal brother when she states plaintively, "you're not paying any attention to me." Lena, speaking as the feminist "other," protests not only power attained solely by virtue of gender, but the white, middle-class family structure that her father foists onto the Dead females as well:

> "When we were little girls, before you were born, he [Macon] took us to the icehouse once. Drove us there in his Hudson. We were all dressed up, and we stood there in front of those sweating black men, sucking ice out of our handkerchiefs, leaning forward a little so as not to drip water on our dresses. There were other children there. Barefoot, naked to the waist, dirty. But we stood apart, near the car, in white stockings, ribbons, and gloves. And when he talked to the men, he kept glancing at us, us and the car. The car and us. You see, he took us there so they could see us, envy us, envy him. Then one of the little boys came over to us and put his hand on Corinthians' hair. She offered him her piece of ice and before we knew it, *he* was running toward us. He knocked the ice out of her hand and into the dirt and shoved us both into the car. First he displayed us, then he splayed us. All our lives were like that: he would parade us like virgins through Babylon, then humiliate us like whores in Babylon." (217–18)

Macon Dead treats his daughters as beautiful objects, as possessions to be admired and envied. Morrison associates this male paternalistic attitude toward women with white America. Morrison writes that "black women have no abiding admiration of white women as competent, complete people" ("WL," 15), implying that black women tend to see white women as children, overprotected by their men and having no real responsibility. In this passage, Lena is protesting Macon's attempt to turn her and Corinthians into this kind of white woman, as he denies them access to what Morrison in *The Bluest Eye* refers to as "funk"—the sounds, sights, smells, and sensations that make up black experi-

ence. Furthermore, Lena goes on to accuse Milkman of following
in his father's footsteps. She calls Milkman a "sad, pitiful, stupid,
selfish, hateful man" (218) and asserts that, like his father, his only
power is derived "from that hog's gut that hangs down" between
his legs (217).

Morrison uses the example of patriarchy to criticize what she
sees as dangerous about the black power movement, about any
political movement for that matter: the tendency to say what
should dominate, what should be given value, ahead of individual
stories and priorities. However, at the same time that Morrison
warns against this erasure of individual needs, she also acknowledges that "unity among minorities is a political necessity" ("WL,"
15). Unlike postmodern authors who often reject both collective
and individual authority, Morrison sees the necessity of each—the
needs of the individual and the authority of individual experience
balanced against social and political realities. Thus, while Lena
speaks for the "other," for the individual ignored by a movement,
Guitar Baines, with his involvement in the radical political group
The Seven Days, speaks for the political necessity of establishing
a black community. Both voices are valuable, and yet both are
incomplete.

While Lena rightfully questions Milkman's disdain for women,
and recognizes that his favored position in the family results from
male prerogative, she is, nevertheless, largely ineffective in
changing her own situation or that of the other women in the
Dead household because hers remains an individual voice. Unlike
African American feminists in the early 1970s who worked to
form a movement, Lena lives an isolated life which renders her
unable to connect with any larger historical or political context.
On the other hand, Guitar Baines, while acutely aware of history
and of political necessity, pushes the idea of social and racial justice to a grotesque extreme. When Guitar tells Milkman that the
purpose of the radical political group The Seven Days is to avenge
murdered blacks by murdering whites, Milkman asks: "Why don't
you just hunt down the ones who did the killing? Why kill innocent people? Why not just those who did it?" (156). Here, Milkman recognizes that acting solely on principles of group identity
and conflict can be dangerously totalizing. Individual lives don't
matter as Guitar places sole emphasis on the large historical picture, on keeping "the ratio the same" (156). Further, Milkman
recognizes the possibility of *himself* becoming the "other" and not
fitting into Guitar's scheme of things:

> "You can off anybody you don't like. You can off me."
> "We don't off Negroes."

"You hear what you said? *Negroes*. Not Milkman. Not 'No, I can't touch *you*, Milkman,' but 'We don't off Negroes.' Shit, man, suppose you all change your parliamentary rules?" (162)

Milkman's response indicates that Guitar has formed a unitary language of his own, similar to the language of the white racist. Milkman is not valued for himself, but only as a member of a particular racial group. Unlike many leaders of the black power movement, who warned against "airing dirty laundry" in public, who advocated group solidarity at the expense of examining women's accusations of sexist rhetoric and practice, Morrison, like other contemporary ethnic women writers, recognizes that communities can both silence members and be sites of resistance at the same time. While the notion of community can suggest group solidarity, inclusion, within the promise of community always lies the possibility for forming a unitary, exclusionary language that suppresses and silences those who do not fit in. Through Guitar's involvement in The Seven Days, Morrison shows that unitary languages, whether oppressive or liberationist, suppress individual difference and personal accountability in similar ways.

Nevertheless, Guitar's vision of racial unity cannot be easily or completely dismissed, just as we should not simply dismiss the fears of black leaders who viewed the success of black feminist writers such as Wallace and Ntozake Shange with suspicion. Such fears were often valid indictments of the willingness of the white media and reading public to accept negative racial stereotypes. And just as Morrison warns against "lump thinking," against viewing individuals solely as members of groups, she also admits that this kind of generalizing is sometimes legitimate, because racial unity can be absolutely necessary politically ("WL," 15). However, as Asian American critic Elaine Kim so convincingly argues, "the solution to the problem of 'cultural misreadings' does not lie in silencing women writers and riveting them back into lopsided gender relationships." Rather, the way out of this problem seems to lie in ensuring that a multiplicity of minority ethnic voices are available and in remembering that, as so many U. S. minority feminists strongly emphasize, for the ethnic American woman writer, "gender and ethnicity cannot be separated."[27] In *Song of Solomon*, Morrison juxtaposes the voices of Lena, Guitar, and Milkman to emphasize both the needs of the individual and the need for a unified community. One should not be pursued to the exclusion of the other; the two must always exist in a dialectical relationship.

It is this dialectic that sends Milkman on his journey in part two of *Song of Solomon*. In order to recreate an identity for himself, Milkman must strive for a kind of manhood based not on the model supplied by his father and accepted by some within the protest movements of the 1960s—a white, middle-class paternalism—but rather on a model suggested by his own unique black history and cultural heritage. Milkman must learn a new language that will help him challenge and subvert the dominant discourse of racism as well as an exclusively individualistic ideology that prevents political cohesion or change. When he finds himself in the forest, hunting with the men of Shalimar, Milkman begins his lessons. In the forest, middle-class materialistic values become meaningless, simply "the shit that weights you down" (180). Similarly, bourgeois emphasis on an isolated individualism—"the cocoon that was 'personality'"—gives way. A new emphasis on community rises to take its place, and this community expands to include both humans as well as their natural environment. The language Milkman learns is one that existed "in the time when men and animals did talk to one another, when a man could sit down with an ape and the two converse; when a tiger and a man could share the same tree, and each understood the other; when man ran *with* wolves, not from or after them" (281). This return to a very old language challenges the authoritative language of the "civilized" white male hegemony in which human beings are separate and distinct from nature. It is made up of many different voices rather than a single, authoritative, unifying language: "all those shrieks, those rapid tumbling barks, the long sustained yells, the tuba sounds, the drumbeat sounds, the low liquid *howm howm*, the reed whistles, the thin *eeeee's* of a cornet, the *unh unh unh* bass chords" (281). Although the voices are not represented as human, Morrison's point is that Milkman is able to accept this multiplicity as language. If the novel ended here, with Milkman's return to cultural roots, the body of criticism emphasizing *Song of Solomon*'s mythic structure might be justified.

However, this "language before language" that Milkman experiences with the men of Shalimar turns out to be inadequate. Although the first step in throwing off white, middle-class values, in writing a new cultural myth, might involve turning to the past, there is always the danger that the past will be romanticized, idealized as some sort of precolonial Edenic utopia. Paula Gunn Allen, a Native American poet and critic, warns against this tendency. Allen argues that this romanticizing is accomplished not only by the dominant culture's stereotyping, but by members of the ethnic

minority group itself: "idealization of a group is the natural consequence of separation from the group: a by-product of alienation."[28] The ideal picture of harmony between men and animals
that Milkman imagines as he rests in the forest is just such a
mystification.[29] Just as Milkman's reverie is interrupted by the
highly political Guitar brutally choking him with a wire drawn
tight around his neck, so the tendency to idealize the past is
checked by political necessity and historical accuracy. Likewise,
although his initiation into the men's group in Shalimar allows
Milkman to discover more about his ancestor Solomon, Morrison
criticizes him for idealizing this ancestor. After hearing the story
of his great-grandfather's ability to fly, Milkman goes swimming
with Sweet, a Shalimar woman who had previously comforted
him. As Milkman jubilantly relates Solomon's story, Sweet remains
calm, finally asking "Who'd he leave behind?" (332). Milkman,
insensitive to her implied criticism, triumphantly answers "every-
body." In his celebration of the past, Milkman still has not learned
to recognize the female in a meaningful way, to criticize his own
patriarchal tendencies. The type of manhood he discovers in the
forest—"the woods, hunters, killing"—allows Milkman to reject
the bourgeois materialism of white America's model of manhood,
yet it still confines him to the type of sexism evident in the thinking
of some of the leaders of the black power movement. Like Lena,
Sweet speaks for the "other," the woman who is forgotten in the
midst of male triumph. The question of who gets left behind in
the quest for "manhood" is not yet important to Milkman.

Not until he turns to Pilate's house, gets hit over the head with
a bottle, and finds himself lying in Pilate's cellar, does Milkman
"wake up" to the issues raised by Lena and Sweet:

> Then he knew. Hagar. Something had happened to Hagar. Where
> was she? Had she run off? Was she sick or . . . Hagar was dead. The
> cords of his neck tightened. How? In Guitar's room, did she. . .?
>
> What difference did it make? He had hurt her, left her, and now
> she was dead—he was certain of it. He had left her. While he dreamt
> of flying, Hagar was dying. Sweet's silvery voice came back to him:
> "Who'd he leave behind?" He left Ryna behind and twenty children.
> Twenty-one, since he dropped the one he tried to take with him. And
> Ryna had thrown herself all over the ground, lost her mind, and was
> still crying in a ditch. Who looked after those twenty children? Jesus
> Christ, he left twenty-one children! (336)

In this moment of epiphany, Milkman takes the final step toward
maturity—he consciously recognizes those females who get left

behind by individualistic male dreams of freedom, of escape.[30] The issue here becomes one of responsibility. In accepting a box of Hagar's hair as a token of his responsibility toward her, Milkman sees through his ancestor Solomon much as Lena saw through Milkman himself in the final scene of part one. Unlike Solomon, who abandons his family, Milkman develops a new commitment to family and community. His early contempt for motherhood, as expressed in his attitude toward Ruth, changes. He now realizes that Pilate's father wasn't telling Pilate to sing, but, as he explains to her, "was calling for his wife—your mother," Sing (337). He also recognizes the importance of children: "it was the children who sang about it and kept the story of his leaving alive" (336).

Milkman's transformation has become complete by the end of the book. When Pilate dies, not only does Milkman recognize and affirm female experience, but he actually lives it. Milkman becomes the "other," the person left behind, as he sings to Pilate: "sugargirl don't leave me here" (340). "Sugarman" in Pilate's song has become "sugargirl" as the traditionally male trades places with the traditionally female. Milkman is now the nurturer as he cradles Pilate in his arms. Further, he recognizes that Pilate was able to fly "without ever leaving the ground" (340). Milkman's own flight at the novel's end is possible only after he learns to value both women and family. Contrary to Brenner's assertions that Milkman's final flight is "but one more gesture of irresponsibility" and that Milkman "flies . . . from the burdens of doing something meaningful in life," Milkman's flight represents an acknowledgment and acceptance of responsibility to others. Neither a suicide attempt resembling Robert Smith's flight at the beginning of the book nor an escape from responsibility resembling Solomon/Shalimar's flight, Milkman jumps *toward* Guitar. The novel's dominant metaphor of flying changes from a "flying away" to a "flying toward." In a departure from traditional *Bildungsroman* form, the quest for identity in Toni Morrison's *Song of Solomon* is rewritten as a search for family and cultural roots. In contrast to the black power movement's struggle to attain "manhood," the novel presents a journey to "personhood" and to community.

Notes

1. Toni Morrison, "Unspeakable Things Unspoken: The Afro-American Presence in American Literature," *Michigan Quarterly Review* 28 (Winter 1989): 29. Hereafter "U," cited in the text.

2. Jacqueline de Weever, "Toni Morrison's Use of Fairy Tale, Folk Tale, and Myth in

Song of Solomon," *Southern Folklore Quarterly* 44 (1980): 131–44; A. Leslie Harris, "Myth as Structure in Toni Morrison's *Song of Solomon,*" *MELUS* 7 (1980): 69–76; Dorothy H. Lee, "*Song of Solomon: to Ride the Air,*" *Black American Literature Forum* 16 (1982): 64–70; Genevieve Fabre, "Genealogical Archeology or the Quest for Legacy in Toni Morrison's *Song of Solomon,*" in *Critical Essays on Toni Morrison,* ed. Nellie Y. McKay (Boston: Hall, 1988), 107; Marilyn Sanders Mobley, *Folk Roots and Mythic Wings in Sarah Orne Jewett and Toni Morrison* (Baton Rouge: Louisiana State University Press, 1991), 132; Trudier Harris, *Fiction and Folklore: The Novels of Toni Morrison* (Knoxville: University of Tennessee Press, 1991); Carolyn Denard, "The Convergence of Feminism and Ethnicity in the Fiction on Toni Morrison," in *Critical Essays on Toni Morrison,* 171–79.

3. Gerry Brenner, "*Song of Solomon:* Rejecting Rank's Monomyth and Feminism," in *Critical Essays on Toni Morrison,* 119. Hereafter "RR," cited in the text.

4. Barbara Hill Rigney, *The Voices of Toni Morrison* (Columbus: Ohio State University Press, 1991), 3.

5. Denise Heinze, *The Dilemma of Double-Consciousness: Toni Morrison's Novels* (Athens: University of Georgia Press, 1993), 83.

6. Michael Awkward, "'Unruly and let loose': Myth, Ideology and Gender in *Song of Solomon,*" *Callaloo* 13 (Summer 1990): 486–87.

7. Cherríe Moraga, *Loving in the War Years* (Boston: South End Press, 1983), 111.

8. Ihab Hassan, "Pluralism in Postmodern Perspective," *Critical Inquiry* 12 (Spring 1986): 503–20.

9. Ramon Saldívar, *Chicano Narrative: The Dialectics of Difference* (Madison: University of Wisconsin Press, 1990), 7.

10. Maxine Hong Kingston, speech delivered at the University of Texas at Austin on 27 March 1990.

11. Diana Fuss, *Essentially Speaking: Feminism, Nature, and Difference* (New York: Routledge, 1989), 95.

12. Patricia Waugh, *Feminine Fictions: Revisiting the Postmodern* (London: Routledge, 1989).

13. Toni Morrison, *Beloved* (New York: Knopf, 1987), 252. Hereafter *B,* cited in the text.

14. Toni Morrison, *Sula* (New York: Knopf, 1973), 118–19. Hereafter *S,* cited in the text.

15. See Michele Wallace, *Black Macho and the Myth of the Superwoman* (New York: Warner Books, 1980).

16. *The Autobiography of Malcolm X* (with assistance of Alex Haley) (1965; reprint, New York: Ballantine Books 1973), 136; 94, emphasis added.

17. In his autobiography, Malcolm analyzes the heavy business he observed taking place every morning among the prostitutes with whom he shared an apartment building: "Domineering, complaining, demanding wives who had just about psychologically castrated their husbands were responsible for the early rush. These wives were so disagreeable and had made their men so tense that they were robbed of the satisfaction of being men. To escape this tension and the chance of being ridiculed by his own wife, each of these men had gotten up early and come to a prostitute. . . . More wives could keep their husbands if they realized their greatest urge is *to be men*" (93).

According to Bell Hooks, "as Sapphires, black women were depicted as evil, treacherous, bitchy, stubborn, and hateful, in short all that the mammy figure was not. . . . Like the biblical figure Eve, black women became the scapegoats for misogynist men and racist women who needed to see some group of women as the embodiment of female evil. See Bell Hooks, *Ain't I a Woman?* (Boston: South End Press, 1981), 85.

18. See Lee Rainwater and William L. Yancy, *The Moynihan Report and the Politics of Controversy* (Cambridge: MIT Press, 1967).

19. Robert Staples, "The Myth of the Black Matriarchy," *Black Scholar* 1 (January-February 1970): 15. Hereafter *"M,"* cited in the text.

20. Calvin Hernton, *Sex and Racism in America* (Garden City, N.Y.: Doubleday, 1965). Hernton tells us that "Negro women who hold up the banner of 'race pride' or of 'unjust rejection' when they see *a* Negro man or *some* Negro men marrying white women are, in essence, not really angry about that at all—usually their anxiety and bitterness stem from the fact that they are rarely successful with men of either race under any conditions. . . . Their fear of competing with white women is generated by their inability to compete successfully with the women of their own race. Predominantly, the women who become most alarmed over interracial marriages are single or victims of unhappy marriages themselves" (141).

21. Manning Marable, *How Capitalism Underdeveloped Black America* (Boston: South End Press, 1983), 93.

22. Eldridge Cleaver, *Soul on Ice* (New York: McGraw-Hill, 1979), 177–78, 110.

23. Linda LaRue, "The Black Movement and Women's Liberation," *Black Scholar* 1 (May 1970): 36–42.

24. Toni Morrison, "What the Black Woman Thinks About Women's Lib," *New York Times Magazine,* 22 August 1971, 15. Hereafter "WL," cited in the text.

25. Toni Morrison, *Song of Solomon* (New York: New American Library, 1977), 79. All subsequent citations to *Song of Solomon* will be to this edition and will be cited parenthetically in the text by page numbers only.

26. Distrust was a common theme in the black sexism debate of the 1970s. As Hernton points out, in 1978 and 1979 "all hell broke loose" over the Broadway production of Ntozake Shange's play *For Colored Girls Who Have Considered Suicide When the Rainbow Is Enuf* and over the publication of Michele Wallace's polemical book *Black Macho and the Myth of the Superwoman:* "the word went out: white males were using black women as a backlash against the black male's dynamic assertion of manhood during the 1960s" (*The Sexual Mountain,* 44). Shange's and Wallace's work was seen as "divisive" to the cohesion of the black community; they were accused of having "fallen prey" to white feminist propaganda or of being the unwitting dupes of an American mass public eager to hear anything negative about black males. The heated exchange reached a peak when, in May-June 1979, *The Black Scholar* devoted a whole issue, titled "The Black Sexism Debate," to black male/female relationships. Though this forum allowed various artists, critics, and movement spokespeople to make their positions explicit, it certainly did not settle anything, as the more recent furor over Steven Spielberg's movie version of Alice Walker's *The Color Purple* shows us. The 1991 U. S. Senate hearings over the confirmation of Supreme Court nominee Judge Clarence Thomas is the latest example of these issues being played out in a public forum. Not only was law professor Anita Hill, who claimed Thomas sexually harassed her when they worked together at the Equal Opportunity Employment Commission, accused of being the tool of white liberal democrats, but, in his defense, Thomas argued that the charges against him replayed centuries of racist stereotypes about the sexual depravity of the black male.

27. Elaine Kim, "Such Opposite Creatures: Men and Women in Asian American Literature," *Michigan Quarterly Review* 29 (Winter 1990):80.

28. Paula Gunn Allen, *The Sacred Hoop: Recovering the Feminine in American Indian Traditions* (Boston: Beacon Press, 1986), 129.

29. Rigney's reading of this "language before language" passage seems to involve such a mystification—she reads this passage as Milkman's initiation into a "mystical," fully "transcendent" language, even using Kristeva's idea of a "mother tongue," which is "beyond and within, more or less than meaning: rhythm, tone, color, and joy, within, through, and across the Word" to characterize it (*The Voices of Toni Morrison,* 10).

30. Awkward notes a similar point in his *Calalloo* article "'Unruly and let loose,'" although he does not place the novel in the context of the 1960s and 1970s black liberation movements. Awkward writes: "It is only at this point, when he learns of the painful consequences of the celebrated male act of flight, that Milkman's comprehension of his familial heritage and the song of Solomon can be said to move toward satisfying completion. Such understanding requires coming to terms with his familial song's complex, sometimes unflattering meaning, and acknowledging both its prideful flight and the lack of a sense of social responsibility in the mythic hero Solomon's leave-taking act" (496). Awkward also includes in his article a moving and insightful reading of Hagar's death, a scene which I do not analyze closely in this essay.

Maxine Hong Kingston and the Dialogic Dilemma of Asian American Writers

Amy Ling
University of Wisconsin-Madison

IN June 1993, at Cornell University during the tenth national conference of the Association for Asian American Studies, Robert Ku, a lecturer at Hunter College, delivered a provocative paper in which he lamented that Asian American writers themselves in writing of the cultural specificities of their own cultural backgrounds are forced into the language of anthropological ethnography and thereby partake of the hierarchical binaries of Same and Other, Normal and Exotic, Advanced and Backward, Superior and Inferior. As "native informants," they naturally fall within the second half of these categories. To demonstrate the similarity of the language used in anthropology, psychology, and literature, Ku read five brief unidentified passages, two by noted social scientists and three by noted Asian American writers. He later identified the authors of these passages as Bronislaw Malinowski, Carlos Bulosan, Younghill Kang, Maxine Hong Kingston, and Sigmund Freud.

What these passages had in common, it seemed to me, was not so much their language as their subject matter. Each passage described an event or ritual, either a marriage or punishment for a violation of a prohibition, that described customs specific to a culture outside of the dominant Anglo-European culture, such as the peasant wedding in the Philippines in the first chapter of *America Is in the Heart,* in which the bride is discovered not to be a virgin and therefore stoned by the villagers, and the similarly brutal treatment of the No Name Woman in Kingston's opening chapter of *The Woman Warrior.* Ku was disturbed and distressed by the "uneasy relationship between literature, ethnography, [and] psychoanalysis"[1] which Asian American writers, by their very position within a dominant society, cannot escape. He was puzzled and paralyzed because he wants to write his own story, presumably a Korean American *Bildungsroman,* but cannot figure out how to do so without sounding like an ethnographic "insider informant."

Moved by this predicament, I tried to console him by remarking that his role and that of all minority writers in this society, if we wish to be understood by a majority audience, cannot help but be that of cultural explainers until such time as everyone is informed on the myriad cultures that make up the United States. Given the size of the task and the inertia or chauvinism of most people, this universal enlightenment is not likely to happen in the near future. We have no choice, except of course, if we choose to speak only to others exactly like ourselves. If Ku wishes to address exclusively a Korean American audience, then, he can feel relieved of what he considers an onerous duty. But he will also be relieved of a great many readers. Moveover, I thought, in my self-righteous missionary mode, as teachers, it is our mission and our privilege to educate.

I suggested also that it is not so much the specificities of what is being conveyed as the tone and manner in which they are conveyed that sets apart the outsider standing aloof and above from the insider standing beside. The outsider creates the sense of otherness; the insider relates the norm.

At the same time, of course, we are all doubly conscious, in the Du Boisian sense, constantly aware of how we are being perceived while we are in the act of perceiving. Readers from outside the Asian American perspective, readers who may be reluctant in the first place, such as students taking a course in Asian American literature because they must satisfy an ethnic studies requirement for graduation, will complain that the material is so foreign and strange that they cannot possibly relate to it. (One would think they'd been asked to read stories written by baboons.) When confronted with several such responses this semester, I finally replied, "What about relating to this material as a human being?" (My sense of mission and privilege as an educator was growing faint.) The other response I found totally exasperating was the "Is-this-characteristic-of-Asian-Americans?" response. For example: "The narration in this text is fragmented. Is this a characteristic of Asian Americans?" Or "These novels devote a lot of time and space to food and family—are these characteristically Asian American concerns?" Where does such lack of comprehension come from? Is it so impossible for such students to think of Asian

Americans as part of the human species? Teaching Asian American literature to white students in the midwest can be at times comparable to handling nitroglycerine; the material, the students, and I are all, for different reasons, volatile.

Kingston herself has published an essay about the cultural misreadings by two-thirds of the reviewers of *The Woman Warrior,* who measured "the book and me against the stereotype of the exotic, inscrutable, mysterious oriental":

> I thought the reality and humanity of my characters would bust through any stereotypes of them. Simple-mindedly, I wore a sweatshirt for the dust-jacket photo, to deny the exotic. I had not calculated how blinding stereotyping is, how stupefying. The critics who said how the book was good because it was, or was not, like the oriental fantasy in their heads might as well have said how weak it was, since it in fact did not break through the fantasy. . . . "How amazing," they may as well be saying. "That she writes like a human being. How unoriental."[2]

It is not just reviewers from other cultures that "misread" an author's intent. Readers from within that very culture feel particularly free to use their own authors for target practice. Perhaps the author has objected to a cultural practice close to the heart of the reader, but such an objection is an author's right. It is bold and courageous, for example, for Kingston to counteract the erasure of her transgressive paternal aunt by writing about her, as it is bold and courageous of Alice Walker to depict the act and the consequences of clitorectomy. It is good and right of Bulosan to sympathize with the bride who did not pass the virginity test and to call her stoning a "cruel" and "backward" custom.

But these bold and courageous stands are also provocative acts which place the multicultural writer in a visible and vulnerable position, susceptible to attack from all sides. All too often the most vociferous slings and arrows are flung from those within the minority culture itself, with such barbs as these: this writer is a traitor to the community and to the cause; she's not telling the story right or she's telling the wrong one; he's hanging out dirty laundry for other people's eyes; she's falling into stereotypes and catering to base appetites for the exotic and the barbaric. Amy Tan, David Henry Hwang, and particularly Maxine Hong Kingston—the best-known Asian American writers—have all been attacked along these lines by Asian American critics.

Sau-ling Wong, a scholar born and reared in Hong Kong, takes American-born Amy Tan to task for mistranslating the Chinese words *tang jieh* as "sugar sister" instead of "older female cousin on the father's side," but Tan's mistake in homonyms may also be seen as poetic license and, further, as affirmation of what it is to be Chinese American. Tan's error in the Chinese language confirms the distance between Chinese and Chinese American, a distinction most Asian Americans are vocal and insistent about maintaining. William Chang has complained that there are no positive images of Asian males for him to identify with in Hwang's *M. Butterfly*. Since the only Asian male in the play is a transvestite, he berates Hwang for not presenting the Asian male in a favorable light. But I haven't heard any French men complaining that they are being portrayed as idiots who after twenty years do not know the sex of their own lovers. The problem is clear: despite the recent efflorescence in Asian American literature, we still do not have enough writers to allow each one the right to write according to his or her own lights.

But most vociferous and persistent among Asian American critics is Frank Chin, who stands out for being uncompromisingly hostile. He has publicly called Kingston a "yellow agent of stereotype" who "falsifies Chinese history" and thereby "vilifies Chinese manhood."[3] When I protested during my only conversation with Frank Chin last fall that Amy Tan and Maxine Hong Kingston were not racists, as he has been asserting, but feminists, his retort—at full volume—was "feminists are racists!" In the "Afterword" to his collection of short stories, *The Chinaman Pacific & Frisco R. R. Co.* (1988), Chin writes a scathing parody of Kingston's *The Woman Warrior*, which he calls "The Unmanly Warrior." As a countermove to Chinese American feminism, and to the effeminization of Chinese American men, Chin offers the Chinese heroic tradition found in *Romance of the Three Kingdoms*, certain of whose heroes he incorporates into his latest novel, *Donald Duk*. But as critic King-Kok Cheung has rightly pointed out: "The refutation of effeminate stereotypes through the glorification of machismo merely perpetuates patriarchal terms and assumptions," and she asks plaintively, "Is is not possible for Chinese American men to recover a cultural space without denigrating or erasing 'the feminine'"?[4]

As a means of putting Chin in his place, though she publicly denies that this was her intent, Kingston has captured Chin's voice and character in her protagonist, Wittman Ah Sing, in her novel *Tripmaster Monkey*. However, instead of placing Chin in the tradition of Gwang Gung, the god of literature and war, one of the one hundred and eight heroes of *Romance of the Three Kingdoms*, which Chin claims for himself, Kingston finds his counterpart in the mischievous and irrepressible Monkey King, a trickster figure from the picaresque Chinese folk novel *Journey to the West*. (Shawn Wong, novelist and colleague of Chin's, told me that he was amazed at how accurately Maxine had caught Frank's voice; he phoned Frank to say, "She must have been a fly on the wall when you were talking!")[5] Kingston, however, claims that the narrative voice in this novel belongs to Gwan Yin, the goddess of mercy, and it is her power that disarms the militant Wittman, transforming him into a pacifist, and her voice that has the last word, "Dear American monkey, don't be afraid. Here, let us tweak your ear, and kiss your other ear."[6] Her tone is slightly mocking and yet loving, like that of an indulgent mother with a naughty but beloved son.

Other Chinese and Chinese American readers have complained that Kingston has mixed up Cantonese and Mandarin romanizations of Chinese words, that she has combined the legends of Fa Mulan and Yueh Fei—*he's* the general who had words carved into his back—that she shouldn't have written about the monkey brain feast, that she mustn't emphasize footbinding and misogynist Chinese sayings because these are only a small part of Chinese culture and tradition. But these complaints seem petty and in no way diminish the considerable achievement of *The Woman Warrior*, which in my opinion stands as the supreme Chinese American feminist text. To read this text as the voice of insider informant, or exotic orientalism, or community historian is to miss the forest for some mosses under certain trees. It is to deny the text its complexity and richness as the embodiment of a multiplicity of perspectives, of reflexivity, dialogism, and heteroglossia. Let us now focus on these aspects of this text.

In the indeterminacy of its narrative style, we find what anthropologists like Barbara Myerhoff are calling reflexivity, the visible sign in the text of the writer's awareness of the act of writing, the writer in dialogue with herself. In "No Name Woman," for example, Kingston tells the aunt's story many times, first giving her mother's brief version, the bare-bone facts, then imagining all the possible narratives behind these bare bones, freely employing the word "perhaps" and the conditional present perfect tense ("A bun could have been contrived") to indicate the tentativeness of these versions. Later, in the story of Moon Orchid's meeting with her long-lost husband, Kingston gives us a detailed version of the encounter in her chapter "At the Western Palace" and in the next chapter undercuts the entire narration by stating, "What my brother actually said was . . ." and correcting herself and becoming even more specific: "In fact, it wasn't me my brother told about going to Los Angeles; one of my sisters told me what he'd told her." In other words, narratives are all created and creative acts; "reality" is created through words, and words are ripe with possibility. In providing her reader with so many possible narratives, Kingston demonstrates her awareness of the act of writing as a reflection of multiple and multiplying images. Where the "truth" lies is not her concern; her delight is in the richness of possibilities and in her own creativity in imagining them.

In applying Bakhtin to *The Woman Warrior*, one may read the entire text as an extended exploration of the internal dialogism of three words: *Chinese, American,* and *female*. Each term carries a multitude of meanings in dialogue, if not open warfare, with each other. To be specific, what does the word *Chinese* mean from the inside, that is, to the people so designated? What does it mean to the first-generation immigrant, to the second-generation American born, to the fourth or fifth generation? At what point does an immigrant Chinese become an American? What does the term mean from the outside, to the designators, to the stereotypers, to whites who feel that their places have been usurped? What are the word's historical, political, and social ramifications, underpinnings, and overlays? How does it differ from other related terms, such as *Japanese* or *Korean?* Similar questions may be applied to the other two terms: *American* and *female*. The entire book is devoted to an exploration of these words in an attempt at a self-definition that, finally, is never definitive in the sense of complete, conclusive, static. Paradox, flux, a "surplus of humanness," a defiance of fixation and categories characterize *The Woman Warrior*, as they characterize life. *The Woman Warrior* has gone further than any other text in exploring the complexities of these terms. Amy Tan's *Joy Luck Club* continues this exploration, but with somewhat less complexity.

We find dialogism and polyphony most apparent in the fissures or fault lines in the narrative, in the places where Kingston's language shifts abruptly and the disrupture is visible. It is these fissures between and overlappings of linguistic plates which are the most revealing and to which we shall direct our attention. One obvious example occurs in the first chapter. Between describing the lengths that women and girls endured to be Chinese beautiful, Kingston interjects this sentence: "I hope that the man my aunt loved appreciated a smooth brow, that he wasn't just a tits-and-ass man."[7] The abruptness of this male-locker-room or fraternity-house lingo in the midst of rather detailed even poetic, if painful, descriptions of Chinese female beauty secrets brings the reader up short. In Bakhtin's terms, Kingston here "exhibits" these American male words as a "unique speech thing,"[8] language that is totally alien and unassimilable in the context, and yet it is a voice, one of thousands, in Kingston's head. That Kingston places this particular sentence in this particular setting is not only a linguistic act with stylistic ramifications but a culturally significant statement as well, for form, style, and content, as Bakhtin noted, are all inextricably linked. The context, the sentences surrounding "tits-and-ass man," show the excruciating pain that Chinese women endure in the removal of eyebrow and forehead hairs and facial freckles in order to win favor from the male gaze, but their attention to such Lilliputian detail is wasted in the United States where the Brobdingnagian male gaze is ostensibly only concerned with gross anatomical parts. The linguistic shift, the insertion of this sentence, emphasizes the contrast between the Chinese women's attention to fine detail and the jock expression's reductionism and objectification.

But Kingston's own position between the two is ambiguous. Is she proud of the "needles of pain" which her mother forced her to endure for the Chinese ideal of beauty or relieved that, in America, a woman is free from these "Chinese tortures"? Does she interject the slang expression to parody its reductionist view or does she appropriate this language to counteract the "demure" and silent Chinese girl stereotype that she hates?

I would argue that Kingston does both and that the ambiguity of her tone in this small episode reflects her tone throughout the entire text. Let us look at another example. In the "White Tigers" chapter, when the young girl, let's call her Maxine, first meets the old couple who will be her teachers on the mountain, we find this dialogue:

> "Have you eaten rice today, little girl?" they greeted me. "Yes, I have," I said out of politeness. "Thank you." ("No, I haven't," I would have said in real life, mad at the Chinese for lying so much. "I'm starved. Do you have any cookies? I like chocolate chip cookies.") (WW, 21)

The first exchange of question and response is pure Chinese convention, valuing politeness, displaying modesty and consideration of the other, saving face. It is, in fact, so conventional a question that it has become a salutation rather than a request for information—much as Americans ask "How are you?" but don't really expect an answer other than "Fine, thanks." The parenthetical addition—what she would have said "in real life"—is, of course, the assimilated American response, valuing honesty and directness, frankly looking out for number one, and tinged with humor. Kingston's words denote impatience with the Chinese way; nonetheless, by the very act of presenting the two opposing ways of greeting strangers, she allows readers to judge for themselves the preferable social code. The expressed fondness for chocolate chip cookies seems a playful and somewhat greedy response, which I'm sure Kingston intended. Can it then be that Kingston is advocating Chinese politeness at the same time that she is complaining about it? Is she subverting American directness while seeming to embrace it? Is she, consciously or unconsciously, displaying the linguistic habit that her mother finally revealed, "That's what Chinese say, We like to say the opposite" (WW, 203). The answer would seem to be yes to all the above, for as Kingston explains, "I learned to make my mind large, as the universe is large, so that there is room for paradoxes" (WW, 29). And in her text, paradoxes abound, and dialogues are continuous.

A third shift in gears, a major one, which certainly every reader of The Woman Warrior cannot help but notice, occurs in the "White Tigers" chapter. After twenty-six pages embroidering on the sixty-two-line Chinese narrative poem "Magnolia Lay," after recounting the young girl's rigorous fifteen-year training in physical, spiritual, and mental self-control in lush, mystical, fantastic language, Kingston concludes the story of this paragon of virtue: "From the words on my back, and how they were fulfilled, the villagers would make a legend about my perfect filiality" (WW, 45). We are given a brief intermission of a narrow blank space and then the prosaic line, "My American life has been such a disappointment." From the rich, colorful heights of Chinese imaginative wish fulfillment, we are suddenly dropped to the depths of mundane American life. Though elsewhere in the text Kingston complains that Chinese is "the language of impossible stories" (WW, 87), in "White Tigers" she clearly indulges herself in embellishing the Chinese story, in making it overwhelmingly beautiful, seductive, and desirable because filled with power and valuation for the usually degraded Chinese girl. The Chinese woman warrior could do it all: excel in the "masculine" sphere of warfare and still return home to take up the "feminine" roles of mother, wife, daughter-in-law.

In fiction, everything is possible. Furthermore, as creator of the fiction, the author has control; she can make the rabbit jump into the fire to provide nourishment; she can have her characters live happily ever after. But "real life" is neither perfect nor controllable. American glories cannot compete with the Chinese glories of Fa Mulan; Maxine's straight A's cannot save her family's laundry, put food on the family table, or eliminate racism. Paradoxically, what Maxine calls "my American life" includes the "binds that China wraps around my feet," which include the misogynist sayings her parents and the other emigrant villagers imported to America: "Feeding girls is feeding cowbirds." "There's no profit in raising girls." "When you raise girls, you're raising children for strangers." "There is a Chinese word for the female I—which is 'slave.' Break the women with their own tongues!" (*WW*, 46–47). Another paradox: the same culture that inspired her with the heroic model of Fa Mulan also oppressed her with hateful sayings that caused her, as a child, to throw tantrums in protest. Words have power. These misogynist sayings of her parents and the racism of her American employers—"Order more of that nigger yellow, willya?" (*WW*, 48)—are the demons that Maxine, the Chinese American woman warrior, must fight. They are what make her American life such a disappointment, for as demons they lack the poetry of swords fighting in midair without hands.

Even in the first portion of "White Tigers" Kingston has not simply retold a Chinese myth, but has given her readers "one transformed by America, a sort of kung fu movie parody" ("CM," 57). The story of Fa Mulan may be a glorious model for a girl to dream about, serving as an antidote to the No Name Woman, but "White Tigers" is also a gross exaggeration, a wish fulfillment which the author indulges in with a smile on her face. The humor and irony are subtle and infrequent, but visible, as in this paragraph:

So the hut became my home, and I found out that the old woman did not arrange the pine needles by hand. She opened the roof; an autumn wind would come up, and the needles fell in braids—brown strands, green strands, yellow strands. The old woman waved her arms in conducting motions; she blew softly with her mouth. I thought, nature certainly works differently on mountains than in valleys. (*WW*, 23)

In the last sentence, of course, we find the dialogic imagination of Kingston at work. She shifts gears and changes tone, moving from serious-poetic to ironic-parodic, interjecting another perspective on the narrative as she progresses, allowing another voice within her head to comment on the one that has up to now held the floor.

That Kingston's perspective fluctuates between Chinese and American is clearly visible in her shifting choice of personal pronouns; sometimes she identifies with the Chinese, using the first-person plural "we"; at other times, she is distanced, referring to the Chinese as "they." Near the end of chapter one, for example, we find these sentences:

> In an attempt to make the Chinese care for people outside the family, Chairman Mao encourages *us* now to give *our* paper replicas to the spirits of outstanding soldiers and workers, no matter whose ancestors they may be. My aunt remains forever hungry. Goods are not distributed evenly among the dead. (*WW*, 16, emphasis added)

Not only is Kingston here assuming the perspective of her father's extended family in China, but, against her frequent assertions of her Americanness, she here identifies with the Chinese living in the People's Republic: "Chairman Mao encourages *us*." In chapter two, in the voice of the woman warrior general nearing the end of her glorious career, Kingston writes:

> I stood on top of the last hill before Peiping and saw the roads below me flow like living rivers. Between roads the woods and plains moved too; the land was peopled—the Han people, the People of One Hundred Surnames, marching with one heart, *our* tatters flying. The depth and width of Joy were exactly known to me: the Chinese population. (*WW*, 42, emphasis added)

Here again, we find the narrator's expression of pride in the land and unity with the people of China; she is the general and though her army has suffered, their tatters are hers.

At the other end of the spectrum, however, are many passages in which the narrator distances herself from the Chinese, speaking of *them* in the third person: "Chinese people are very weird" (*WW*, 158), Maxine and her brothers and sisters tell each other, rejecting their connection with their mother's incomprehensible sister, Moon Orchid, and asserting their difference. In another significant passage, Maxine clearly situates herself between Chinese and American, attributing an identity to herself through the modulation of voice:

> Normal Chinese women's voices are strong and bossy. We American-Chinese girls had to whisper to make ourselves American-feminine.

Apparently we whispered even more softly than the Americans. (*WW*, 172)

Volume here is a trope for confidence and power. In the social hierarchy of Maxine's world, Chinese mothers have the loudest voices, the most power; American girls are next, with voices softer and more feminine. Chinese American girls have the softest voices of all, the least power. From Maxine's perspective, Chinese mothers are tyrannical forces to be struggled against; American girls are the enviable models to emulate; and Chinese American girls, straining to reject one model and to imitate the other, have no confident sense of self, for to whisper is to have no voice, and to have no voice is to be powerless. "Most of us eventually found some voice, however faltering. We invented an American-feminine speaking personality, except for that one girl who could not speak up even in Chinese school" (*WW*, 172). "If you don't talk, you can't have a personality" (*WW*, 180), Maxine screams at this totally silent Chinese girl whom she shockingly and unsuccessfully bullies. Maxine lashes out at this girl in a fury of self-hatred and also of rage against the powerless position of all Chinese American girls. As she punishes the silent girl for not conforming to the American norm, Maxine simultaneously uses her as a scapegoat for her own rage over her necessity to "invent an American-feminine speaking personality." Caught in a double bind, Maxine has been simultaneously silenced by a misogynist Chinese society, including a loud-voiced, domineering mother who may have cut her frenum, and also forced by American social pressures to assume an "invented" personality and voice.

In still another passage, the narrator spurns Chinese ways and seeks refuge in an American identity:

To make my waking life American-normal, I turn on the lights before anything untoward makes an appearance. I push the deformed into my dreams, which are in Chinese, the language of impossible stories. Before we can leave our parents, they stuff our heads like the suitcases which they jam-pack with homemade underwear. (*WW*, 87)

"Homemade underwear" is itself a multivalent trope, bursting with an internal dialogism encompassing both humiliation at these ill-fitting economy measures and, at the same time, pride in the determined parental love that defies poverty and hardship. On the one hand, one senses that the child leaving home is embarrassed by the homemade underwear packed into her suitcase; on the other hand, she knows that the parents who "jam-packed" and "stuffed" the suitcases were motivated by a surplus of love. As far as the parent is concerned, the beloved child leaving home to brave the world alone cannot be overprotected, cannot have too much to cushion her from the cold she is certain to encounter. One cannot help but be touched by this concern. But who wants awkward, ill-fitting homemade underwear? On still another hand, isn't it good to be loved so well, and who sees one's underwear anyway? The words "jam-packed" and "stuffed" also carry countervailing forces. These are parents who overwhelm with their undesired shows of love. It is no matter that their grown children will not wear this homemade underwear; these parental offerings cannot be refused. (Amy Tan calls parental gifts of food "stern offerings of love.")

Just before this passage, Kingston had been retelling her mother's monster stories: the ape-man that attacked her, the baby born without an anus. In reaction to these frightening tales that haunt her nightmares, she clings to what seems "American-normal"—the illuminated, the rational and logical, plastic, neon, and periodic tables. A few pages later, "I would live on plastic" (WW, 92), Kingston says in disgust over the objects her mother has placed on her dinner plate. But here again is a dialogic passage. As plastic does not nourish the body, so periodic tables do not nourish the imagination. Although her mother's stories may have frightened her as a child, these stories, now that she is adult and a writer, are her mother's legacy, for they provide the color, texture, and substance of the daughter's text. Although the daughter/ narrator states a preference for the clean, the illuminated, and the plastic, she weaves her actual text from the monstrous, the frightening, the powerful—her mother's stories. The words say one thing; the text does another.

In fact, though the working out of a whole range of meanings around both ethnicity and gender is located in the Chinese/ American dichotomy, it is most particularly situated in the mother-daughter relationship. Much of The Woman Warrior deals with the oppression of silencing and the liberation of speaking out.[9] And this theme is embodied in the problematic, dialogic mother-daughter relationship which informs the entire book. The mother's voice is so overpowering the daughter cannot speak, even believing that her mother has cut her frenum and, by extension, her vocal cords. Maxine's reaction to this act, imagined or real, is again ambivalent and overtly expressed: "Sometimes I felt very proud that my mother committed such a powerful act upon me. At other times, I was terrified—the first thing my mother did when she saw me was to cut my tongue" (*WW*, 164). Identifying with her mother, she is proud of such strength and power; however, considering herself the recipient of the operation, she is terrified. Is it an act of tyranny and silencing, as she fears, or an act of love, as her mother claims? "I cut it so you would not be tongue-tied. Your tongue would be able to move in any language . . . You'll be able to pronounce anything," her mother explains (*WW*, 164). Later, Kingston writes, "I shut my teeth together, vocal cords cut, they hurt so. I would not speak words to give her pain. All her children gnash their teeth" (*WW*, 101). The daughter is both the pained and angry victim of her mother's powerful act of mutilation, or freeing, as well as the considerate daughter who will not speak words to give her mother pain. (Writing them, however, is another matter, because "the reporting is the vengeance," *WW*, 53).

Describing the trip to Los Angeles to regain Moon Orchid's straying husband, Kingston writes, "Brave Orchid gave her sister last-minute advice for five hundred miles" (*WW*, 143). Note the dialogue within this sentence between the earnestness of the mother—"last minute advice" and the ironic context supplied by the daughter/author "for five hundred miles." Throughout *The Woman Warrior* we find the dialogue between anger/bitterness and love/tenderness as the daughter seeks self-definition apart from the mother. Since the struggle is defined as one of words and voice between one who is a powerful talker with many stories and one who has yet to find her voice, so the resolution of this struggle, and of the book, is a verbal and narrative one in that the final story of Ts'ai Yen is a collaborative effort between mother and daughter: "Here is a story my mother told me, not when I was young, but recently, when I told her I also am a story-talker. The beginning is hers, the ending, mine" (*WW*, 206). It is, however, impossible to tell in this story where the beginning ends and the ending begins, which part of T'sai Yen's story is the mother's, which part the daughter's. Thus, the daughter's journey for her own voice is a struggle in which the "mother-tongue" must be both refused and embraced, both preserved and modified, both acknowledged and gone beyond.

In the critical scene when Maxine finally "confesses" to her mother the two hundred plus items that had been weighing on her conscience "that I had to tell my mother so that she would know the true things about me and to stop the pain in my throat" (*WW*, 197), when her voice so long repressed finally erupts before the person in whom she had invested all power and authority, she finds "no higher listener. No listener but myself" (*WW*, 204). This scene is critical because in it Maxine comes into her own voice at the expense of her mother's voice, her mother's authority. She makes an existential discovery—that she must be her own voice, her own listener, her own authority. This discovery is both frightening and liberating, both humiliating and exhilarating. And the voice that she reveals in this book is a composite of many voices: her mother's, her own physical voice, her imaginative voice, the Chinese culture's, American males', and American females' voices. The tonal range is broad, encompassing complaint, confusion, anger, bitterness, pride, resignation, poetry, resolution.

Kingston eventually sees the similarities between herself and her mother, "a dragoness ('my totem, your totem')" (*WW*, 67). "At last I saw that I too had been in the presence of great power, my mother talking-story" (*WW*, 19–20). The Chinese customs that had been oppressive and incomprehensible for the child Maxine, the Chinese stories that had frightened and haunted her waking and sleeping, are now seen by the adult Maxine, the writer Kingston, to be a rich source of inspiration, unique materials for her pen, a legacy to show off at the same time one complains about it.

In her last chapter, "A Song for a Barbarian Reed Pipe," Kingston writes of the Chinese rituals her mother followed without bothering to explain, leaving a confused Maxine to hypothesize about the Chinese in the alienated third-person plural:

> "I don't see how they kept up a continuous culture for five thousand years. Maybe they didn't; maybe everyone makes it up as they go along." (*WW*, 185)

This sentence sums up the dialogic style of Kingston's book; both impulses—the pride of inheritance and a revisionist compulsion—are in dialogue. Her surface tone is complaining and disparaging, but there is an underlying pride in the inclusion of "five thousand years"—this length of time cannot help but be impressive. "Maybe everyone makes it up as they go along" seems to belittle Chinese culture, but for the daughter of a story-talker who is herself a masterful story-talker, as testified to throughout this text, what could be more wonderful than making up stories as one goes along?

In asserting racial and cultural difference, we Asian Americans run the risk of being dismissed as irretrievably and irrevocably "other." We also run the risk of falling into the stereotypes of difference created by the dominant culture. The obverse, however, is that if we assert our similarity to others, our humanness above our cultural specificities, we would seem to be eliminating the reason for multicultural studies in the first place. That Asian Americans are seen as irrevocably "other" was forcibly brought home to me again last fall when our Wisconsin congressman Scott Klug was campaigning on the campus of the University of Wisconsin; he handed fliers to all students except those with Asian faces. His reasoning apparently went something like this: these fliers cost money; Asian students are foreigners who can't vote; therefore, why waste money on foreigners? As Elaine Kim wrote in a recent issue of *A Magazine*, "While we don't generally ask European Americans how come they speak such fluent English, how long they've been here, and when they are going back, these are common questions for Asian Americans."[10] These are what novelist Joy Kogowa has called "ice breaker questions that create an awareness of ice."[11] They are so frequently asked that we've come up with our own answers for them. When I'm complimented on how good my English is, I usually retort, "It should be, I teach it." Maxine Hong Kingston's standard response is kinder and wittier, "Thanks. So's yours."

In *Woman, Native, Other,* Trinh T. Minh-ha expresses the Third World writer's dilemma thus:

> Every path I/i take is edged with thorns. On the one hand, i play into the Savior's hands by concentrating on authenticity, for my attention is numbered by it and diverted from other, important issues; on the other hand, I do feel the necessity to return to my so-called roots, since they are the fount of my strength, the guiding arrow to which i constantly refer before heading for a new direction.[12]

This passage vividly delineates the dialogic dilemma of a person of color: we are identified anthropologically by the outside world according to external physical characteristics and expected by virtue of these characteristics to be "authentic," "the real thing." I note in Minh-ha's expression, "i play into the Savior's hands," that by being singled out for attention from the First World, we are being lifted up and saved from the Third World status into which we were born. Should we be grateful or angry? Are we being rescued or insulted? To be rebellious and subversive, we could, as some of us do, reveal the deceptiveness of exterior signs by asserting our ignorance of that which we are thought to have inside knowledge of and to demonstrate how much we belong to the First World by showing off our ability to employ its "discursive" jargon and by displaying our "inside" knowledge of its canonical texts. On the other hand, are we not then also demonstrating how thoroughly we have been colonized, how disadvantaged and depleted we've grown in being so cut off from our "roots"? Further complication is added when those "roots," as in the case of Chinese American women, are not nurturing but devaluing. As a small example, my father said to me years ago, "Why do you need to go to college, you're only a girl; you'll only get married." What sustenance can we get from such traditions? How can they be "the fount of [our] strength"? These are questions that Maxine Hong Kingston wrestled with in *The Woman Warrior* and she answered them as well as anyone can, I believe, in her line: "I learned to make my mind large, as the universe is large so that it can contain paradoxes."

I conclude with another quote: "I write to show myself showing people who show me my own showing" (*WNO*, 22), writes Trinh Minh-ha to emphasize the multiple reflexivity, the many-mirrored images bouncing back and forth in dialogue with one another when an Asian American speaks and when she writes.

Notes

1. Robert Ji-Song Ku, "Can the Native Informant Write?: The Ethnographic Gaze and Asian American Literature," paper delivered at the Association for Asian American Studies Conference, 3 June 1993.

2. Maxine Hong Kingston, "Cultural Mis-readings by American Reviewers," in *Asian and Western Writers in Dialogue: New Cultural Identities*, ed. Guy Amirthanayagam (New York: Macmillan, 1982), 55–57. Hereafter "CM," cited in the text.

3. Frank Chin, lecture, Oakland, California, 15 September 1989; quoted by Elaine H. Kim in "'Such Opposite Creatures': Men and Women in Asian American Literature," *Michigan Quarterly* 29 (Winter 1990):76.

4. King-Kok Cheung, "The Woman Warrior versus the Chinaman Pacific: Must a Chinese American Critic Choose between Feminism and Heroism?" in *Conflicts in Feminism*, ed. Marianne Hirsch and Evelyn Fox Keller (New York: Routledge, 1991), 242.

5. Conversation with Shawn Wong, Madison, Wisconsin, October 1991.

6. Maxine Hong Kingston, *Tripmaster Monkey: His Fake Book* (New York: Knopf, 1989), 340.

7. Maxine Hong Kingston, *The Woman Warrior: Memoir of a Girlhood among Ghosts* (New York: Knopf, 1976), 9. Hereafter *WW*, cited in the text.

8. Mikhail M. Bakhtin, *The Dialogic Imagination: Four Essays*, trans. Michael Holquist (Austin: University of Texas Press, 1981), 299. Hereafter *DI*, cited in the text.

9. See King-Kok Cheung, "Don't Tell: Imposed Silences in *The Color Purple* and *The Woman Warrior*," *PMLA* 103 (1988):162–74 and her recent book, *Articulate Silences: Hisaye Yamamoto, Maxine Hong Kingston, Joy Kogawa* (Ithaca: Cornell University Press, 1993).

10. Elaine H. Kim, "Business: The Color of Money," *A Magazine* 2 (Spring 1993):30.

11. Joy Kogawa, *Obasan* (1981; reprint, New York: Doubleday, 1992), 271.

12. Trinh T. Minh-ha, *Woman, Native, Other: Writing Postcoloniality and Feminism* (Bloomington: Indiana University Press, 1989), 89. Hereafter *WNO*, cited in the text.

Power Lines: The Motif of Twins and the Medicine Women of *Tracks* and *Love Medicine*

Kristan Sarvé-Gorham
Emory University

THE figures of the sacred twins appear in the pantheons of several American Indian cultures. Although often male, the twins also recur as sisters, for example, Ic'sts'ity and Nau'ts'ity of the Laguna Pueblo people, the Navajos' Changing Woman and White Shell Woman, and in the Anishinabe culture, Matchikwewis and Oshkikwe, the daughters of Nanabozho, or Nanabush. Louise Erdrich draws on this mythological tradition for her portrayal of the two medicine woman figures in *Tracks:* Fleur Pillager and Pauline Puyat. Erdrich veers away from a simple recasting of the myth, for in the novel the two women are not genetically related. Instead, she confirms their twinship through their possession of supernatural power and by their representing alternative religions. Through these medicine women, Erdrich establishes two lines of power in *Tracks* which flow generationally through the characters in *Love Medicine*. Paula Gunn Allen associates the idea of twinning in American Indian spiritual traditions with that "of complementarity, of duality that is not the same as opposition,"[1] a concept of balance that perceives the integration of two diversities as creating a whole. Erdrich portrays Fleur and Pauline as extremes—one an ultratraditionalist and the other an ultra-assimilationist. Yet the twinship of these two medicine women represents the dilemma confronting modern Native Americans. And it is a harmonious resolution of these two competing traditions toward which the great-grandchildren of the medicine women—Lipsha Morrissey, Albertine Johnson, and King Kashpaw—struggle.

Instead of drawing on the events of the Matchikwewis/Oshkikwe myths to shape her novel, Erdrich extracts motifs from these myths and maintains the basic character traits of the sisters in her portrayal of Pauline and Fleur. Allen describes Matchikwewis as a mutable personality: "She blew hot and cold. She was excitable, changeable, subject to sudden bursts of gaiety or curiosity, and to as sudden bursts of anger" (*GL*, 143). Like Matchikwewis, Pauline exhibits sudden emotional transformations. Nanapush calls her "a quick brittle thing, all nerves"[2]—and these nerves often flare under his routine teasing. Pauline also vacillates emotionally as when she first spurns Napoleon Morrissey's advances then encourages them, and when, at one birthing, she shoots an intruding bear, yet at another lacks the presence of mind to prevent premature delivery. As Pauline's character develops, mutability changes into a psychotic imbalance. In contrast to Matchikwewis, Allen describes Oshkikwe as more stable: "Where her sister was boisterous or seductive, Oshkikwe was reserved and modest. She was steady in her affections and loyalties, clear in her taste and purpose, calm and self-contained in her demeanor, and altogether of a reasonable and practical turn of mind. She provided the grounding . . . her mercurial sister . . . needed" (*GL*, 143–44). Oshkikwe's reserve and modesty translate to Fleur's magnetic and commanding presence and to her relative muteness within the novel, for in contrast to Pauline's narrative and dialogue, the lines Fleur speaks within the novel are short and few. Instead of emphasizing the duality of the two women by having each tell her own story, Erdrich skews the relationship by giving Nanapush a narrative voice, thus injecting subtlety in the twinship. Fleur may not provide the ballast in her counterpart's life that Oshkikwe does, yet she remains a major focus for Pauline. Pauline, first dazzled by Fleur's effect on the Argus poker players and then consumed with guilt by her failure to avert their revenge, gravitates around Fleur and her cabin at Matchimanito.

Sacred twins do not always appear in myths as actual twins. The mothers of Monster Slayer and Born For Water—respectively Changing Woman and White Shell Woman—become pregnant from different sources. Although Matchikwewis and Oshkikwe share the same parents—Nanabozho and a human woman—Matchikwewis is the older by about a year (*GL*, 143). Similarly, Erdrich's "twins" are born at different times and from different families. Erdrich's pairing reverses the seniority of the sisters, making the Oshkikwe-like Fleur older. Nanapush estimates Fleur to be "about seventeen years old" in winter 1912 (*T*, 3), slightly older than Pauline, who mentions that she herself is fifteen when

Fleur joins her in Argus the following summer. Fleur, born into the bear clan, is a member of a shamanistic family which, Nanapush states, "knew the secret ways to cure or kill" (*T*, 2) and whose name elicits fear across the reservation. In contrast, Pauline, a mixed-blood, comes from an undistinguished family of "skinners" and a clan "for which the name was lost" (*T*, 14). Neither woman is related to Nanapush, yet each shares a special relationship with him. He addresses Fleur as "daughter" and, although she calls him "uncle," she regards him as her surrogate father. Through Eli Kashpaw, Nanapush passes his most treasured possessions to his "daughter." And at Lulu's birth, Nanapush maneuvers the baptism records to join himself to the Pillagers in a family relationship when he gives his "granddaughter" the surname of Nanapush. No such close and loving relationship exists between Nanapush and Pauline, however. He disparages her as "the crow of the reservation" who was "born a liar" (*T*, 54, 53). Yet Erdrich links Nanapush and Pauline as two generations of storytellers through their role as co-narrators. One, the elder with the mythic voice who sees the past, present, and future of his people, alternates with the other, an impetuous self-centered child with limited vision, as both tell the tale of the woman they regard respectively as daughter and surrogate sister.

Erdrich begins to bond Fleur and Pauline in a symbolic twinhood when Fleur arrives in Argus. Both are young single Indian women working together in a butcher shop and both have been recently orphaned. Although Pauline, having abandoned her own family to come to town, lives with her aunt, she draws closer to Fleur than to her true kin. Fascinated by Fleur, Pauline begins to ease her into her life in the place of the sisters she lost: "I tried to stop myself from remembering what it was like to have my mother and sisters around me, but when Fleur came to us . . . I remembered. I made excuses to work next to her . . . followed her close . . . stayed with her" (*T*, 15, 23). And Pauline is deeply touched by Fleur's occasional sororal gentleness. Fleur soothes Pauline's uneasiness over her missing family: "She touched my face once, as if by accident, or to quiet me, and said that perhaps my family had moved north to avoid the sickness" (*T*, 15). And when Pauline falls asleep during a marathon poker game, Fleur puts her to bed in a closet: "I was lifted, soothed, cradled in a woman's arms and rocked so quiet that I kept my eyes shut while Fleur rolled first me, then Russell into a closet of grimy ledgers, oiled paper, balls of string, and thick files that fit beneath us like a mattress" (*T*, 20).

This latter act becomes a significant memory for Pauline because it constitutes a rare moment of care for the unloved and unlovable young woman. This moment of nurturing seems to symbolize family to her. Catherine Rainwater writes that "the Native American 'family' allows for various ties of kinship—including spiritual kinship and . . . ties of friendship and love."[3] In the wake of a devastating epidemic, Pauline yearns to be included. But as Fleur's family expands to encompass, in addition to Nanapush, Eli, his mother Margaret, Lulu, and finally a second child, Pauline feels increasingly sidelined: "Fleur thought so little about me it was almost like being despised. Since that night she had carried me to bed in her arms, laid me among the ledgers and balls of twine, I had been no more to her than a piece of wall. Any of her attention that spilled past Eli, she had turned on her child. . . . I could feel the distance rush between us like cold water from a broken dam" (*T,* 76). And when Pauline appears at Fleur's cabin malodorous from her self-imposed penance of unwashed body and clothing, she again recalls the closet as Fleur and Lulu begin to bathe her: "I gave myself up . . . and decided not to question Fleur's habit of sudden tenderness. It was like that night she carried me to Fritzie's closet and lay me among the ledgers" (*T,* 154). Ironically, these memories of Fleur's caring impel Pauline to commit two acts seemingly designed to disband Fleur's family. First, as Pauline recalls the closet and notes the discrepancy between past nurturing and present neglect, she begins to court Fleur's husband. As Annette Van Dyke observes, Pauline, who "feels excluded from the clan which the others have formed," is motivated by jealousy.[4] And second, when Fleur starts premature labor following Pauline's bath, Pauline demonstrates an incompetence that leads to the death of Fleur's infant. A sisterly love-hate quality continues throughout the relationship of the two women as Pauline both craves Fleur's attention and, like a younger sister trying to establish both autonomy and recognition in her older sister's eyes, competes with her in terms of power.

Although Erdrich initiates the idea of twinning through Fleur's and Pauline's employment and experiences in Argus, she enhances this relationship through the two women's association with power. In *Tracks* Erdrich establishes two lines of power which Fleur's and Pauline's daughters will inherit. Although other characters such as Nanapush, Margaret Kashpaw, and Moses Pillager demonstrate various degrees of power, with the possible exception of Moses, a minor character, the possession of power is not their raison d'être as it is for Fleur and Pauline. Erdrich develops each woman's experience with power in a unique manner. Fleur's power as an Anishinabe shaman and sorcerer peaks toward the middle of the novel, then wanes and surges again at the end. In contrast, Pauline possesses a latent power not immediately apparent. She channels her pursuit of power through Christianity rather than the indigenous religion, but by using Native American techniques. Finally this renegade medicine woman amasses enough power to battle the supernatural figure which is the source of her twin's power. Thus the complementary nature of the twinship evolves into an oppositional one as Erdrich pits the power of one religion against the power of another as Pauline, constructing herself as a Christian warrior, combats an Anishinabe manitou.

For the Anishinabe, securing the aegis of a guardian spirit, usually attained through a vision quest, was the primary objective of young adulthood. Patron spirits appeared most commonly as birds or animals, but Misshepeshu, the water spirit of Matchiman-ito, is, as Van Dyke notes, the source of Fleur's power ("Q," 15). Although Ruth Landes categorizes underwater spirit helpers as being "calamitous for their protégés,"[5] Pauline contends that he is "neither good nor bad, but simply had an appetite" (*T*, 139). In either case, Fleur handles Misshepeshu adeptly. This lake spirit is part of the Pillager heritage, for Nanapush comments that "when that family came here, driven from the east, Misshepeshu had appeared because of the Old Man's connection" (*T*, 175). Even before Old Man Pillager's death, Misshepeshu sought out Fleur because, Pauline explains, "he's a devil . . . love hungry with desire and maddened for the touch of young girls, the strong and daring especially, the ones like Fleur" (*T*, 11). Although Landes remarks that "water monsters represented a sexually romantic obsession and turned their protégés into celibates, mated only to the manito," or spirit (*ORM*, 31), Fleur's powers over Misshepeshu allow her to take a human lover—one whom, after his dalliance with Sophie Morrissey, Fleur taunts by walking naked into the ice-encrusted lake to consort, he believes, with her spirit helper.

In addition to the possession of a guardian spirit, certain individuals with special faculties were invited to extend their power by training as medicine women or men. Although Erdrich identifies Fleur's cousin Moses as a Jeesekeewinini (*T*, 188), a person who has attained the third level in the Midéwewin, or Medicine Society, she does not designate Fleur as one of this rank. Yet Fleur demonstrates the abilities attendant to this rank. According to Basil Johnston's description of the four orders of the Midéwewin, a novice Midewequae, or medicine woman, spends the first year learning herbal lore before induction into the first order. Attaining the second order yields the abilities to "see far, even beyond the scope of sight," to "hear matters beyond the range of hearing," and to "touch and sense" good and evil.[6] Initiation into the third order involves communion with the incorporeal world, learning to "summon supernatural powers and beings, cause vibrations in things," to acquire skills in weather control, and to "extract hidden things and meanings" (*OH*, 58, 91–92). After a fourth year of study, a medicine woman becomes qualified to instruct and to initiate apprentices into the society.

One common element of the four initiation ceremonies is the rite of death and renewal during which the candidate is shot with the Midemegis, the sacred shell (*OH*, 87). Whether or not Fleur formally undergoes these rites, as the novel opens she has symbolically experienced death and rebirth three times—twice by drowning and once from consumption as Nanapush brings her back from feverish delirium to consciousness—and she consequently demonstrates the skills of the first three orders of the Midéwewin. Her well-stocked lean-to attests to her knowledge of herbal medicine. When Eli approaches Fleur following his adultery with Sophie, Fleur appears to use her ability to touch and sense the truth and extract hidden meanings: "The expression on Fleur's face was open lines. Then she saw. The lines shaded in, the pattern darkened" (*T*, 90). And she amply demonstrates her talents in weather control through the cyclone she summons to destroy Argus and the winds that fell the sawed trees around Matchimanito.

Fleur's powers, however, supersede those of a Midewequae. Pauline reports that, after recovering from consumption, Fleur "messed with evil. . . . She got herself into some half-forgotten medicine, studied ways we shouldn't talk about" (*T*, 12). Both rumors of Fleur's shape-changing and her acts of revenge suggest that she has become a sorcerer. Among various groups of the Anishinabe, sorcerers either attain four additional grades of the Midéwewin or form a separate society, the Waubunowin, or Society of the Dawn.[7] Johnston emphasizes that, because of the secrecy surrounding this society, hearsay flourishes:

> It was said that the Waubunowin was dedicated to the practice of sorcery, and that its members were inspired by evil. No one was quite sure. The uncertainty bred many rumors. . . . . One thing that was constant was the people's fear of the Waubunowin. . . . The members

of the Waubunowin were reputed to summon the spirits of evil and to use conjuring to inflict harm on others. (*OC*, 115)

Whether or not Fleur formally belongs to the Waubunowin, she has acquired both the reputation and the skills of one of its members. Initially, she is able to direct this power against those who are complicit with Euro-American domination of the reservation: Jean Hat, a guide, "got himself run over by his own surveyor's cart" (*T*, 10); George Many Women, who led "the mappers back into the bush" near Matchimanito, drowned in his bathtub (*T*, 11); Edgar Pukwan *père*, the tribal policeman responsible for carrying out the Agency's quarantine procedures at the Pillager cabin, "came home, crawled into bed, and took no food from that moment until his last breath passed" (*T*, 4); and even the Agent himself, while trying to collect fee money from Fleur for Pillager land allotments, first "spent a whole night following the moving lights and lamps of people who would not answer him," and then asked again and ended up "living in the woods and eating roots, gambling with ghosts" (*T*, 9). Erdrich adds complexity to Fleur's character and heightens the quality of her power through ambiguity. In some cases, reservation rumors ascribe events for which Fleur is not responsible, such as Napoleon Morrissey's death, to her malevolent influence. In other instances, Erdrich deliberately obscures a clear cause. For example, Fleur collects snips of Boy Lazarre's fingernails and hair, and he believes that she is responsible for his inflamed arm, yet Nanapush asserts that Boy's blood poisoning results from Margaret's bite rather than Fleur's use of "bad medicine" (*T*, 120). Despite Fleur's power, Erdrich generally portrays her as a positive character as seen through Nanapush's eyes, yet even he regards her as dangerous.

Landes observes that common injuries inflicted by sorcerers include the use of love medicine and paralysis of various parts of the body, particularly the mouth and legs (*ORM*, 62). Nanapush refutes the rumors that Fleur uses love medicine to capture Eli, yet she demonstrates her ability to impose paralysis on her victims, which establishes her as a sorcerer. When Boy, hired by Margaret as a spy, returns from Matchimanito "talking backwards, garbled, mixing his words," people assume that Fleur had "tied him up, cut his tongue out, then sewn it in reversed" (*T*, 49). Although Landes notes that sorcerers reportedly collected the tongues of the dead, she mentions nothing about the tongues of the living (*ORM*, 64–65). An alternative explanation might be partial paralysis of the mouth, such as that which later occurs to Clarence

Morrissey. Although Nanapush claims credit for the permanent "drag of Clarence's mouth" (*T*, 123)—the result of Clarence remaining frozen in a precarious balance on the brink of a pit with a noose encircling his neck—Landes comments that sorcerers were notorious for inflicting a "twisted mouth" on their victims (*ORM*, 62). And this incident follows Fleur's visit to the Morrisseys' house, which involves her "touching here, touching there, sprinkling powders that ignited and stank on the hot stove" and cutting a hank of Clarence's hair to take home with her (*T*, 119).

Whether or not Fleur is responsible for Clarence's paralysis, she definitely takes credit for that of his sister. Just as Fleur draws the deer Eli wounded to her cabin, she similarly ensnares Sophie, for as Pauline relates, "it was Fleur's purpose that the girl plunged" through the brush toward Matchimanito, "unaware of pain and helpless, drawn there against herself" (*T*, 87–88). Pauline discovers her kneeling, rigid in the pose of a supplicant, mute, unblinking, and insensate. Fleur not only paralyzes Sophie, but roots her to the ground, for when her brother and uncle attempt to dislodge her, they cannot: "They . . . tried to pick her up and found she would not budge. They put their weight to her, tried at least to tip her so they could drag her, but they could not shift her one small inch" (*T*, 91–92). Erdrich's treatment of Fleur's powers therefore includes observable acts, such as Sophie's paralysis and the manipulation of weather, which become fueled by reservation gossip and tempered by Pauline's unreliability as a narrator and Fleur's own silence in the novel. Fleur, consequently surrounded by ambiguity, becomes as much an enigma to the reader as she does to those in the novel who interact with her. Erdrich thus establishes her as a mythic figure whose acts storytellers chronicle. Therefore, when her power begins to decline, she does not seem more human because of failure, but through the journeys she takes down the four-day road of the dead into the lake, more superhuman, although bereft.

While Fleur's power remains potent during her capture of Sophie and throughout the ensuing Morrissey revenge, it ebbs following the birth of her second child. Nanapush states that "power dies, power goes under and gutters out. It is momentary, quick of flight and liable to deceive. As soon as you rely on the possession it is gone" (*T*, 177). Yet Fleur's journey with her dying baby and Pauline into the spirit world of the dead marks the point at which her power fades. Erdrich portrays this realm of the dead as containing not only people, but also symbols of the precontact Indian world, for, as Pauline relates, "we passed dark and vast seas of moving buffalo and not one torn field, but only earth, as it was before. . . . There were no fences, no poles, no lines, no tracks" (*T*, 159). The presence of buffalo and the undisturbed earth in the afterworld suggests not only that the death of one source of traditional power—the old physical world—has occurred, but also that the demise of its interdependent other—Indian cosmology which fused together natural and supernatural, myth and ritual, language and action, human and animal, female and male into a dynamic and intelligent universe—is imminent. Thus one universal cycle is ending and evolving into another in which the old medicine power becomes ineffective in combating new forms of power: secular ones based on Euro-American concepts such as the authority of hierarchical government and land as personal property to be purchased and exploited. Neither Pauline nor Fleur seem to be consciously aware of the significance of the death of the old physical world, yet an unconscious imbibing of its presence here may explain Fleur's subsequent reluctance to restore her waning power and Pauline's determination to hasten the turning of the old cycle into the new.

Only Pauline recounts this pilgrimage down the four-day road, with no corroboration from Fleur, yet two details suggest that they share this experience. First, such an expedition is not beyond a shaman's powers, and second, after their return, when Fleur sees the lock of Lulu's hair—over which she gambles for her daughter's life—she panics: "Fleur screamed at the sight and tore it from [Margaret's] hand. . . . She would only be comforted by [Lulu's] present" (*T*, 169). For while Fleur and Pauline make their mythic journey, Lulu hovers perilously close to death from exposure at Nanapush's cabin. Unlike the Matchikwewis/Oshkikwe myths, when, after Oshkikwe's childbirth, "Matchikwewis took good care of her sister, and everything was going fine,"[8] Pauline's incompetence results both in Fleur's baby's death as well as Lulu's near death.

Allen writes that "there are a number of physical locations on the earth we usually inhabit that serve as crossing points between the mundane and supernatural planes of existence" (*GL*, 18). Erdrich portrays one of these spots as a path near Matchimanito which leads into the realm of the dead. Landes remarks that "the world of the dead was . . . believed to lie beyond the western horizon because the sun dips there nightly" (*ORM*, 190), and, Pauline recalls, "we glided west, following the fall of night in a constant dusk" (*T*, 159). Numerous North American Indian peoples, including the Anishinabe, believe that each person has two souls:

the free soul which leaves the body at death and enters into the spirit world, and the body soul which remains with the corpse.[9] Åke Hultkrantz mentions that "while the free soul finds its way at random" to the land of the dead, "the medicine man may intentionally direct his free soul there and, contrary to the layman, he generally may then return to the world of the living."[10] Fleur, through Misshepeshu's patronage, wields this power, for before they embark on their journey, Pauline glimpses the water man. But whereas Misshepeshu's influence may have enabled Fleur to win precisely one dollar each evening gambling with the living, his power has less effect as she gambles with the dead for the lives of her children and loses her baby. Unlike Oshkikwe who enters an otherworld and reclaims her baby from a sorcerer, Fleur returns unsuccessful.

After the revelation of the death of the Indian world, the loss of her infant appears to be the first instance in which Fleur's power, which is related to this world, fails. A second instance rapidly follows when Fleur dreams of the location of a deer, but when Eli goes to that spot to hunt it, he finds no tracks. Fleur's realization that "her dreams lied, her vision was obscured, her helper slept deep in the lake" (T, 177) casts her into despondency. Nanapush describes her as uncharacteristically "hesitant in speaking, false in her gestures, anxious to cover her fear" (T, 177), and she rejects his plea to "go down to the shore. . . . Make your face black and cry out until your helpers listen" (T, 177). However, the stimulus of another catastrophe—the loss of her land—spurs her into action. Although Catherine Catt believes that Fleur intends to drown herself when she walks into the lake after hearing of Margaret's treachery,[11] the process of death and renewal thrusts the Midéwewin initiate into the next level of power, and, after Eli pulls her from the lake, Misshepeshu begins to stir: "The ground beneath us was trembling, I felt it shake, and it was not the felling of the trees or a storm gathering beyond sight, it was what was in the water, which I didn't dare to name" (T, 213). Fleur's fourth "drowning" renews her power enough to enable her to perform a final dramatic display of weather control and the summoning of spirits. Nanapush notes that "there was a long period of unusual calm . . . days in which no air stirred, no breeze foamed the lake" (T, 219), a time during which Fleur prepares the trees around her cabin. On the day the lumber crew prepares to evict Fleur and fell the last of Matchimanito's trees, Nanapush observes an eerie climatic change—"Nothing about this weather seemed proper" (T, 219)—plus unusual spirit activity: "I heard the hum of a thousand conversations. . . . The spirits in the western stands had been faced together. The shadows of the trees were crowded with their forms" (*T*, 220). As soon as Fleur gives the signal—"she said nothing, just glanced into the sky and let her eyes drop" (*T*, 222)—she loosens both the winds and the spirits.

Although Erdrich portrays Fleur as a masterful medicine woman/sorcerer, her powers are limited to the traditional Anishinabe world. She can save neither her land nor her people from the encroachment of Anglo landgrabbers and their commercial values. As one of two twins, then, she represents the old Indian world of animism, community, and affinity with nature. In contrast, Pauline rejects tradition and identifies herself with the Euro-American world: "I saw that to hang back was to perish. I saw through the eyes of the world outside of us" (*T*, 14). She completely enters this world through the avenue of Christianity, jettisoning her identity as an Indian to become white. As the second of two twins, she represents the modern world of Christianity, money, property deeds, and bureaucracy.

Despite her white aspirations, Pauline, like Fleur, argues Van Dyke, "also embodies traditional Chippewa powers" ("Q," 21). But unlike Fleur, who comes from both a powerful clan and family, Pauline is an aberration in an unremarkable family. "Except for me," Pauline admits, "the Puyats were known as a quiet family with little to say" (*T*, 14). And Nanapush agrees that Pauline differs from the Puyats, "who were always an uncertain people, shy, never leaders in our dances and cures" (*T*, 38). Whereas Fleur enters the novel already possessing strong medicine power, Pauline's story shows her gradual acquisition of power. The first sign occurs at Mary Pepewas's deathbed. En route to the Pepewas's house, Bernadette Morrissey and Pauline encounter an owl which "floated off a branch like smoke and called" (*T*, 67). According to Landes, both the sight of an owl and the sound of its hooting warn of sorcery afoot (*ORM*, 61), and Bernadette and Pauline cross themselves to ward off misfortunes. Landes remarks that should the sorcerer's victim also be a shaman, a battle followed with each antagonist in the semblance of her or his guardian spirit (*ORM*, 61). In *Tracks*, however, Pauline's glimpse of the owl serves as a catalyst that frees her power for a future showdown, "a spiritual battle" which, James Stripes believes, "lies at the heart of *Tracks*."[12] At Mary's side, Pauline first enters a hyperconscious state—"I began to doze in waking, and in waking to dream with clear sight" (*T*, 67)—which enables her to hover between the world of the living and the world of the dead and to cut Mary loose to enter the latter. Minutes later, Pauline acquires the power of flight: "Twirling dizzily, my wings raked the air, and I rose in three powerful beats and saw what lay below" (*T*, 68). The next morning, they find Pauline nestled in an unclimbable tree: "The trunk was smooth for seven feet and there were no hand- or footholds of any sort" (*T*, 68).

Although Pauline rejects elements of her culture such as her mother tongue and customary women's work, she accepts what traditional medicine can offer. When nightmares plague her sleep, she hangs a dreamcatcher "alongside the crucifix in my corner" (*T*, 66). And she purchases love medicine to ensnare Eli Kashpaw. Speaking of Fleur, Nanapush mentions that "all she had was raw power" (*T*, 7). Similarly, Pauline possesses raw power, but unlike Fleur, she cannot actively direct and control it. And although Van Dyke calls her "a powerful sorcerer" ("Q," 21), Pauline never demonstrates the mastery over the supernatural world that Fleur does. Yet once she procures the love medicine from Moses, Pauline is able to channel her power both to derive physical pleasure through Sophie's and Eli's lovemaking and to control the actions of the lovers. Even as Pauline devises her scheme to capture Eli through Sophie, she realizes she can project herself into Sophie's body and, because of this, decides to activate her plan: "I could almost feel what it was like to be inside Sophie's form, not hunched in mine. . . . It was because of that . . . that I went to the trader a few days later and bought the blue material" for Sophie's provocative dress (*T*, 78). And indeed, when the couple begin to make love, Pauline can experience Eli through Sophie: "She shivered and I . . . shrank backward into her pleasure" (*T*, 83). Simultaneously, through this thread of connection with Sophie and because of her own hand in administering the love medicine, Pauline can also control both lovers:

> I turned my thoughts on the girl and entered her and made her do what she could never have dreamed of herself. . . . They were not allowed to stop. . . . I drove Eli to the peak and took his relief away and made him start again. I don't know how long, how many hours. . . . I was pitiless. They were mechanical things, toys, dolls wound past their limits. I let them stop eventually. . . . As if cut from puppet strings, Eli lunged to the bank . . . and staggered past me. (*T*, 83–84)

Although both Fleur and Nanapush establish Pauline as one who lies and embroiders stories, Erdrich supports Pauline's claim to power. Afterwards, Pauline worries that she may have been too blatant about experimenting with her power: "I had gone too far.

The last part, where I had not let them stop, where I had tested my influence, must have surely given it away" (*T*, 85). And it has. Both Sophie and Eli are aware of Pauline's power, for Sophie says "it's you should ask for mercy . . . death's bony whore" (*T*, 86), and Eli confesses to Nanapush that "I was witched" (*T*, 98). Again the twinship of Fleur and Pauline appears, for Pauline's use of sorcery for unscrupulous purposes resembles Fleur's infliction of paralysis, for love medicine, Landes writes, being a "sneak [assault] on human will . . . was considered the ugliest sorcery" (*ORM*, 65).

The aftermath of Pauline's use of love medicine propels her into seeking an alternative source of power, for, as Pauline learns when finding Sophie paralyzed, the power of the Catholic religion supersedes Fleur's power. For only the miracle of the Virgin's tears releases Sophie. Erdrich establishes parallel icons of Misshepeshu and the Virgin Mary through the motif of hardened tears. Earlier Pauline mentions that Misshepeshu "weeps gleaming chips that harden into mica on your breasts" (*T*, 11), and now she becomes transfixed by the Virgin's tears which harden on the ground, thus resembling "ordinary pebbles of frozen quartz" (*T*, 95). Pauline repeatedly associates the colors of copper, gold, and green with Misshepeshu and describes the water manitou as being able to assume the body of "a fat brown worm" (*T*, 11). The statue of the Virgin depicts Mary standing on "a lively serpent . . . colored a poison green" (*T*, 92). Although the connection between brown worm and green snake is loose, the statue seems to represent a combination of Indian and Christian figures, for at the moment the Virgin's tears touch the serpent, Sophie is freed from Fleur's power: "Her tears . . . rolled down the stiff folds of Her gown and struck the poisoned snake. It was then that the commotion took place . . . over Sophie, who tried to rise" (*T*, 94). Although Pauline says "for many months afterward I brooded on what I'd seen" (*T*, 95), she mentions only her preoccupation with the sexual nature of the Virgin's relationship with God. Yet, determined to compete with Fleur, Pauline must simultaneously recognize that only the power of the Christian religion can rival and defeat the medicine power that Fleur possesses.

Both Nanapush and Margaret exhibit what Edward Dozier terms "compartmentalization": participation in "two mutually distinct and separate socioceremonial systems, each containing patterns not found in the other."[13] Quite unintentionally, Pauline does too, for her search for power through divine revelation resembles a perverted form of the vision quest. Anishinabe parents habitually encouraged their young children to charcoal their eyes in order to attract a spirit helper and to fast in order to receive a vision through dreams, as Erdrich describes Fleur's cousin's family as having done: "Moses took the charcoal from his mother's hand too often. He blackened his face and fasted for visions until he grew gaunt" (*T*, 36). Later, during adolescence, a ritual vision quest occurs, during which the seeker, isolated away from the village, abstains from food and drink and encourages supernatural favor through prayer and meditation.[14] Like the vision seeker, Pauline sequesters herself away from the Indian community in the convent. She customarily chooses to go hungry, reporting "I had starved myself for so long" during pregnancy (*T*, 131) and, at the convent, claiming "my stomach never filled. . . . Every time I sat to eat [I] halved my bread. . . . I drank only hot water, took the thinnest cut of bread" (*T*, 136–37, 152). Soon she devises a way to forgo water: she allows herself to urinate only twice a day, at dawn and at dusk, and thus can drink only minimal amounts in order to "last the final hours" until sunset (*T*, 148). Johnston observes that both physical and mental preparation were necessary before undertaking the vision quest: "Preparation rendered the body worthy through physical testings, and the inner being worthy through dreaming and vigils ready for vision. . . . For the body there was to be strength, endurance, agility; for the inner being, patience, discipline, silence, and peace" (*OH*, 120). Yet Pauline, perhaps trusting in the Mother Superior's praise for her piety, focuses entirely on the body, inventing numerous physical testings, from breaking ice in buckets of water with her hands, to placing burrs and nettles in her clothing and wearing her shoes on the wrong feet. "I grew strong," she asserts; "My shoulders hardened and I gained in height. I could kneel hour upon hour" (*T*, 136). Although Pauline cites the examples of saints, she admits that her own martyrdom "took another form" (*T*, 152). Rather than receiving the tortures of others, Pauline inflicts her own torments on herself in order, like the vision seeker, to invite supernatural visitation.

Johnston writes that "for the Anishinabe the vision became the theme and quest in his life that attained the character of force; as a force, it could alter the course of individuals, bend the nature of living, enhance the tone of life, and change character" (*OH*, 119–20). In short, the vision became the driving philosophy of one's life. When Christ perches on the convent stove, Pauline undergoes a transformation like that of the vision seeker: "I grew in knowledge. Skins were stripped from my eyes. Every day I saw more clearly and I marveled at what He showed me" (*T*, 137). As

Pauline follows this new path, Erdrich increasingly sets her up as a complement to Fleur. Whereas Fleur doggedly remains a traditionalist, Pauline aligns herself with whites. Her father's prophecy that, in town, Pauline will "fade out," plus her own desire "to be like my mother, who showed her half white" (*T*, 14), become fulfilled as her new spirit helper erases her Native American background—a convenience which allows her to join an order of nuns that refuses to admit Indians: "He said that I was not whom I had supposed. I was an orphan and . . . despite my deceptive features, I was not one speck of Indian but wholly white" (*T*, 137). And those at Matchimanito acquiesce in this transformation: "They treated me as they would a white. I was ignored most of the time. When they did address me they usually spoke English" (*T*, 145–46). Simultaneously, Pauline's vision path allows her to compete with Fleur in an entirely new arena as agents of their respective religions.

Louis Owens calls Pauline "the Christian who never relinquished her belief in Misshepeshu"[15] and Catherine Rainwater claims that "despite her scorn for her Native American upbringing, Pauline . . . cannot quite escape her old way of constructing experience."[16] Although Pauline aspires to eradicate her Indian roots, she maintains a basic Anishinabe belief in the manitou. Whereas the Anishinabe in the past regarded spirits such as Misshepeshu as being tremendously powerful, Pauline senses a change occurring: "It was clear that Indians were not protected by the thing in the lake or by the other Manitous. . . . There would have to come a turning" (139). And Pauline regards herself as the one appointed to hasten that turning. Consequently, through Pauline's conception of herself and Fleur as representatives of two alternative paths and through the imagery of doors and hinges, Erdrich recreates the structure of the twin stories.

Following Christ's visits, Pauline constructs Misshepeshu as her own patron's competitor for souls. Simultaneously she regards Fleur as the agent who ushers those souls to Misshepeshu: "She was the one who closed the door or swung it open. Between the people and the gold-eyed creature in the lake . . . Fleur was the hinge" (*T*, 139). Pauline feels, though, that the power of the old ways is waning, evidenced by the Indians who "receded and coughed to death and drank" and by the "animals that were hunted so scarce they became discouraged and did not mate" (*T*, 139). Pauline anticipates a shift in spiritual power in which Christianity ascends in influence to save the Anishinabe people while their indigenous religion fades. Thus Pauline envisions "an-

other door. And it would be Pauline who opened it" (*T*, 139).
Instead of the Anishinabe four-day road, Pauline sees "a new
road" leading to "the great shining doors, beaten of air and gold,
swung open on soundless oiled fretwork" with Christ there to
greet the travelers (*T*, 140). And apparently she believes this "turning" has already occurred. While claiming "I'm sent to prove
Christ's ways" (*T*, 190), she again tests her influence. But instead
of directly confronting Fleur, which Pauline never does, she challenges the power of her rival's religion by emulating Nanapush
and thrusting her arms into a boiling kettle.

By Pauline's subsequent reasoning, Fleur's guardian spirit is
more powerful than her own since Christ failed to protect her.
And although she does not articulate it, Pauline may regard her
own power as now stronger than Fleur's since, raised on the reservation, she likely recognizes that the ceremony she aborted was
intended to restore Fleur's powers. Following this incident, Pauline
receives a vision of herself wandering to Matchimanito where Misshepeshu rises in all his horrific splendor from the water. And,
like the Anishinabe vision seeker, Pauline interprets this dream
and follows its direction. She deduces that since "Christ had hud-
dled out of frailty, overcome by the glitter of copper scales, ap-
palled at the creature's unwinding length and luxury" (*T*, 195),
she herself was the one to battle the enemy: "Because my own
God was lamblike and meek and I had strengthened, daily, on
his test and privations, it was I who was armored and armed"
(*T*, 195). Thus the medicine woman, perceiving herself to be
stronger than her spirit helper, prepares to battle the manitou.

In this battle, Erdrich draws diverse elements of *Tracks* together.
Early in the novel Erdrich raises the possibility of Pauline's mental
imbalance. Nanapush reports: "There was some question if she
wasn't afflicted, touched in the mind" (*T*, 39). And later Margaret
calls her a "half-mad thing" (*T*, 189). Interestingly, Pauline recognizes a schizophrenia within herself resulting from her guilt over
incidents in Argus: "I was cleft down the middle by my sin"
(*T*, 195). She believes that her victory over Misshepeshu will heal
that split: "If I did not forsake Jesus in this extremity, then He
would have no other choice but to make me whole" (*T*, 195). Both
the manitou Pauline thinks she battles turning into Napoleon
Morrissey plus her denial of responsibility for his death support
her mental imbalance. Simultaneously, Pauline expects her victory
over Fleur's spirit helper to eliminate her craving for Fleur's atten-
tions—"I would be . . . wiped clean of Fleur's cool even hand on
my brow" (*T*, 196)—and Fleur's power. For Erdrich returns to the

image of doors as Pauline, standing in the boat, feels herself sucked in through Fleur's door then released: "Her heavy black clothes, her shawl, the way she held herself so rigid, suggested a door into blackness. I stood before it and then she turned, so slowly I heard the hinges creak. A moment and I was inside where I could not breathe. . . . I thought I would be shut there but she turned again and off she walked . . . a passage into herself" (*T*, 200). Pauline does not comment, yet, back outside the door, she must feel free of Fleur's influence.

Another element Erdrich integrates into this battle is a mythological thread. Erdrich seems to draw on two epic battles, one in which Odysseus fights the shape-changer Proteus, and an Anishinabe myth concerning the giant leech of Leech Lake. In the latter, two young women venture out onto the lake in a canoe. While one makes offerings, the other does not and is consequently seized by the leech.[17] Although the two women are not identified as Matchikwewis and Oshkikwe, Barnouw both includes it in his section of Matchikwewis/Oshkikwe myths and likens its teachings to those which appear in the myths of the sisters.[18] Just as one young woman challenges the leech by not making an offering, Pauline dares Misshepeshu to react by not offering him tobacco as Margaret once did. On the lake, Pauline senses Misshepeshu's presence: "I lowered the rock. Down it went . . . to where the thing was coiled, half-sluggish from the winter. In my mind, I saw the stone glance off its shoulder. One gold eye opened" (*T*, 197). Yet Misshepeshu does not immediately respond. In fact, his inactivity recalls Fleur's reaction when Eli first challenges her over the deer and she "scorned him as though he were nothing" (*T*, 43). However, hours later, Pauline reports that "the thing below severed the rope of my anchor with its long saw-tooth tail, and began to tow me towards shore" (*T*, 201). The fact that Pauline's boat is towed, plus the specific reference that a creature "crawled from the water to confront" Pauline (*T*, 201), suggests that this figure perhaps is not Napoleon, for the lake is frigid with "slow-melting cakes and plates of ice in the waves" (*T*, 197). As in her treatment of Fleur, Erdrich's use of ambiguity surrounding the battle between Pauline and Misshepeshu preserves its mythic character. Yet the identity of the corpse as Napoleon's comments both on Misshepeshu's power to evade her—which is not an impossibility for a supernatural being—and Pauline's inability to destroy him. For even Pauline admits that Misshepeshu still lives: "I believe that the monster was tamed that night, sent to the bottom of the lake and chained there by my deed" (*T*, 204).

Like Fleur, Pauline undergoes repeated symbolic death and renewal which Erdrich portrays through the image of skins. Her first "death" occurs when Christ cleanses her of her Indian past, suggesting a symbolic exchange of red skin for white, which is accompanied by her mention of skins being stripped from her eyes (*T*, 137). Her second "death" happens following her disillusionment with Christ's power as her burned hands heal. Simultaneously, as she reinvents herself as God's warrior in lieu of Christ, she sheds and regrows skin: "When the binding was excruciatingly changed, I shed a skin with the dirty wrapping. Every few days I shed another, yet another. . . . New flesh grew upon my hands, smooth and pink as a baby's" (*T*, 195–96). And following her battle with Misshepeshu, she again experiences "death." Unlike the young woman in the Leech Lake myth, Pauline does not drown, but she does acquire a new skin—"I rolled in dead leaves, in moss, in defecation of animals. I plastered myself with dry leaves and the feathers of a torn bird" (*T*, 203)—and is subsequently reborn as a nun when she takes her vows, prays "to leave Pauline behind, to remember that name . . . was no more than a crumbling skin" (*T*, 205), and becomes Leopolda.

Despite their rites of death and renewal, the possession of power helps neither Pauline nor Fleur at the end of the novel. Instead of eradicating the Anishinabe religion and achieving sainthood, Pauline is destined to become a teaching nun. Although Fleur's powers temporarily stay the lumber company's rape of Matchimanito, a generation later the lake is known by the company's name: Lake Turcot. Yet each medicine woman bears one daughter, and although their own power plays out, it survives in traces within their daughters. Simultaneously, Erdrich advances the trope of twinship one generation forward, for, by the end of *Love Medicine*, Marie and Lulu reconcile and, Van Dyke writes, "together they become respected elders on the reservation . . . [who] have been able to use their inherited powers to ensure the continuance of the nation" ("Q," 24).

Like Pauline, her daughter Marie leans heavily toward Euro-American culture. Pale-skinned and, like her mother, proud of her white blood, Marie claims "I don't have that much Indian blood" and asserts that the nuns "were not any lighter than me. . . . I looked white."[19] Marie also finds the white religion appealing, possibly unconsciously sensing that her aspirations toward sainthood are one way to channel the touch of power she inherited. For despite the fact that the Puyat family lacks an inherent association with power, Pauline passes down some of her first-

generation power to her child. But the Puyat power plays out as
Marie moves even further than her mother from the old ways.
Unlike Pauline, Marie seems unaware that she possesses power.
Perhaps it has become too weak to recognize, or perhaps, as a
woman who "will not admit she has a scrap of Indian blood in
her" (*LM*, 198), she refuses to acknowledge this vestige of power.
Nevertheless, at a time of heightened emotion, she taps this power
which ultimately enables her to capture Nector Kashpaw.

Marie's first experience with supernatural power occurs at the
convent, where she wants to prove herself superior to the nuns:
"They never thought they'd have a girl from the reservation as a
saint they'd have to kneel to. But they'd have me" (*LM*, 40). When
her daydreams inadvertently come true through the nuns' wor-
ship of the ersatz stigmata, Marie at first experiences a sense of
power before her disillusionment: "I couldn't tell why they were
praying to me. But I'll tell you this: it seemed natural. . . . I lifted
up my hand as in my dream. It was completely limp with sacred-
ness" (*LM*, 54). Minutes later, when Nector tackles Marie on the
dusty road outside the convent, some of that power seems to linger
and arise again to trap him, and thus Nora Berry and Mary Prescott comment that "her vision appears to have left Marie with
enormous power, for she immediately snares Nector."[20] For, from
Nector's perspective, he seems caught up in a weaker version of
that same power that Pauline long ago used on his brother:
"Something happens. The bones of her hips lock to either side
of my hips, and I am held in a tight vise. I stiffen like I am
shocked. . . . And then I am caught. I give way. I cannot help
myself. . . . When I come back and when I look down on her I
know how badly I have been weakened. . . . Somehow I have been
beaten at what I started on the hill" (*LM*, 60–61). When Nector
turns to Marie to accuse her—"You made me! You forced me!"
(*LM*, 62)—he seems to acknowledge that he was acting under a
force outside of himself, just as, long ago, Eli recognized Pauline's
sorcery. The Puyat power seems to grip Nector as Marie leads the
man who loves Lulu Nanapush down the hill: "Her hand grows
thick and fevered, heavy in my own, and I don't want her, but I
want her, and I cannot let go" (*LM*, 62). Yet, with the exception
of this incident and occasional divinings from her household ap-
pliances, Marie lets the power inherited from Pauline lie dormant.
Instead, she uses the power assigned by white culture to the role
of a wife as the means by which she coerces her husband into
becoming a tribal leader and a successful man as defined by Euro-
American society.

Whereas the Puyat power rises and dies within two generations, the Pillager power, strong in Fleur's ancestors, extends through her great-grandson. Power, states Pauline, "comes down through the hands, which in the Pillagers are strong and knotted, big, spidery and rough, with sensitive fingertips good at dealing cards. It comes through the eyes, too, belligerent, darkest brown, the eyes of those in the bear clan, impolite as they gaze directly at a person" (*T*, 31). Although Lulu, who may be part white, has green eyes rather than the power-carrying Pillager brown eyes, she inherits certain aspects of Fleur's power. Lulu, raised in the traditional way and brought home from school by Nanapush and Margaret when about age ten, maintains stronger ties to the old ways than does her contemporary, Marie, whose foster parents have become alcoholics and thus dependent on Euro-American culture. Lulu's generation stands one step further from the mythic past than Fleur's does, and, instead of depicting supernatural feats, Erdrich tends to ascribe power to Lulu by association. To Beverly Lamartine, dazed by Lulu's sexual advances, magic seems to abound in her house: "She seemed to fill pots of food by pointing at them and take things from the oven that she'd never put in. The table jumped to set itself. The pop foamed into glasses, and the milk sighed to the lip" (*LM*, 86). Years later, her grandson Lipsha Morrissey reports that Lulu exerts an uneasy influence over her fellow residents in Senior Citizens:

> She scared people after the bandages came off her eyes, because she seemed to know everybody else's business. . . . That time the Defender girl was less than two months pregnant Lulu knew about it just from touching her hand. When Old Man Bunachs got a mistaken thousand-dollar credit from the government in his social security check, she asked him for a tiding-over loan. He had been keeping it a secret. (*LM*, 241)

Although Lipsha attributes Lulu's talent to "insight" and Lulu herself explains that after her vision began to fail, "my ears had seemed to grow like radar" (*LM*, 231), Lipsha's conclusion—"It was as though Lulu knew by looking at you what was the true bare-bone elements of your life. . . . She saw too clear for comfort" (*LM*, 241)—suggests that Lulu possesses traces of the Pillager power. Occasionally Erdrich allows glimpses of Lulu's natural power to stand alone without realistic explanation, as when Lulu recalls how she knew who burned her house: "How can I say it was Kashpaw who lit my house? I can say so because of what I saw in his eyes when I looked deeply through them after I told him about my marriage. . . . My house was burning in his eyes, and I was trapped there, alone, on fire with my own fire" (*LM*, 225). Within Lulu, then, lurks a spark of the medicine woman's ability to use her power.

Whereas Pauline's power seems to die out with Marie, both the Puyat and Pillager lines of power symbolically fuse in Lipsha Morrissey, who is Marie's foster grandson and Lulu's biological one. Like her mother, Marie resorts to using love medicine, yet unlike Pauline, Marie distances herself from the process. Possibly because, as a modern Christian woman, she hesitates to use pagan charms, and partly because, despite her Christianity, she believes in Lipsha's "touch," Marie delegates him to procure the love medicine. But unlike the complicated love medicines known by the older generation in *Tracks,* or even the simpler ones Lipsha has heard about—"a charm of seeds that looked like baby pearls. They was attracted to a metal knife which made them powerful" and another involving frogs caught "in the act" (*LM*, 200)—he devises one out of turkey hearts, holy water, and his own "touch."

Even before he begins, Lipsha, who, Rainwater argues, is "born with the shaman's healing touch,"[21] senses the hazards of playing with the ancient powers. When Marie even mentions love medicine, Lipsha claims "I feel my back prickle at the danger" (*LM*, 199). He understands the perils that amateurs might encounter: "Love medicines is not for the layman to handle. . . . Before you get one, even, you should go through one hell of a lot of mental condensation. You got to think it over. Choose the right one. You could really mess up your life grinding up the wrong little thing" (*LM*, 199). Nevertheless, he disregards his own advice. Bullied by Marie, Lipsha learns from experience. Later he admits "I played with fire. I told myself love medicine was simple. I told myself the old superstitions was just that—strange beliefs. . . . What I did . . . made the medicine backfire. I took an evil shortcut" (*LM*, 203). However, the turkey hearts he uses come not from wild birds, but from animals raised in captivity on a poultry farm, mass slaughtered, and packaged for the supermarket. Thus they seem innocuous. Yet, when sprinkled with holy water and sparked by Lipsha's shamanistic touch, the hearts become edible dynamite and result in Nector's death. A positive result ensues, for with the man they both love gone, his wife and mistress, daughters of rival medicine women, begin to bond.

Simultaneously, as Lulu and Marie unite, the traces of their mothers' sacred medicine power become transformed into secular political power. As James McKenzie points out, Lulu becomes "an

effective spokeswoman for traditional Indian values. She fights
the sale of Indian land for a factory that would manufacture
bangle beads and plastic tomahawks . . . and testifies in an important land claims case" while Marie, "who earlier denied any
Indian identity, makes common cause with Lulu, joining her in
'running things.'"[22] The fusing of the power lines results in a
transformation of the nature of power. Whereas medicine power,
grounded in the old ways, served the needs of the traditional
Indian world, it proves ineffective in confronting a changed post-
contact world. Erdrich's endings of both *Tracks* and *Love Medicine*
therefore indicate that power itself evolves along with universal
cycles, for Nanapush, a medicine man, becomes a tribal bureau-
crat in order to reclaim Lulu, while the daughters of the medicine
women become political activists who address the hybridized ac-
culturated world of contemporary Indians to ensure the preserva-
tion of Anishinabe land.

Sacred twins often give rise to the advent of a new era and
symbolize change. In *Tracks,* Erdrich's twin medicine women
usher in a new age in which living by the old ways becomes increasingly unfeasible as the Indians are forced to rely ever more
heavily on white culture. As Nanapush relates, his people subsequently become "a tribe of file cabinets and triplicates, a tribe of
single-space documents, directives, policy" (*T*, 225). Unlike Nanapush and Margaret, Fleur refuses to adapt to the imminent
change. Although portrayed as a powerful and frequently positive
character, Fleur remains myopically a traditionalist who, unlike
Nanapush, refuses to recognize the power of Anglo money and
documents in a changing culture: "She spoke with contempt for
the map, for those who drew it, for the money required, even for
the priest. She said the paper had no bearing or sense, as no one
would be reckless enough to try collecting for land where Pillagers
were buried" (*T*, 174). Through Nanapush and Margaret, Erdrich
emphasizes how recalcitrant her position is. Margaret comments
that "she's living in the old days" (*T*, 174), and Nanapush regards
Fleur's confidence as "pitiful and false" (*T*, 175). Fleur's failure
to recognize the reality of white encroachment undermines her
functioning as a role model. Similarly, Pauline's embrace of Euro-
American religion and culture to the effacement of her Indian-
ness represents another radical position: that of complete assimilation. Even more than Fleur, Pauline's fanaticism and mental
imbalance eliminate her as a viable role model. Each twin, then,
represents an extreme. Yet each subsequent generation must define a position within these extremes. An essential tenet of Native

American thought concerns the concept of balanced bipolarity or twinness which "emphasizes complementarity rather than opposition" and which is reflected in Indian social, political, and ceremonial structures.[23] And for each individual to find the balance between tradition and assimilation, between conflicting religious beliefs of animism and Christianity, becomes the dilemma of the descendants of these medicine women.

Notes

1. Paula Gunn Allen, *Grandmothers of the Light* (Boston: Beacon Press, 1991), 141. Hereafter *GL*, cited in the text.

2. Louise Erdrich, *Tracks* (New York: Henry Holt, 1988), 52. Hereafter *T*, cited in the text.

3. Catherine Rainwater, "Reading between Worlds: Narrativity in the Fiction of Louise Erdrich," *American Literature* 62 (1990): 419, 421.

4. Annette Van Dyke, "Questions of the Spirit: Bloodlines in Louise Erdrich's Chippewa Landscape," *Studies in American Indian Literature* 4 (1992): 21. Hereafter "Q," cited in the text.

5. Ruth Landes, *The Ojibwa Religion and the Midéwewin* (Madison: University of Wisconsin Press, 1968), 31. Hereafter *ORM*, cited in the text.

6. Basil Johnston, *Ojibway Heritage* (New York: Columbia University Press, 1976), 90. Hereafter *OH*, cited in the text.

7. Landes, *Ojibwa Religion*, 59; Basil Johnston, *Ojibway Ceremonies* (New York: AMS Press, 1990), 115. Hereafter *OC*, cited in the text.

8. Victor Barnouw, *Wisconsin Chippewa Myths and Tales and Their Relation to Chippewa Life* (Madison: University of Wisconsin Press, 1977), 113.

9. Landes, *Ojibwa Religion*, n.190–91; Åke Hultkrantz, *The Religions of the American Indians*, trans. Monica Setterwall (Berkeley: University of California Press, 1979), 131.

10. Hultkrantz, *Religions*, 131.

11. Catherine Catt, "Ancient Myth in Modern America: The Trickster in the Fiction of Louise Erdrich," *Platte Valley Review* 19 (1991): 72.

12. James Stripes, "The Problem(s) of (Anishinaabe) History in the Fiction of Louise Erdrich: Voices and Contexts," *Wicazo Sa Review* 7, no.2 (1991): 28.

13. Edward P. Dozier, *The Pueblo Indians of North America* (Prospect Heights, Ill.: Waveland Press, 1983), 24.

14. Johnston, *Ojibwa Heritage*, 125–26; Ruth Landes, *The Ojibwa Woman* (New York: AMS Press, 1969), 3–4.

15. Louis Owens, *Other Destinies: Understanding the American Indian Novel* (Norman: University of Oklahoma Press, 1992), 204.

16. Rainwater, "Reading," 409.

17. Barnouw, *Wisconsin Chippewa Myths*, 111–12.

18. Ibid., 112.

19. Louise Erdrich, *Love Medicine* (New York: Holt, 1984), 40, 45. Hereafter *LM*, cited in the text.

20. Nora Barry and Mary Prescott, "The Triumph of the Brave: *Love Medicine*'s Holistic Vision," *Critique* 30 (1989): 128.

21. Rainwater, "Reading," 405.

22. James McKenzie, "Lipsha's Good Road Home: The Renewal of Chippewa Culture in *Love Medicine*," *American Indian Culture and Research Journal* 10, no.3 (1986): 61.

23. Hultkrantz, *Religions*, 112–14; Paula Gunn Allen, *The Sacred Hoop* (Boston: Beacon Press, 1986), 19.

"Chambers of Consciousness": Sandra Cisneros and the Development of the Self in the BIG House on Mango Street

Andrea O'Reilly Herrera

SUNY—College at Fredonia

> One writes to make a home for oneself, on paper.
> —Alfred Kazin

BEFORE we even open her book, the very first image that we encounter in Sandra Cisneros's novel *The House on Mango Street* (1984) is the house. With it, Cisneros enters a tradition, adding to a wide array of houses that throughout literary history have provided writers with rich, protean metaphors. As the phenomenologist Gaston Bachelard reminds us, the house "constitutes a body of images that give mankind proofs or illusions of stability. We are always re-imagining its reality."[1] From a post-Freudian vantage point, the architectural layout of the house, with its various levels, has been made to parallel the different layers of the psyche, and with its multiple openings and passageways and its interior and exterior design, to suggest the body. In both the East and the West mystics and philosophers have linked the human soul with the image of the house: frequently, the body is figured as the house of the soul. Teresa of Avila envisaged the "way of perfection" as a dynamic progression through the seven mansions of the soul. The English Romantic poet John Keats compared life to "a large Mansion of Many Apartments" and described the development of the human thought process as a journey through the "chambers" of consciousness. Writers have also used the metaphor of the house to represent (quite literally) "structures" of economic, political, and social power. In the eighteenth- and nineteenth-century "big house novel" the old manor house signified social and economic status; it was either bequeathed from generation to generation or acquired and maintained through venture capitalist enterprises. In the same vein, the image of the decaying house has been employed as a symbol of political or social instability and decline by writers as various as William Faulkner, Virginia Woolf, Emilia Pardo Bazán, and Isabel Allende. Women's experience has especially been linked to the home, the domestic sphere as it were, and within that sphere there are clear-cut spatial boundaries which are designated as male and female. For example, the kitchen has traditionally been regarded as woman's place, whereas the study is male preserve. For scores of women writers the house is simultaneously a symbol of female enslavement and male privilege or guardianship. Finally, the metaphor of the house has been implemented to represent both the literary canon and the art of fiction-writing itself.[2] Referring, presumably, to Euro-(Anglo)American literature, in the preface to his *Portrait of a Lady* Henry James writes:

> The house of fiction has in short not one window, but a million—a number of possible windows not to be reckoned, rather; every one of which has been pierced, or is still pierceable, in its vast front, by the need of the individual vision and by the pressure of the individual will.[3]

The image of the house looms large in American literature. As Marilyn R. Chandler observes, the "prominence" that houses have occupied in American novels is directly related to the fact that the United States is "a country whose history has been focused ... on the business of settlement and 'development.' ... 'The American Dream' still expresses itself in the hope of owning a freestanding ... dwelling."[4] Traditionally, establishing, maintaining, or possessing houses has been, in fiction and in life, a male enterprise; the house, therefore, has often been a symbol of male success or failure. Rather than using the image of the house as a measure of "cultural enfranchisement," many American women writers of the twentieth century have employed the image of the house as a symbol of cultural disenfranchisement.[5] More specifically, they have used this architectural metaphor in order to define and articulate the (female) self in relation to the larger community. For Edith Wharton (*The House of Mirth*) houses symbolize the materialistic, patriarchal ideology that entraps both men and women and prescribes limited and repressive behavioral patterns to females, offering them few options outside the context of marriage. The house is the metaphor through which Paule Marshall *(Brown Girl, Brownstones)* explores the relationship of beauty, identity, and self-perception; but the house that the heroine seeks to possess reveals the "ugliness" of the culture which she wants to enter in light of its association with the ideas of power and appropriation, as well as self-creation and identity. And in Toni Morrison's work *(Beloved)* the house functions as a symbol of white supremacy; it is haunted by a past which all of the characters must confront and come to terms with before they can join as a community and, together, forge their future.

For Sandra Cisneros the house on Mango Street simultaneously represents all of the systems that oppose or challenge her as a woman, a minority, and a writer. In the last ten or fifteen years Chicana writing has been dedicated to examining the question of personal identity; frequently, not unlike African American and Native American literature, the process of private inquiry therein dilates into an exploration of self in terms of the community and in relation to the wider world. In their writing, Chicanas have attempted to pierce new windows into "the house of fiction." *The House on Mango Street* has as its central subject the Chicana writer's struggle for female, communal, and literary identity; the house that Sandra Cisneros constructs stands as her attempt to better understand, define, and synthesize the (interior) self in terms of the (exterior) Chicano and Anglo-American community. Simply, Cisneros has reinscribed the age-old metaphor of the house in order to explore the themes of sexism, racism, and the struggle of the female minority writer to appropriate the word in the Anglo-American "house of fiction."

Recent criticism has focused on the idea that Chicanas, like African American women, are caught in a kind of double bind. First and foremost, they are discriminated against and marginalized by both Anglo-American and Mexican culture, an idea subtly emphasized in Cisneros's novel by the fact that a house in Esperanza's and Nenny's neighborhood (in America) reminds them, for no particular reason, of houses they had seen as toddlers in Mexico.[6] In Gloria Anzaldua's words, Chicanos live "on the border," the "fault line," the "wound" between two cultures; although they share aspects of each, ultimately they are dispossessed from both. Further complicating the issue is the idea that Chicanos must come to terms with their fractured Mexican past before they can begin to negotiate their present.[7] The struggle to synthesize this bifurcated sense of personal and communal identity is frequently depicted in Chicana literature by the blending and intertwining of the Spanish and English languages. This idea is illustrated in *The House on Mango Street* by the fact that many of the characters have two names: Nenny's real name is Magdalena (a name that also resounds with biblical connotations); Meme Ortiz's name is actually Juan, and his sheepdog has one name in Spanish and one name in English.

In attempting to establish self-identity in relation to the larger Chicano community, the Chicana's task is further complicated by the fact that she is subordinated, because of her gender, within her own culture. The skewed sexual politics within the *movimiento Chicano* during the sixties exposed the asymmetry of the male-female relationship in Chicano culture and prompted the development of a specifically Chicana aesthetic. In effect, the Chicana is a minority within a minority, for women are endowed with a secondary status in Chicano culture. The dual struggle against (external) racism and (internal) sexism, a subject which also informs the writing of female African American authors, surfaces again and again in Chicana literature; it is one of the central concerns of Cisneros's novel.

Aiming to create an aesthetic that addresses her particular needs and concerns, the Chicana writer is faced with other obstacles as well. In attempting to explore her identity through the written word, both as a Chicana and as a woman, she is faced with a difficulty that all female American writers (and readers) encounter when attempting to write with (or read) a language or a literary tradition that is essentially male. Moreover, the Chicana must battle with the fact that the American "house of fiction" has been "dedicated," as Judith Fetterly observes, "to defining what is peculiarly American about experience"—in other words, white, male, Anglo-Saxon experience.[8] Cisneros combats these problems in several ways.

Throughout *The House on Mango Street* Esperanza longs for a "real" house of her own, signifying, perhaps, Cisneros's desire for a "legitimate" literary formula or pattern with which she can adequately express herself.[9] While Cisneros seeks Virginia Woolf's literary "room of one's own," Esperanza finds her father's house on Mango Street neither fulfills her needs nor her expectations. The longed-for house that Esperanza describes at the close of the novel is much more than a single room:

Not a flat. Not an apartment in the back. Not a man's house. Not a daddy's. A house all my own. With my porch and my pillow, my pretty purple petunias. My books and my stories. My two shoes waiting beside the bed. Nobody to shake a stick at. Nobody's garbage to pick up.

Only a house quiet as snow, a space for myself to go, clean as paper before the poem.[10]

Though it is altered and transformed, the house is an imaginative vision of Mango Street resurrected, reconstructed, and rendered through language: "Mango Street, sad red house I belong but do not belong to. I put it down on paper" (101). The vision expresses the desire on the author's part (Esperanza–Cisneros) to reconstruct the uncomfortable dimensions of her father's house in response to the desire its partial adequacy awakens.

Although Cisneros fashions a house from ordinary paper and ink—the materials most frequently used by writers—it is the scaffolding of her design that draws our attention. In a word, Cisneros invokes and implements traditional narrative patterns and motifs only to disrupt and reconstruct them. Simply, she uses "the master's tools" not to disassemble the master's house, as Audre Lorde suggests, but to remodel it according to her own aesthetic purpose. This idea is cleverly underscored by the fact that practically everything that Esperanza "inherits," from a bag full of shoes to her great-grandmother's name, is second-hand.

The overarching narrative formula in *The House on Mango Street* is a conflation of the *Bildungsroman* (the novel of formation) and its correspondent variant the *Kunstlerroman* (a novel that "culminates in the artist's" literal or imaginative "withdrawal to the inner life which leads to a discovery of his or her vocation").[11] Yet *The House on Mango Street* is a transformed, expanded variant of the novel of development. Unlike traditional nineteenth-century patterns of female development and character formation, Cisneros's narrative takes into account variables such as language, history, gender, and particular cultural practices. In the same vein, unlike the traditional female *Bildung,* such as Maria Luisa Bombal's "The Tree" or Charlotte Lennox's *The Female Quixote,* which almost always concludes with the heroine's psychic or physical death or her "consolidation" with cultural expectations, *The House on Mango Street* comes to a close with the heroine's self-discovery and, moreover, social involvement. It is a cathartic process which is made possible through the act of writing. In Cisneros's re-visionary novel the heroine, Esperanza, synthesizes and harmonizes her public and private lives; in the process she is endowed with a significance that has traditionally been denied to female characters. Moreover, her inner development is transformed into a public, creative response to stultifying and seemingly untenable circumstances. Further defying the conventions of the female *Bildung,* Cisneros adopts a typically male picaresque formula in order to chart Esperanza's development, something which is evidenced in both the form and the setting of the novel. One need only glance at the table of contents to see that *The House on Mango Street* is a discursive, episodic novel which displays the peripatetic quality of the picaresque.[12] Moreover, not unlike the picaro, Esperanza tests her self-image in the wider world: her adventures and education take place in the streets of her neighborhood. Her experience of the world is anything but vicarious, unlike the scores of women depicted in her novel, who gaze longingly outside their windows entrapped in their domestic roles. Finally, Cisneros avoids the flat circularity of the female *Bildung* by writing beyond traditional plot endings: marriage or death. Esperanza's projected mental return to Mango Street is spiral rather than circular. Derivative of the male *Bildungsroman,* her discovery and validation of an inner life, realized outside the context of marriage and motherhood, leads to a vision of social integration rather than death, madness, or isolation.

Cisneros's adaptation of the *Bildungsroman* charts the growing sexual and social consciousness of Esperanza as she grows up in her father's house; we learn at the conclusion of the book that she is a Chicana writer who has rejected the Chicano definition of woman's role and status. In her discussion of Chicana poetry, Elizabeth Ordoñez states, "the theme of sexuality consistently serves as a poetic vehicle whereby the Chicana comes to the authentic core of her being and creativity."[13] One could easily apply Ordoñez's statement to Cisneros's novel, for to borrow Barbara Christian's terminology, Esperanza's "trajectory of self-hood," which culminates in artistic expression, is defined in sexual terms.[14] Carefully choosing the experiences she wishes to represent, at the outset Esperanza depicts herself as an innocent child on the threshold of sexual awakening. In her own words, she is "a red balloon, a balloon tied to an anchor" (11). She is not totally unaware of the things which distinguish her from others, and in the opening chapter Esperanza discontentedly perceives both her own difference and lack. It is the house on Mango Street, the house that somehow falls short of her dreams—her "T.V." image of a "real" house—that evokes her dissatisfaction and disappointment. As the novel progresses, Cisneros carefully traces Esperanza's increasing ability to differentiate between herself and others. At first her observations are somewhat simplistic. She notes, for example, that each of her family members "have different hair"; she is aware that "boys and . . . girls live in separate worlds" and that her name has a different meaning, a different sound, depending on where it is spoken. Yet she soon learns that there are distinctions between people, and thus her mother forbids her to play with the "bad" Vargas children, who were "without respect for all living things, including themselves" (30). Again she enunciates her consciousness of her own inferior social status: Cathy, a neighborhood "friend" whose family is just a rung above Esperanza's on the economic ladder, thoughtlessly tells her, "as if she forgot" Esperanza had just moved in, that they were moving "a little farther *north* from Mango Street" (emphasis added) because "the neighborhood [was] getting bad" (14–15).[15]

As Esperanza matures she becomes increasingly conscious of her changing body and her sexuality; it is at this time that she begins to grow apart from her younger sister, Nenny. In the chapter entitled "Hips," Rachel, Lucy, and Esperanza discuss the possible functions of their widening hips. Nenny innocently points out that they distinguish men and women and "rock the baby asleep inside you," an idea Esperanza ascertains and explains in scientific terms that Alicia, a young college student, has taught her (47–48). Yet Lucy quickly adds that "you need [hips] to dance"; in other words, you need hips to attract men. Indicating their transitional level of maturity, the three older girls conclude their discussion by weaving the sexual themes of their "adult" conversation with nonsensical, rhythmic verse which they chant while skipping rope:

> Skip, skip,
> snake in your hips.
> Wiggle around
> and break your lip.

Aside from obvious physical changes, the girls also discover the social significance of clothing. Reminiscent of Marguerite Duras's novel *L'Amante*, Cisneros uses shoes as a metonym for female power and sexuality. Gleefully receiving a bag full of old high heels, Esperanza and her girlfriends find that they are somehow transformed the moment that they put on the shoes; for the first time they become conscious of their legs, despite the fact that they are thin and covered with satiny scars. "Today we are like

Cinderella," Esperanza happily comments, yet in the next breath she acknowledges that "it is scary to look down at your foot that is no longer yours and see attached a long long leg" (38). Strutting through the neighborhood wearing the "magic high heels"—outside of their fathers' houses—the three girls become immediately attuned to the fact that the shoes attract the male gaze (38). "The men cannot take their eyes off us," Esperanza observes; the grocer, Mr. Benny, warns them that the shoes are "dangerous" and threatens to call the police; and a drunken bum on a stoop tells Rachel that she is "prettier than a yellow taxi cab" in her lemon-colored heels and offers her a dollar in return for a kiss (38–39).[16] Yet Esperanza finds that she can be beautiful, she can attract attention, wearing "ordinary" shoes as well. She recalls that as she moved across the dance floor with her Uncle Nacho, "like in the movies," "my mother watches and my little cousins watch and . . . all night the boy who is a man watches me dance. He watched me dance" (46).

Despite her growing consciousness, Esperanza remains largely innocent and naive. She skips rope in her high heels, moving her hips in steady rhythm to the "double dutch" (48).[17] It isn't until Sally is led into the "monkey garden" with Tito's "grinning" buddies, on the pretense of retrieving her key, that she falls from innocence. It is a scene which reverberates with mingled Darwinian and biblical overtones.[18] Of course the garden that her family "took over" is, on one level, a symbol of America as the new Eden; the disillusion and perhaps failure of the Chicano to domesticate or shape the garden—property that is clearly attached to, and an extension of, the father's property (the house)—is signified by the fact that the garden soon grows unkempt. But it is also the locus of Esperanza's sexual awakening. Armed with three sticks and a brick she discovers, much to her consternation, that Sally does not want to be saved.[19] Throwing herself on the grass in tears, she realizes all at once that the garden "isn't a place to play any more" (91).[20] Esperanza longs for the androgynous state of childhood when she could run in the garden "fast as the boys" (89).[21] Symbolically, she longs for her own (sexual) death and observes that when she got up her dress was stained green (an obvious symbol of growth) and her feet "in their white socks and ugly round shoes . . . seemed far away": "They didn't seem to be my feet any more" (90). Her conscious awareness of the potentially perverse aspect of human sexuality commences in the episode in which she takes her first job at *Peter Pan* Photo Finishers; yet her sexual awakening brutally culminates in the scene at the amusement park in which she is (presumably) raped behind the tilt-a-whirl with the laughing red clowns.[22]

The House on Mango Street raises disturbing questions regarding both female nature and the realities and the fictions of development for women in general, and Chicanas in particular. Cisneros's novel reverberates with mythic allusions and fairy-tale motifs. Yet her reformulation of Christian models and fairy tales, reminiscent of writers such as Anne Sexton and Olga Broumas, not only underscores the developmental and psychological changes Esperanza undergoes in her passage from childhood to womanhood, but it forces us to recontextualize and revise her original sources. The self which Cisneros defines is, in effect, defined both in relation and resistance to conventional plot formulas. Cisneros refashions archetypal paradigms, such as the Fall, the Peter Pan syndrome, and the Cinderella cycle; in this way, she exposes the limited narrative strategies and "patterns for maturation and behavior," to borrow Karen Rowe's terminology, available to female authors writing in, and against, a male tradition.[23]

Like the narrative formula of the *Bildung,* myths and fairy tales enable Cisneros to underscore and reiterate her major themes and investigate or bring to light the limited maturation and behavioral patterns that fiction has offered to women. Repeatedly, she emphasizes the fact that Esperanza wishes to belong, to fit in; the theme of friendship is woven throughout the novel. Yet as she grows older she not only becomes conscious of her own sexual identity, but she becomes aware of the fact that the romantic vision offered to Chicanas in "storybooks and movies" is a debilitating, self-diminishing myth that fails (93). In effect, Esperanza becomes conscious of the fact that her interior sense of self does not correspond with the accepted self that her culture has carved out for her; in fact it collides with the image offered to her by society. *The House on Mango Street* is a virtual portrait gallery of disillusioned, passive women who are victimized, or victimize themselves, because of their sexuality; Cisneros interweaves their narratives with mythic, fairy-tale motifs. Rosa Vargas is a single parent who, like the old woman in the shoe, has "too many" kids; Lois, who can't tie her own shoes and smells "pink like babies do," laughs and drinks beer and follows her boyfriend Sire into dark alleys; Ruthie whistles "like the Emperor's nightingale," recites poetry from *Alice in Wonderland,* used to write children's books, and sleeps on her mother's couch, despite the fact that she married a man who gave her a "real" house of her own; locked in her bedroom by a jealous husband, Rafaela leans out of her window "dream[ing] her hair is like Rapunzel's" and drinks coconut and papaya juice because she wishes there were sweeter drinks; and finally Sally, "the girl with eyes like Egypt" and paints her eyes "like Cleopatra," marries at thirteen and sits at home alone staring at the "linoleum roses" on her kitchen floor in her "wedding cake" house (28, 30, 64, 76). Ironically, even the women within her own house bear a similar destiny; Esperanza is literally surrounded by women who "consolidate" their subservient nurturing role by exchanging "one domestic sphere for another"; in effect, they have fulfilled what Abel, Hirsch, and Langland call "the conventional expectations of marriage and motherhood."[24] Her great-grandmother, whose name she has "inherited," was carried off like a "fancy chandelier" to her husband's house and spent her life looking out the window; her mother sings *Madame Butterfly* with "velvety lungs" and sadly tells her daughter that she "could've been somebody"; and her aunt, the swimmer-surviver, dies a blind invalid with only a photograph as a testimony to her strength (12, 83).[25] Through their negative example, Esperanza learns that the institution of marriage—the big wedding cake "house"—is not all that it seems. Only Alicia, the girl who sees mice late at night because she sits up studying and refuses to "inherit her mother's rollingpin," provides Esperanza with a female mentor (32).[26] Unlike Marin, who dances on the street corner waiting for someone to "change her life," Esperanza rejects the role models which her society offers her and consciously chooses to forge her own identity through writing; and in so doing, she symbolically chooses the American translation of her name (hope) over the Spanish (waiting).

In addition to being an exploration into the way in which the Chicano community deters the Chicana's exploration and discovery of selfhood, Cisneros's novel emphatically stresses the role of writing in the process of self-definition. In *The House on Mango Street* gender is inextricably linked to artistic development. Cisneros's novel is, in some sense, a work in process, a growing experience "recollected" in a kind of uneasy Wordsworthian "tranquility." As readers, we are acutely aware that Esperanza (alias Cassandra, Alexis, Maritza, Lisandra, or Zeze the X) is constantly, and consciously, fashioning and refashioning her identity, her history, an idea underscored by the chapter in which Lucy, Rachel, Nenny, and Esperanza name and rename the clouds. As she matures, she learns the power of language and discovers that naming creates and dispels fear.[27] Not only is she empowered by the scientific words that she gleans from her library books or learns from Alicia, but she is empowered by her fiction, unlike Minerva who writes visionary poetry on scraps of paper but "is always sad like a house on fire" (80). As an adult, she discovers the meaning of her dying aunt's words: "You just remember to keep writing, Esperanza. You must keep writing. It will keep you free" (56). The psychic freedom embodied in the written word is tantamount to freedom; yet it is a truth that Esperanza comes to understand only when she has managed to free herself, if only imaginatively, from Mango Street. Only then can she become an independent, self-determining agent. Yet independence does not imply isolation. For Esperanza the act of writing and recollecting (perhaps something akin to Toni Morrison's concept of "remem-ory") enables her to synthesize, critique, and recuperate her own personal history and, by correlation, the history of her culture. Writing enables her to realize the redemptive vision of the mystical sister with marble hands:

> When you leave you must remember always to come back . . . for the others. A circle, understand? You will always be Esperanza. You will always be Mango Street. You can't erase what you know: You can't forget who you are. . . . You must remember to come back. (97–98)

Significantly, the old woman imparts her message at Rachel's and Lucy's baby sister's funeral; it perhaps foreshadows Esperanza's eventual rejection of marriage and motherhood. Only in retrospect does she realize her redemptive role, a role almost mystically signified by her name Esperanza (Hope) Cordero (sacrificial? Lamb).

Widely characteristic of contemporary American minority fiction, the final vision of *The House on Mango Street* is the individual defined within the context of the larger community; it is an idea that is evidenced by the fact that we gradually acquire a fuller understanding of Esperanza's identity as she acquaints us with the various members of her family and neighborhood. In effect, Esperanza's development is thrown into high relief against both her family's and her community's history. Simone de Beauvoir once commented, "The ideal of happiness has always taken material form in the house, whether cottage or castle; it stands for permanence and separation from the world."[28] Unlike de Beauvoir's isolated, idealized house, the house that Cisneros built is a meeting place, hospitable and inviting. It is, to borrow Bachelard's vocabulary, "better built, lighter, and larger than all of the houses of the past"; and though it stands in "symmetrical relation" to the houses of the past, the house she was born in, it is living, and protean, and impermanent.[29] Cisneros seemed to know that "it is better to live in a state of impermanence than in one of finality."[30]

That Sandra Cisneros drew on an established tradition to accomplish her own ends is readily apparent in *The House on Mango Street*. Cisneros's adaptation and reinscription of established narrative patterns enabled her to explore the psychological, historical, and cultural forces which shape individual and collective identity. At the same time, her revisions reveal the way in which the writer can shape and reshape not only personal history, but cultural history as well. Ultimately, *The House on Mango Street* calls attention to the near impossibility of rendering, and thus harnessing, human experience and human nature with language, for in the process of refashioning, Cisneros points up the artificial, subjective, and often political nature of artistic creation. Nevertheless, rearranging the furniture in the house of fiction becomes for her both an act of defiance and, in Adrienne Rich's words, "an act of survival."[31] Unlike Mamacita "no speak English," Esperanza refuses to preserve some fixed image, some photograph, of home. On the contrary, at the end of her narrative—her (his)story—she affirms the idea that home resides within the individual "heart." Like the four skinny trees in her neighborhood, she "reaches" and does not forget, despite the bricks and concrete (71). As we close her book we are left with the feeling that Cisneros's "house" of paper and ink, her "house made of heart," is extraordinarily resistant and durable.

—garigots—

Notes

1. Gaston Bachelard, *The Poetics of Space* (New York: Orion Books, 1964), 17.

2. It is impossible to overlook the fact that nowadays the word "canon" has virtually lost its currency. In effect, it has become a kind of a pregnant form, expanding and contracting according to the individual will.

3. Henry James, *The Art of the Novel* (New York: Scribner's, 1962), 46.

4. Marilyn R. Chandler, *Dwelling in the Text: Houses in American Fiction* (Berkeley: University of California Press, 1991), 1.

5. Ibid.

6. This notion is later emphasized in the episode with "Geraldo no name," the man who has no name or address in America and is never heard of again at home in Mexico.

7. Gloria Anzaldua, *La Frontera: The New Mestizo* (San Francisco, Calif.: Spinsters, 1987).

8. Judith Fetterley, "Introduction: On the Politics of Literature," in *The Resisting Reader* (Bloomington: Indiana University Press, 1977).

9. Of course the question of what is real or what is perceived to be real is thrown into high relief in Cisneros's novel.

10. Sandra Cisneros, *The House on Mango Street* (Houston, Tex.: Arte Publico Press, 1985), 100. All subsequent quotations from the novel are taken from this edition and citations will appear parenthetically in the text by page number only.

11. I am using Marianne Hirsch's definition of the *Kunstlerroman;* it appears in her essay "Spiritual *Bildung:* The Beautiful Soul as Paradigm," in *The Voyage In* (Hanover, N.H.: University Press of New England, 1983), 46. I must also add that the essays in *The Voyage In* provided both the inspiration and the narrative framework for my own investigation of Cisneros's novel.

12. One might also suggest that the narrative gaps in the fractured chronological plot not only challenge the conventions of the linear or "realistic" plot, but, in the tradition of *écriture féminine*, gaps signify women's absence or omission from cultural productions such as writing.

13. Elizabeth Ordoñez, "Sexual Politics and the Theme of Sexuality in Chicana Poetry," in *Women in Hispanic Literature*, ed. Beth Miller (Berkeley: University of California Press, 1983), 318.

14. Barbara Christian, "Trajectories of Self-Definition: Placing Contemporary Afro-American Women's Fiction," *Black Feminist Criticism: Perspectives on Black Women Writers* (Elmsford, N.Y.: Pergamon Press, 1985).

15. The chapter entitled "Papa Who Wakes Up Tired in the Dark" signals Esperanza's first encounter with death and her consequent realization that her father is vulnerable.

16. Symbollically there are three pairs of high heels—three is a kind of mystical, quasi-religious number that recurs in folklore and fairy tales. The colors of the shoes are significant as well: red suggests female sexuality and passion (it also recalls the image of Dorothy's ruby slippers); yellow seems to signify fetishized, even prostituted, sexuality (as the bum points out, it is also the color of a taxi cab, a vehicle that can take you anywhere you want to go as long as you're willing to pay the price); and the pale blue shoes that used to be white symbolize lost innocence (the fact that it is lost in the dance, an obvious symbol of unrestrained sexuality in Cisneros's novel, is worthy of attention).

17. Cisneros underscores this theme by including a number of parallel sequences in her novel which trace Esperanza's maturation process; for example, in the beginning of the novel she contributes five dollars toward the purchase of a used bicycle, and at the end she pays Elenita, a fortune-teller who, like Jean Rhys's character Christophine, mingles Christian superstition with voodoo-like practices to read her fortune.

18. The Darwinian leitmotif resurfaces in the scene in which Esperanza reads Charles Kingsley's *The Waterbabies* (1863) to her dying aunt.

19. The kiss that the boys demand from Sally recalls the episodes with Rachel and the "bum man" and Esperanza and the old Chinese man at the photo finishers.

20. While playing in the garden Eddie Vargas falls asleep beneath a hibiscus tree "like a Rip Van Winkle," the archetypally henpecked husband, a detail that reinforces the overall mythic atmosphere of the garden.

21. The overtly phallic gesture of shaking the stick at Sally underscores this theme. This theme is also developed later in the novel when Esperanza "wages a quiet war" against pretty women who "wait on the threshold waiting for the ball and the chain": she adopts chauvinistic male behavior such as "leaving the table like a man, without putting back the chair or picking up the plate" (82).

22. The scene in the "photo lab" parallels the episode with Rachel and the "bum man."

23. Karen E. Rowe, "'Fairy-born and human-bred': Jane Eyre's Education in Romance," *The Voyage In,* 69.

24. Abel, Hirsch, and Langland, *The Voyage In,* 7–8.

25. Cisneros repeatedly uses the photograph in her novel. Esperanza, for example, works at a photo finishers and the photograph taken at her *abuelito's* tomb is a photograph of a pink house in Mexico. In Cisneros's work, photographs represent the attempt to preserve memory and, in Roland Barthes's terminology, make oneself historically significant.

26. At this junction in the text Esperanza also becomes conscious both of her own "ugly" physical appearance and of her mother's "shame" (82–84).

27. This notion is emphasized in the chapter entitled "Those Who Don't" in which she demonstrates that fear and danger are relative.

28. Simone de Beauvoir, *The Second Sex* (1953; reprint, New York: Vintage Books, 1989), 501.

29. Bachelard, *Poetics of Space,* 61.

30. Ibid.

31. Adrienne Rich, "When We Dead Awaken: Writing as Revision," in *On Lies, Secrets, and Silences* (New York: Norton, 1975), 35.